# VICTOR HUGO'S DRAMA

# VICTOR HUGO'S DRAMA

## AN ANNOTATED BIBLIOGRAPHY 1900–1980

COMPILED BY
RUTH LESTHA DOYLE

**Greenwood Press**
WESTPORT, CONNECTICUT ● LONDON, ENGLAND

**Library of Congress Cataloging in Publication Data**

Doyle, Ruth Lestha.
    Victor Hugo's drama.

    Includes indexes.
    1. Hugo, Victor Marie, comte, 1802-1885--
Dramatic works--Bibliography.    I.   Title.
Z8424.D69   [PQ2301]        016.842'7        80-29680
ISBN 0-313-22884-1 (lib. bdg.)

Library of Congress Catalog Card Number: 80-29680
ISBN: 0-313-22884-1

First published in 1981

Greenwood Press
A division of Congressional Information Service, Inc.
88 Post Road West, Westport, Connecticut 06881

Printed in the United States of America

10 9 8 7 6 5 4 3 2 1

To Alfred Garvin Engstrom

*with gratitude for his inspiration and guidance*

# Contents

# Preface

The purpose of this annotated bibliography is to list the books, parts of books, articles, and reviews that have appeared since 1900 concerning aspects of Victor Hugo's theatre. An attempt has been made to comment objectively on every item available and to include direct quotations in order to indicate the style and critical approach of each author. During the course of this compilation, the holdings of thirty-nine libraries in the United States, the Bibliothèque Nationale, and the Arsenal were consulted. More than eight hundred books, periodical and newspaper articles, and reviews are listed. Available items in English, French, German, Italian, and Spanish have been commented upon.

Preceding the bibliography is an introductory section containing an analysis of the trends in critical thought on Hugo's theatre. The first part, organized chronologically, deals with general criticism. The second part covers criticism of the individual plays.

The bibliography section is divided into three parts. The first part lists editions and translations of Hugo's plays alphabetically by play or, in the case of selected or complete Hugo works, by date of publication. The second part contains a list of general critical works, arranged alphabetically by author. Pertinent items on individual plays, listed chronologically by composition and performance date, are found in the third part. All three parts contain critical annotation. Author and subject indexes for all entries conclude the volume.

A standard bibliographical form has been adopted to furnish as much information as possible for each listing. Specific references to Hugo's theatre are included in the main portion of the bibliographical entry or in parentheses after it. The original edition of a book has been consulted, except where otherwise indicated, and whenever possible, a comparison of later editions with the original is included in the annotation.

Pertinent unpublished dissertations and theses, both European and American, have been included though, for the most part, not consulted. Some literary histories from various countries have been included to provide an overview of standard opinion throughout the period in question. Book review references are intended to supplement the necessarily brief comments in the bibliography. It has been impossible to consult every review of every performance of every Hugo play since 1900. Included are a sufficient number, however, to indicate the trends of popular and critical reaction.

It is the author's hope that these 826 entries will provide useful information to the interested scholar. This bibliography has been a labor of love, and the author hopes that it will contribute to the renaissance of interest in Hugo's works and, more specifically, to a sensitive reappraisal of Hugo's dramatic writings.

# INTRODUCTION

# General Trends of Criticism

Victor Hugo's theatre has generally been considered the weakest part of his total work. The highest praise for it has often been that the poet and novelist can be recognized in the dramatist's work. Throughout the twentieth century, however, dedicated Hugophiles have battled Hugophobes over Hugo's talents as a dramatic author and his contributions to French dramatic history. Most critics and literary historians are willing to agree that *Hernani*'s premiere in 1830 marked the triumph of something—be it that of an innovative, liberating poetic style in drama or simply that of the outdated aesthetic of Pixérécourt's melodrama—and most recognize, begrudgingly or cheerfully, Hugo's lyrical magic in *Hernani* and *Ruy Blas*. Yet there is little agreement beyond these few clichés among the many writers who have expressed their views on Hugo's plays since 1900.

A plethora of newspaper and periodical articles have appeared on Hugo's theatre and on his individual plays, particularly concerning theatrical productions, sources, unpublished material, and influences. Quite a few separate, annotated editions of the plays, especially of *Hernani* and *Ruy Blas*, intended for school use in many cases, have been published in the United States, England, and France. Chapters concerning Hugo's plays are included in the many books on the French Romantic theatre, on Victor Hugo's life and works, and on studies of the influence of England, Spain, and other countries on French Romanticism and vice versa. At the same time, however, there has been a dearth of books devoted solely to the theatre of Victor Hugo. With the renaissance of Hugo studies and the renewed productions of his plays, which began in the late 1940s and, fortunately, continued in full force through the 1970s, Hugo's theatre has received increasing attention and has profited from the new scrutiny. It is hoped that the impetus will remain strong to produce a synthesis of new information and fresh ideas in this somewhat neglected area of Hugo scholarship.

## 1900-1926

The early years of the twentieth century were marked by several attempts to renovate Hugo's plays for modern audiences. *Les Burgraves* was solemnly performed at the Comédie-Française to mark the centenary of the poet's birth. Many of the plays enjoyed reprises, even *Angelo* and *Le Roi s'amuse. Mangeront-ils?* received its Paris premiere in 1919 and *Les Deux Trouvailles de Gallus* its world premiere in 1923. Both played to enthusiastic audiences and received largely favorable reviews. Scholastic editions of *Hernani* and *Ruy Blas*, especially in America and England, already recognized the plays as French classics.

The scholars and critics evaluating Hugo's theatre as a whole, however, were often less generous during the first twenty-five years of this century. Biré (91), Brunetière (99), Lanson (206), and Strachey (295) all deplored Hugo's weaknesses—his lack of psychological realism, his overabundance of antithesis, his somewhat childish dramatic techniques. That Hugo's marvelous lyricism could save some of his plays was often added in the evaluations almost as an afterthought. Hugo's champions during this period included Richepin (264) and Hervieu (183), dramatists themselves. Le Breton (211) selected *Ruy Blas* as Hugo's finest play, one which illustrates that Hugo is the best poet among the Romantic dramatists but a weak playwright. Smith's study (287) emphasized that Hugo is chiefly a destructive force in the theatre, clearing the stage of the dying imitations of Voltaire rather than offering a lasting new model of his own. Bédier and Hazard (83) expressed fond admiration for Hugo's theatre, in which they saw a skillful combination of lyric, epic, and dramatic poetry.

During this first period of twentieth-century criticism, several important studies on specific aspects of Hugo's theatre also appeared. The number of German investigations indicates that country's sustained interest. Degenhardt (127) studied metaphors in the plays; Sleumer (283) compiled critical opinions on the dramas; Martini (225) examined Hugo's dramatic techniques; Mrodzinski (238) analyzed the many German translations of the plays; Harden (178) offered a brief comparison of the theatres of Goethe and Hugo.

Hugo's theatre and its relation to society came under Guex's (171) scrutiny while Pellissier (255) identified the realistic elements Hugo introduced on the stage. Sand (274) traced the evolution of Hugo's *drame romantique* into two genres that he felt had outlived it—the *drame réaliste* and the Wagnerian opera. Le Breton (211) and Coeuroy (119) suggested Hugo's influence on Wagner, but Weil's detailed comparison (326) of the two men's works led him to reject this thesis. Mason (226) and Lacey (200) tried to prove the importance of melodrama in Hugo's theories and composition, while Lanson (205), on the other hand, claimed that Hugo's *Hernani* struck the first note of real tragedy on the French stage since *Athalie*. Kammel (198) looked at the plays' heroes and heroines, and Carter (104) concentrated on Hugo's women characters.

Two very fine studies on the many parodies to which Hugo's plays fell prey were offered by Blanchard (92) and Bersaucourt (89). Also during this fruitful period, Gustave Simon, Paul Meurice's successor as Hugo's executor, tirelessly published a vast amount of unpublished material on the specific plays and on general topics like Hugo's friendly relationships with his interpreters (281, 280). In one year, Rudwin published a bibliography on Hugo (270) and a study of Satan and Satanism in Hugo's works (363). A word must be said about Lasserre's strongly anti-Romantic tome (208), in which he accused Hugo of causing the decadence of the French drama through his introduction of "l'emphase au théâtre" ("bombast in the theatre"). A certain current of anti-Romanticism, similar to that expressed by Lasserre, runs through Hugo criticism from this time into the 1950s.

Various studies on the French Romantic theatre during these years highlighted different areas of information about Hugo. Le Roy (214) concentrated on the dawn of the Romantic theatre. Ginisty (161) was strongest on parodies, portraits, and actors. Draper (133) stressed the influence of English authors—Scott, Byron, and Shakespeare—while Evans (140, 139) attributed the failure of the *drame romantique* to the lack of a theatre open to experimental plays and to the gross materialism of the new industrial age.

A number of works shed light on international literary relations. In his study on the English theatre in Paris under the Restoration, Borgerhoff (418) rejected substantial Shakespearian influence in *Hernani*. Partridge (252), however, identified echoes of Shakespeare in various Hugo plays as well as traces of Byron, Scott, and Bulwer-Lytton. Moraud (234) said Hugo was closer to Shakespeare than was Dumas. Ayer (72) found that Hugo's dramas have been more successful on the English than on the American stage. Bowley (96) offered a list of the English versions of Hugo's dramas that he had located and described the main changes made in these adaptations. Spain's influence on Hugo's theatre was treated by Huszár (190) and even more solidly by Martinenche (495). Galletti (152) investigated Italy's contributions to Hugo's plays and their influence, in turn, on Italy. Of particular interest to Franchetti (146) and Primo (261) was the long, fertile history of Italian operas based on Hugo's plays. In assessing the impact of French Romanticism in Holland, Panne (247) considered Dutch translations of Hugo's plays. In his massive tomes on Schiller and French Romanticism, Eggli (138) included attention to Hugo's borrowings in his plays and theories from the great German.

It seems at times that a researcher finds anything he looks for in Hugo's theatre. In the wide range of offerings during this first quarter-century of criticism, however, the most useful and important work produced, still of value today, was the two-volume study, published in 1902-1903 by Paul and Victor Glachant (163), of the manuscripts and variants of Hugo's plays. Their painstaking descriptions and suggested genesis for each verse and prose play were quite informative, and it is interesting that they chose *Ruy Blas*, as so many other critics have done, as Hugo's masterpiece.

## 1927-1939

In 1927 the centenary of Romanticism was celebrated officially by a reprise of *Les Burgraves* at the Comédie-Française, beginning more than a decade of centennial celebrations for *Hernani*, especially, and for plays from *Marion de Lorme* through *Ruy Blas*. During this period of proud homage, the general studies on Hugo's theatre by Berret (88), Clément-Janin (117), Bellessort (84), and Gregh (167) selected *Ruy Blas* as Hugo's most lyrical and best play. All except Bellessort were enthusiastic about Hugo's verse dramas; yet Gregh and Clément-Janin conceded that Musset was a more lasting, modern playwright. Hermann Hugi (189) attempted to explain Hugo's dramas through psychoanalysis and managed to identify in them strong Oedipus and Cain complexes and several personal myths from Hugo's psyche.

Comments from literary histories, works on Romantic theatre, studies of Hugo, and brief evaluations tended to mirror the polite salute to Hugo as a lyric genius expressed in the more comprehensive treatments described above. The comic excellence of act IV of *Ruy Blas* is also underscored by Truffier (540), Dubech (134), and Henriot (180). Thibaudet (302, 303) wrote, perhaps, the best evaluation of Hugo in judging that Hugo was a man of monologue, not of dialogue, and that he was a victim of his own lived "théâtromanie." Thibaudet also anticipated future critical common-places in praising *Cromwell* and suggesting that *Antony*, not *Hernani*, won the real stage victory for Romanticism.

As in the first quarter-century of criticism, an amazing variety of dimensions of Hugo's plays was examined in this fertile period. Lyonnet's informative but occasionally inaccurate book on Hugo's premieres (222) gave many details and was one in a series dealing also with the premieres of Corneille, Racine, Molière, and Musset, elegant company for Hugo. Maurice Souriau's seminal work (292) on the history of French Romanticism offered solid facts and logical interpretations. As Joussain (196) examined a neglected area of Hugo's work, humor, he found a great deal of it in *Crom-*

*well*, *Ruy Blas*, and *Le Théâtre en liberté*. One of the most important works of this period was that of Allevy (67), in which she showed Hugo's extension of the role of author to encompass those of director, stage and costume designer, and rehearsal coordinator.

Hugo's thought and art in the plays were not ignored. Rousseaux (515) examined his Pan-European ideal. Heimbacher (179) was interested in Hugo's artistic expression of the ideas of the French Revolution. Moreau's fine study on the classicism of the Romantics (236) characterized Hugo's *drame romantique* as less innovative and more linked to classical tragedy than Hugo wished. Sacher (272) attributed Hugo's lack of psychological depth in his plays to his reliance upon the formulae of melodrama. Treille (538) traced the impact of the dramatic conflict in France during the 1820s upon the young Hugo. By surveying the critical opinions of the *Gazette de France* in the 1830s, Wood (328) suggested that the negative reaction to Hugo's plays had a political, as well as literary, basis.

Works identifying a variety of influences on Hugo's plays dealt with both French and foreign history and literature. Rozelaar (362) traced the influence of the Napoleonic *Mémorial de Sainte-Hélène* in plays from *Cromwell* through *Les Burgraves*. Hugo's ignorance of Italy, as displayed in his dramas, infuriated De Carli (621). Thomas (305) ferreted out many English sources for *Amy Robsart*, *Cromwell*, and *Marie Tudor* and berated Hugo's superficial concept of historical truth.

Quite an intriguing series of works on Hugo's influence in other countries showed that it was first as a dramatist that Hugo made an impression outside of France. George found this to be true in America (156), and Ware's discussion of French adaptations on the Philadelphia and New York stages until the Civil War (324) supported the claim. Parker and Peers found Hugo's vogue in Spain (250, 251) to last just as long as his dramas reigned there in popularity. Moraud (235) included some amusing early criticism of Hugo's plays in England in his book on French Romanticism in England. It was Hooker's conclusion after examining Hugo's fortune in England (184) that his plays were never really accepted seriously there.

## 1940-1948

The period from 1940 through 1948 is poor in both the quantity and quality of material on Hugo's theatre. World War II explains this situation in part and also influenced, perhaps, the negative, condescending tone of much of the criticism available for those years. Typical of the critics of this period is Philippe Van Tieghem (319), who said that only *Hernani* and *Ruy Blas* remain playable, and even they lack psychological intuition. The only positive appreciations were offered by Grant (164), who credited Hugo with breaking the rigidity of the traditional theatre and with creating the concept of "useful theatre," and by Froment-Guiyesse (147), who saw Hugo's *Hernani, Ruy Blas, Cromwell,* and its preface as major forces determining the development of French theatre.

Psychoanalytic interpretations abounded in the 1940s. Baudouin's study (80) surely was the most reliable of such efforts. Besides the Oedipus and Cain complexes previously indicated by Hugi (189), Baudouin added the themes of fatality and the redemptive power of love.

A very few other studies of note which contained information on Hugo's plays complete this period of neglect and underestimation. Travers (310) catalogued all nineteenth-century French theatrical parodies that he had discovered, and Hugo was the target of a considerable number of them. Hervier (182) offered a very helpful compilation of contemporary critical opinions of Hugo. Pendell's more specific examination of press reaction to Hugo's acted dramas (256) indicated that opinions varied from newspaper to newspaper and from critic to critic. In a different vein, Picard (258) expressed in his work on social romanticism the view that Hugo's sympathy for "le peuple" and defense of the outcast in his plays had a beneficial effect on social attitudes. In evaluating Hugo's fortune in Croatia, Dzakula (137) found *Lucrèce Borgia* Hugo's most popular drama there!

## 1949 – Present

With the publication of the first volume of Barrère's *La Fantaisie de Victor Hugo* (75) in 1949 began the revival of Hugo studies that has spread from academic circles to the general public and from France abroad. Several important studies have appeared on Hugo's theatre and a certain reevaluation of Hugo as dramatist seems to be taking place. It is also noteworthy that revivals of many of Hugo's plays have been undertaken consistently over the quarter-century beginning in the late 1940s. This encouraging trend continued through the 1974 reprises of *Hernani* and *Ruy Blas*—both received with considerable popular and critical success—and through such experimental productions as Vitez's *Les Burgraves* in 1978 and Lewinson's *L'Intervention*. The comments on Hugo's plays from such men of the theatre as Jouvet (197), Vilar (719), and Vigo-Fazio (323, 786) indicate the plays' strengths and weaknesses from the point of view of mounting them for a modern audience. The numerous annotated and critical editions of his plays published since 1950 provide another indication of vigorous activity as well as of the renewed playability of Hugo's dramas.

Central in most criticism during this period has been the question of Hugo's intended goals for his theatre and his attainment of them. The traditional complaints lodged against Hugo as dramatist were repeated in conservative literary histories, like those of Picon (259) and Fuchs (148), and in studies of Hugo's life and works, like those of Maurois (228).

Tephany (301) offered a view that was to become commonplace in critical circles—that, although Hugo failed to "métamorphoser la foule en public" ("metamorphose the crowd into an audience") in his dramas, he did accomplish this objective in *Les Misérables*.

Gaudon's valuable but highly personal book on Hugo's theatre (154) contained the opinion that Hugo's vision of a popular theatre ultimately failed because of his poor dramatic techniques. In a series of perceptive articles, Butor (100) focused upon those same highly criticized dramatic procedures—gestures, asides, and the use of objects to perform dramatic functions—and reevaluated them as part of Hugo's search for "la transparence." Barrère (77), Carlson (102, 103), and Chahine (107) all attempted to understand the originality and effectiveness of Hugo's dramaturgy.

Affron (65) argued that since the theatre of Musset and Hugo is essentially lyrical, it should be judged accordingly and not solely from the viewpoint of traditional psychological drama. John Houston's 1974 book on Hugo's life and works (186) elevated *Marion de Lorme* and *Cromwell* above *Hernani* while affirming that *Ruy Blas* stood out for its coherence, style, and tightly structured plot. His perceptions, those of Schafer (276), and those of Howarth (187) offered a valid reappraisal of Hugo's contributions to a renewed poetic style and invigorated vocabulary on the French stage. Howarth's 1976 article on Hugo's dominant role in the history of the *drame romantique* (188) is excellent.

In Barrère's summary of the state of scholarship on Hugo of 1961 (78), the author observed that Hugo's theatre has not attracted scholars despite the fact that "il offre pourtant encore beaucoup à trouver" ("it still offers, however, a lot to be found"). Mme. Ubersfeld-Maille has since then become the acknowledged expert on Hugo's theatre and has offered a number of original interpretations of various Hugo plays, often through the application of techniques of the New Criticism. Her fine edition of *Cromwell* (3) and two-volume edition of *Ruy Blas* (58) are very well researched and useful. She has also collaborated on the excellent Massin chronological edition of the *Oeuvres complètes* (43) and brought out separate articles on diverse aspects of Hugo's plays, such as his symbolic use of objects (314) and contemporary press rejection of the ideology of his plays (313). Her *Le Roi et le bouffon* (317) surely will remain for some time the major study of Hugo's dramatic production from 1830 to 1839. Her tireless efforts have made her one of the most articulate and productive Hugo scholars at work today and responsible to a large degree for the higher esteem Hugo's theatre enjoyed in the 1970s.

Important work by other researchers on Hugo's sources and influence has continued throughout this period. Laplane (207) described the general nature of Hugo's *españolismo*, while Piétri (260) found faults in Hugo's knowledge of the language, geography, and history of Spain. Both Lombard

(220) and Lebreton-Savigny (212) discovered that adaptations of Hugo's plays were more popular on the American stage than previously thought. Oliver (244) treated the general question of the *drame romantique*'s relation to opera, while Franceschetti (144) offered the definitive study on Hugo's dramas and the *melodramma italiano*. Hugo's heavy debt to Schiller, among other German authors, was Dédéyan's contribution (125).

Hugo's French sources have not been neglected, nor has French critical reaction. Patterson (254) identified the strong influence of Sébastien Mercier on Hugo's theories as well as on certain scenes, characters, and the style of his dramas. Balzac's unfashionable refusal to regard *Hernani* as a success in 1830 was taken by Etiemble (447) as a measure of Balzac's astute critical judgment. Bach (73) offered the opinion that Sainte-Beuve was bitterly disappointed by the gap between Hugo's theory and his practice. Ripoll (266) presented Zola's warnings to young dramatic actors not to follow Hugo's example in *Marion de Lorme* and *Marie Tudor*. Gély's fine sampling of Hugo's "fortune littéraire" in France (155) encompassed a wider perspective of general trends in Hugo criticism. Two well-known French men of letters, Gide (160) and Claudel (432), recalled their reactions, past and present, to Hugo's theatre.

The year 1952, the 150th year after Hugo's birth, was celebrated officially by a reprise of *Hernani* at the Comédie-Française and by a Hugo exhibition at the Bibliothèque Nationale. The revival seems to have brought about a new battle, described amusingly by Bernard (410) and won once more by enthusiastic youth. Chancérel (108) found that the exhibition revealed to his surprise Hugo's genius as a director and designer of stage sets and costumes. Descotes (130) examined in detail every aspect of the productions of the *drames romantiques* and stressed the role of the actors and actresses in their creation. Triaire (312) discussed Hugo's original mises-en-scene. Ihrig (191) selected doña Sol as the perfect heroine of French Romantic drama, while Ridge (512) included Hernani and Ruy Blas in his discussion of the French Romantic hero. An interesting "psychocritique" of Hugo's characters by Mauron (229) formed one of the introductory essays in the Massin edition of the *Oeuvres complètes*.

In the late 1960s and early 1970s, it became fashionable to examine Hugo's political development and the ideology in his works. An illustration of this critical point of view was furnished by much of Ubersfeld-Maille's work along this line—for example, her discussion (315) of Hugo's theatre for the Abraham and Desné new literary history—and by Halbswachs's article on the battle of Hernani (470). Dereeper (129) focused on the democratic idea in Hugo's plays, while John (194) looked at violence and identity. Ward (776) saw Hugo's use of the Middle Ages as a metaphor for his political ideals and found this especially true in *Les Burgraves*.

Other thematic studies on the plays included Oyerbide's treatment of religion (246), Cryer's dissertation on the trap, mask, death, and liberty (122), and Van Eerde's article on death (318). Another recent finding is that Hugo's theatre seems, at least in theory, to lend itself particularly well to the cinematic art. Fernández-Cuenca (141) listed the fifty films made of Hugo's works through 1953, including four versions of *Marie Tudor*, three of *Le Roi s'amuse* and, of course, Jean Cocteau's creative 1948 film of *Ruy Blas* (657). Chiaromonte (114) wrote a general discussion of the plays' ready adaptability to film, and Lemaître et al. (213) tried to show film possibilities for the important *Cromwell*. In addition, several television productions (381, 394, 798) have been made of Hugo plays with some success.

It is obvious from these numerous studies, from widely varying comments, and from recent revivals, that Hugo's theatre is very much alive, and it continues to attract critical interest. Yet there is still much work to be done. It would be helpful to have critical editions of the plays that presently lack such apparatus (*Hernani* in particular). The great amount of research and commentary today on the period of Hugo's exile, his fantasy, mythological creation, metaphysical writings, and delvings into the supernatural should bring attention to and a thorough study of the neglected *Théâtre en liberté* and other plays from the exile years. Hugo's lifelong devotion to the theatre from his earliest writings to his last creations is also deserving of a careful analysis. A comprehensive examination of recent reprises, premieres and adaptations could possibly furnish new views on Hugo's dramaturgy and concept of a "théâtre uni et populaire." Another interesting subject of investigation would be the influence of Hugo on those dramatists mentioned by various critics such as Kirton (199) as Hugo's direct descendants —Sardou, Rostand, Artaud, Salacrou, Montherlant, Brecht, Ionesco, and Beckett. Surely the rich, varied dramatic efforts of the genius that was Hugo merit continuing consideration.

# Critical Trends of Individual Plays

## Juvenilia

**H**ugo's dramatic attempts in his youth have attracted relatively little attention. Jean Montargis (336) published Hugo's first play, *Le Château du diable* (1812), in 1939. This text was given by Hugo to Juliette Drouet in 1834 with that of another 1812 playlet, *L'Enfer sur terre*, a comedy first published by Koch (335) in 1959. Billy (332) wondered if the devoted mistress perhaps corrected Hugo's youthful spelling and errors in grammar in copying the manuscript and if we have, indeed, the original version. Fargher (333) suggested a source for *Le Château du diable* in Loaisel de Tréogate's 1793 melodrama of the same name.

Gustave Simon published *Irtamène* (1816) first in his 1904 study on Hugo's youth (338). His analysis of it and of Hugo's next play chronologically, *Athélie, ou les Scandinaves* (1817), stressed the Racinian and Voltairian qualities apparent in these more regular tragedies.

Simon also briefly examined A.Q.C.H.E.B., Hugo's 1818 *opéra-comique*, approved by the actors at the Théâtre Feydeau but never performed. *Inez de Castro*, a perfect melodrama with musical interludes and all the standard trappings, was accepted for performance at the Panorama-Dramatique in 1822, but was banned subsequently by the official censor. Simon discussed this last play only superficially, but he did an excellent job in analyzing *Pierre Corneille*, which he published for the first time in 1909 (339). This unfinished verse drama of 1825 is shown to represent Hugo's intended identification of himself with the young seventeenth-century dramatist at the troublesome time of the quarrel over *Le Cid*. Its importance in the genesis of *Marion de Lorme* was also indicated.

In his study of Hugo's youth, Benoît-Lévy (331) examined most of these early plays in a general manner and pointed out their neoclassical framework already combined with a tendency toward freedom. Nozick (337) saw Houdart de la Motte's *Inès de Castro* (1823) as a strong influence on Hugo's play of the same name, and saw Hugo's version as an "apprenticeship" for *Hernani*.

Further study of these early products of Hugo's dramatic inspiration would be profitable in tracing the dual currents of melodrama and neoclassical drama in Hugo's developing techniques of composition and dramaturgy. Another interesting area to investigate would be Hugo's struggle, as early as 1818, to have his plays performed and the obstacles he met, especially the official censor, with whom he clashed over *Inez de Castro*, *Marion de Lorme*, and *Le Roi s'amuse*.

## *Amy Robsart* (1822, 1828)

This prose melodrama has received more critical examination than its literary merit warrants. Yet it has provided an interesting problem in literary history and an example of the need for sufficient, accurate information in determining authorship.

Allais (341) in 1902 compared the purported 1822 and 1828 versions of the play published by Paul Meurice and concluded that Hugo was not the author of the 1828 one-night failure at the Odéon. Allais attributed it to Paul Foucher, Hugo's brother-in-law, whose name was circulated publicly as the play's author. Allais minimized the fact that Hugo claimed authorship himself in a press article the day after the disastrous premiere. Allais did provide, however, a good summary of Hugo's collaboration with Soumet in 1822 on the play drawn from Scott's *Kenilworth*.

In 1903 Pavie (345) tried to shed some light on the problem of authorship by publishing a previously unpublished letter written to his grandfather, Victor Pavie, by Paul Foucher; in this letter the latter took full credit for *Amy Robsart*. It was not until 1928 that Curzon (343) located in the Theatrical Censor's collection in the National Archives the missing manuscript used for the play's unique performance. The handwriting was that of Hugo alone; so Curzon ended speculation and, further, compared the 1828 version with that of 1822 and with Soumet's *Emilia* on the same subject to show the genesis and qualities of Hugo's mature version.

Besides the question of authorship, the play's complete failure on the stage has attracted comment. Emile Faguet (344) in 1907 found it a rather good "petit mélodrame" but chided Hugo for sacrificing character to "pur guignol" ("pure Punch and Judy"). In a very good 1931 study synthesizing all previous work, Ascoli (342) characterized the play as a deliberate experiment by Hugo to see how much "grotesque" the Parisian audience would accept in a play. In 1933 appeared the Imprimerie Nationale edition of *Amy Robsart*, along with *Torquemada* and *Les Jumeaux*. Henriot (181) took this occasion to discuss the genesis of and his personal evaluation of these plays. He found *Amy Robsart* among Hugo's lesser plays. In the same year appeared an English translation of the play (1), in the preface to which basic background information was given along with a comparison of the historical Amy with Hugo's heroine. After this year the play seems to have inspired no further special critical interest beyond general information on its place in literary history and in Hugo's works. No one has yet explained satisfactorily why Hugo had the play performed under Foucher's name.

### Cromwell (1827)

One of the major questions investigated in criticism on *Cromwell* has been whether or not the 7,500-verse drama is actually performable. Two attempts, in 1902 and 1927, to celebrate respectively the centenaries of Hugo's birth and of Romanticism, had to be scrapped in favor of mounting *Les Burgraves*. On July 4, 1956, director Alain Trutal finally managed to have his adaptation performed in the cour carrée of the Louvre. In an interview with Yves Benot (349), he explained that he wanted to emphasize the "cape and dagger" effects of the play. Generally mixed reviews followed the premiere, as critics like Triolet (371) found the setting too distracting. The problem of adapting the play successfully to the stage, then, has not yet been resolved.

Early criticism of *Cromwell* focused on sources, genesis, and unpublished material. In 1911-1912, Léon Séché (365, 366) published letters from Sainte-Beuve to Hugo before the play's completion in which the critic astutely urged the poet to tone down the grotesque and excesses in the play. In 1914 Ruinat (364) rejected the anecdote that Hugo wrote the play for the great tragedian Talma and deliberately exaggerated the Romantic qualities of the play after Talma's death in 1826.

The play's centenary in 1927 encouraged several fine investigations of *Cromwell*'s sources and influences. Sée (367), Tournier (370), and later Fecarotta (356) found the play historically inaccurate, especially in the depiction of Cromwell himself. They also agreed that Hugo did not consult the large number of sources he claimed to have studied. The centenary also encouraged Qualia (360) to show the influence of Hugo's play on the English dramatist Bulwer-Lytton in his *Richelieu*. In the same year, Roth (361) discussed the first stage adaptation made of the play, an 1859 English version that enjoyed relative success. Two years later, Baldensperger (347) identified *Cromwell* and its year of composition as the turning point in the ultimate liberation of dramatic language and form in France. In 1937, Jules Marsan (359) saw *Cromwell* as a transitional work uniting Stendhalian chronicle with lyrical melodrama.

*Cromwell* seems not to have generated much interest again until the general revival of Hugo studies beginning around 1950. The 1956 premiere is one indication of the revival. Another is the suggestion by Courville (351) and Beck (348) of an additional source or forerunner of both the preface and the play in Graziani's 1671 *Cromuele*. The year 1967 produced an excellent study by Descotes (353) on Hugo's obsession with Napoleon in the play, Seebacher's fine analysis of the character Milton in *Cromwell* (368), and Duchet's perceptive introduction to the play in the Massin chronological edition of the *Oeuvres complètes* (355). All three articles stress political ideas and themes dominating *Cromwell* that recur in later works. Lemaître et al. (213) explored *Cromwell* as the best example in Hugo's theatre of his use of "l'espace cinématographique."

The very fine edition of *Cromwell* by Annie Ubersfeld-Maille (3) is also indicative of renewed critical interest in this play. The *pittoresque biblique*, studied by l'abbé Grillet (357) in 1910, received expanded treatment in Houston's 1974 book on Hugo's works (186). Another aspect of the play being explored now is the grotesque. Ubersfeld-Maille's 1971 article (372) is perhaps the most comprehensive study of this subject.

*Cromwell* has, until recently, been overshadowed by its preface. The criticism since 1956 on the play itself has rectified this situation somewhat in pointing out the play's central position in Hugo's dramatic efforts.

### Marion de Lorme (1829, 1831)

Criticism has been rather consistently sparse on this play despite its interesting history as Hugo's intended battle-horse for conquering the stage in 1829. Performances of it have been few in this century. The 1907 reprise after twenty years drew largely favorable reviews. Critics were more divided over the quality of Jean Kerchbron's 1967 television production of the play. Brincourt (381) found Romanticism deadly on "le petit écran," while Saurel (394) approved this "grand 'western' de l'injustice et de l'amour."

Sources, historical inaccuracies, and unpublished materials were the subjects of several early articles on *Marion de Lorme*. The 1907 reprise inspired Batiffol (378) to examine Hugo's historical characters, and he concluded that Hugo erred considerably in his portrayals, especially of Louis XIII and Richelieu. The same year Simon (397) published several interesting unpublished documents concerning the play and including Soumet's complimentary letter to Hugo and what Hugo cut out of act IV to try to get the play by the censor. Also in honor of the reprise, Séché and Bertaut (395) treated the events leading up to the play's 1829 ban, its premiere at the Porte-Saint-Martin in 1831, and the changes in title and ending. The centenary of the play's composition produced an article by Aegerter (375) on the literary history surrounding the play and its premiere. Citoleux (386) offered an extensive comparison of Hugo's play with Vigny's *Cinq-Mars* and concluded that Hugo used elements from the novel in his play. Another possible source was suggested by Nauta (392) from a Sanskrit play, *Le Chariot d'enfant* (A.D. 400), a translation of which is known to have been circulating in 1829. Nineteen thirty-four marked the first and only edition of the play annotated in English (33). In 1947 Braun (380) devoted a large portion of his chapter on the historical courtesan in the French theatre to Marion de Lorme.

Since 1950 criticism has largely centered around influence and literary relations. In 1956 Pommier (393) investigated the similarities between Hugo's play and Balzac's *La Torpille*. In 1967 Cabanis (383) published a letter of 1840 in which the young Baudelaire expressed his great admiration for the established poet and author of *Marion de Lorme*. Cabanis used Baudelaire's changing comments on the play to measure his attitude at various stages towards Hugo. Cellier (384) took this interesting study a step further in examining echoes of the play in various works of Baudelaire.

*Marion de Lorme* has apparently suffered more from neglect on the part of directors and researchers than from negative comments. In his fine 1975 study of French Romantic drama, Howarth (187) called for a new production of the play, which he judged superior to *Hernani* and *Ruy Blas* because it embodies the lyrical essence of Romantic drama. A critical edition complete with variants would also be most useful.

### Hernani (1830)

*Hernani* is by far Hugo's most popular play in number of theatrical productions, editions, translations, and critical comments. According to Collins (24), *Hernani* was performed at the Comédie-Française during every theatrical season from 1884 to 1914. The performances of 1930 to mark *Hernani*'s centenary and those of 1952 to celebrate Hugo's 150th anniversary were the outstanding reprises of *Hernani* in this century.

Generally favorable comments on revivals of the play were voiced by Larroumet (482) in 1900, Bauër (409) in 1922, and Berton (412) in 1927. The special 1930 centenary production featured a fond personal tribute to *Hernani* by Gregh (466); yet the majority of reviewers, like Brisson (421) and Giraudoux (461), were dissatisfied with the ceremony and disappointed in the play.

A generation more in tune with the panache of *Hernani* seems to have been produced in 1952, as reviews like those of Bernard (410), Gandrey-Rety (458), and Plinval (506) expressed the feeling that the play's youth and enthusiasm had won a new political and literary battle. Gandon (457), however, dissented, calling Henri Rollan's production a failure.

*Hernani*'s revival by the Comédie-Française at the Théâtre Marigny in the fall of 1974 was again fairly well received. Galey (456) agreed that *Hernani* is "un monument d'enflure et de ridicule grandiloquent" ("a monument of turgidity and grandiloquent ridiculousness"), yet he and the audience still found something "irrésistible" in the play where "on bascule dans la démesure d'un mauvais goût . . . proche de génie" ("one swings in the immoderation of bad taste . . . close to genius"). Much the same tone of admiration mixed with exasperation characterized the anonymous review (471), which praised especially Robert Hossein's directing, scenery, and use of music. A special issue of *Comédie-Française* contained informative articles by Mme. Chevalley, the bibliothécaire-archiviste at the Comédie-Française (112, 113), Maillard (491), and Ubersfeld-Maille (541). Also in 1974, *Hernani* was presented for the first time in 103 years in New York City. According to Thompson (536), Takazauckas's modernistic off-off Broadway production was outstanding. These successful revivals amply demonstrated that *Hernani* still could muster appreciative support and thrill audiences.

Critics have discussed the famous battle and premiere more than any other aspect of the play. The articles of Brisson (420), Régnier (511), and Palache (502) preceded the plethora of articles published in 1930 for the centenary. Alméras (401) briefly reviewed the parodies that immediately followed the premiere. The "enemy" camp of the *perruques* (old fogies) was amusingly examined by Bertaut (411) and Passillé (504). Perhaps the best articles seeking to reinterpret the battle, especially from the political viewpoint, were those by Jasinski (476) and Souriau (528). The effects of the battle of *Hernani* in various provinces were explored in 1927 by an anonymous author (510) on the 1834 premiere in Lons-le-Saunier, by Spinelli (529) on Marseille's reaction, by Thomas (535) on Montpellier in 1830, and by Fourcassié (143) on Toulouse in the Romantic epoch.

The events leading up to the premiere continued to be recounted fondly by Achard (398) in 1940 and by the outstanding theatre critic Kemp (478) in 1952. The real contributions of *Hernani* in theatre history, however, were reexamined beginning in the 1950s. Revel (263) claimed that the "vittoria romantica" marked by *Hernani* was the hollow triumph of the melodrama and not the true victory of a new aesthetic. In stressing the battle as one of ideological conflict, Halbswachs (470) saw Hugo's liberalism, as represented by *Hernani*, attacked by political and literary conservatives; yet he, too, thought Hugo defended an already outdated aesthetic program. The revisionist criticism continued with Yarrow's 1969 article (549), in which 1829 became the year of real Romantic victory with *Henri III et sa cour, Marino Faliero*, and *Le More de Venise*. Bassan (79) agreed that Dumas père really accomplished the triumph of the *drame romantique* in 1829 with *Henri III et sa cour*.

The centenary also saw a special issue of the theatrical periodical *Bravo* containing intriguing articles by Allan (400), Bauër (408), Kemp (479), and Pannetier (503). Marsan (493) reminded the reader that Romanticism was the great literary fact of the nineteenth century and that *Hernani* was its greatest dramatic accomplishment. Praviel (509) agreed that *Hernani* was the outstanding symbol of the *zeitgeist* of 1830, yet he called the play a melodramatic museum piece. After a vivid re-creation of the premiere, Van Tieghem (542) evaluated Hugo's contribution in *Hernani* as one of great poetry. Geneva, too, put on a special centenary performance, complete with reenactment of the battle. It was greeted with much enthusiasm by Roger (513), quite in contrast to the cold reception for the original premiere in Geneva (514). Lote's book (488), *En préface à Hernani: Cent ans après*, was a fine summation of all the literary history surrounding *Hernani*, but it was disappointing in its rather limited, condescending view of the play as simply a melodrama with two denouements whose only superior quality is its lyric poetry.

There has been a steady flow of suggested sources for *Hernani* from Duval's 1904 depiction of the play as a *"Cinna* romantique" (444) to McLean's 1962 complaint that Hugo's historical inaccuracies totally distorted his purported Spanish sources (489). Other fascinating influences identified in *Hernani* include Alfieri's *Filippo* (423), Shiel's *Eviradne* (517), Balzac's *Argow le pirate* (497), the Bible (481), Goethe's *Egmont* (472), Alarcón, Calderón, and Schiller (462), Racine's *Les Plaideurs* (436), Casimir Delavigne's *Le Paria* (450), Pousset de Montauban's *Les Aventures et le mariage de Panurge* (534), Victor Cousin's *Cours de philosophie* (448), Shakespeare (405, 424), perhaps Anthony and Léopold's *Le Corregidor* (546) and, of course, Hugo himself (446, 449, 463, 469, 544).

Hernani's qualities as a rogue-hero and *homme fatal* were examined by Frick (453, 454) and by Bruner (422), who also offered his thoughts on doña Sol, don Carlos, and Ruy Gomez. Rousseaux (268) found Hernani's panache and moral grandeur still appealing to the young in 1952. Tronquart (539) argued that the metaphor "lion superbe et généreux" was perfectly suited to Hernani's character. Don Carlos recently has come under scrutiny by Bertrand (413) and Clark (431), both of whom find him true to life historically and psychologically.

Various previously unpublished materials, published from 1902 through 1952, have thrown light upon different aspects of *Hernani*. Salomon (518), Pavie (505), and Séché (346, 525) published letters from Hugo and his contemporaries describing the exciting events of 1830. Levaillant (484) proved by printing box-office receipts that *Hernani* was, indeed, a moderate financial success. Guillot de Saix (468), Delorme (437), and Levaillant

(485) discussed the play's manuscript and first edition with an eye to variants. Hugo's contract for publishing *Hernani* indicated to Stock (530) that the poet was also a good businessman. The letters published by Schaffer (521) and Guillemin (467) had to do with the brilliant 1867 reprise of *Hernani* and Hugo's relationship with Soumet in 1830. That *Hernani* was particularly subject to parody has been well established. The parodies of it continued with Bastia (406) in 1927 and Oudon (500) in 1931.

Allevy's 1938 study on the mise-en-scene in France (67) pointed up the technical innovations that Hugo introduced with *Hernani*. This neglected aspect of Hugo's accomplishments has only recently been thoroughly researched by Carlson (102, 426) and Chahine (107).

Some attention has been given to the themes and structure of *Hernani*, although there is still much to be investigated. Schinz (522) viewed *Hernani* as the first expression of Hugo's political ideas and his vision of a "United States of Europe." Hernani's love is examined by Falk (452) and by Baguley (404). Maillet (490) identified the play's structure as based on a "moule classique" ("classical mold"), upon which Hugo piled up word after word.

A few attempts have been made to sample critical opinion on *Hernani* and to investigate the play's success. In 1930 there appeared two brief articles on this subject by Alguazils (399) and Bauër (408). Schneider's comprehensive examination (523) was complete up to 1930, and he concluded that *Hernani*'s lyrical youthfulness and beautiful poetry are its most appreciated qualities. An explanation is offered by Charlier (428, 429) for the negative 1830 article in *Le Figaro* on *Hernani*. Koçiecka (480) investigated *Hernani*'s fortune in Poland. Three other articles treated *Hernani*'s effect on well-known foreign authors. Stremoukhoff (532) described Turgenev's preference for its parodies to *Hernani* itself. Pollin (507) suggested the influence of *Zanthe*, an English adaptation of *Hernani*, on Poe's "Masque of the Red Death." Bertrand de Muñoz (414) offered a comparative study of *Hernani* and Martínez de la Rosa's *La Conjuración de Venecia* and Garciá Gutiérrez's *El Trovador*.

Verdi's opera *Ernani*, based on Hugo's play, has had a successful life of its own. Gara (459) described the leading ladies involved in the premieres of both productions. Two fine recent articles by Stocker (531) and Stringham (533) compared the two lyrical masterpieces and signaled changes Verdi made in adapting Hugo's drama.

*Hernani* has been through an amazing number of annotated editions, for the most part scholastic texts. The 1927 "reconstitution intégrale, minutieuse et fidèle du manuscrit" ("integral, thorough, and faithful reconstruction of the manuscript") by Daniel Jacomet (10) and Maurice Levaillant's "édition classique" (13) are very informative, but neither fills the role of a complete critical edition of the play. Other commented editions in France came out in 1930, (5), 1941 (16), 1950 (19), 1963 (22), 1964 (23), and 1969 (25). This last edition, put out in the Livre de Poche series, contains *Ruy Blas* also and is a handy volume for the general reader.

Even abroad, *Hernani* has enjoyed considerable success in print. The relatively large number of British and American commented editions testifies to the play's perceived importance in French literary history. Of all these editions with commentary in English—1900 (45), 1902 (6), 1906 (7, 8), 1910 (9), 1929 (11, 12), 1936 (14), and 1968 (24)—Collins's (24) is perhaps the best. There also appeared a Belgian edition in 1941 (15), a Swiss edition in 1945 (17), a Dutch edition in 1946 (18), and an Italian edition in 1961 (21).

Schneider (523) concluded that only a French-speaking audience could truly appreciate *Hernani*. It would appear that the inevitable loss of lyrical beauty and vitality through translation explains the dearth of translations and performances of *Hernani* outside of France in the twentieth century. Galdemar (455) discussed a performance of *Hernani* in the Spanish city which furnished the play's title. Avrett (403) offered Ochoa's translation into Spanish as a study of different "racial psychologies." Engel (445) treated one of the more popular early English adaptations of *Hernani*, that of Kenney. In 1924 (26) and again in 1964 (64) new editions appeared of Slous and Crosland's weak 1887 blank-verse translation into English. Linda Asher's 1963 version (29) is not much better. A Polish translation of 1953 (27) and a German verse translation of 1968 (30) are both preceded by long introductions, and it is presumed that they are designed for reading rather than performance.

*Hernani*, then, would seem still to be a national classic in France. Since this *drame romantique par excellence* appears tied to the language and taste of francophones, it is perhaps destined to be, unfortunately, only a date and name in literary history for much of the rest of the world.

### *Le Roi s'amuse* (1832)

The strange history of this play, banned by the censor immediately after its premiere, was adequately recounted by Du Bos (559) and Bertaut (553) in their articles for the play's centenary in 1932. Du Bos characterized the play as a "médiocre mélodrame," and the relatively unsuccessful reprises in 1882, 1909, and 1911 support the contention that the play best survives in Verdi's *Rigoletto*.

The 1911 reprise caused Péladan (565) to complain about the play's historical inaccuracies. Much later, Du Bos (560) identified one of Hugo's sources for the play in Paul Lacroix's novel, *Les Deux Fous*, and attributed to it some of Hugo's historical errors. Richer (566) proved through letters from Hugo to Lacroix that Hugo had read the novel. In 1964 Lambert's very fine, painstaking study of the manuscript variations of the play appeared, with a thorough introductory essay on sources and genesis (563).

Guichard supplemented known sources for the play with his article of 1965 (562), in which he also discussed details of rehearsals and the failure. Two peripheral but interesting areas explored by critics are Verdi's adaptation and Hugo's lawsuit to try to have his play performed after the ban. Trompeo (568) traced François I's famous "souvent femme varie" song from its origin in Vergil through Verdi's version. Abram (550) presented a lucid comparison of the play and the opera. Hugo's loss in the lawsuit was adequately treated first by Girault (162), then by Alméras (551), who concentrated on Hugo's lawyer Barrot, and by Cadroy (556), who published transcripts from the trial to highlight the events.

Recent criticism has tended to focus on the interior structure of the play, its meaning, or its influence. Vandegans's 1969 article (716) isolated certain themes in the play that seem to have influenced the playwright Ghelderode, especially in *Escurial*. Tyler offered a sociological interpretation of the play (569) and linked it with works of Shakespeare and Calderón. Ubersfeld-Maille (570) treated *Le Roi s'amuse* and *Lucrèce Borgia* together as separate creations sharing the same basic inspiration and pointed out the two plays as simultaneous attempts by Hugo to create his own unified public.

There is as yet no complete critical edition of *Le Roi s'amuse*. The edition of the Imprimerie Nationale, when taken with Lambert's edition of manuscript variants (563), serves the function but is awkward to use. Helen Gaubert's 1964 edition of the old nineteenth-century translation (64) does not, unfortunately, add much to appreciation of the play for speakers of English.

## Lucrèce Borgia (1833)

Although this play was Hugo's greatest success on stage, it has shared the same fate of neglect as his other prose plays. The few major revivals during this century have elicited more negative than positive reactions from reviewers. The 1918 reprise at the Théâtre-Français induced Poizat (588) to criticize the play's tone, style, and historical inaccuracies. Martin du Gard (581) found the 1935 revival at the Comédie-Française laughable. The Odéon's revival in 1948 was greeted by more favorable reviews from Parrot (584) and Roux (590). Julien Green (579), however, characterized *Lucrèce Borgia* as "ce texte aujourd'hui impossible" ("this text that is impossible today"). Raymond Rouleau's production of 1964 caused mixed reactions. Silvia Monfort's 1976 production at the Avignon Festival and later at le Nouveau Carré occasioned an issue of *L'Avant-Scène* (572).

The play's centenary in 1933 produced two fine articles giving complete details in the composition and production of the play by Augustin-Thierry (571) and Du Bos (575); the latter found the play "d'un attrait singulièrement fascinateur" ("of a singularly fascinating appeal").

It is in this play especially that Hugo has been criticized for being untrue to life. Bruner (98) examined the play's characters and found Lucrèce a "dramatic impossibility," psychologically false. Funck-Brentano (577), furthermore, said that Hugo's version of the legendary Borgia lacked all authenticity when compared to contemporary descriptions of her in historical sources. Historical accounts, however, argued Crump (620), furnished Hugo only with local color, and literary sources supplied him with prototypes for every important scene in this play and in *Angelo*. Cheek (111) agreed that Hugo's prose plays were not accurate in historical fact.

Hugo's prose style was the subject of two intriguing studies. Le duc de la Force (580) found in *Lucrèce Borgia* forty-nine perfect alexandrines and concluded that Hugo composed in verse form naturally. Brun's work on the prose styles of Hugo and Musset (97) evaluated Musset as the real innovator in prose style for the stage. He found Hugo's prose too much oriented toward rhetoric and effects.

The recent work by Ubersfeld-Maille (570) has been mentioned in connection with *Le Roi s'amuse*. Ubersfeld-Maille also has published an article (594) on the grotesque in Gubetta's song in the play's original version as the embodiment of Hugo's revolutionary ideology, destined to rejection for its threatening iconoclasm.

No critical edition of *Lucrèce Borgia* has appeared. Büchner's nineteenth-century German translation is examined by Furness (578) and Bell (573). Miard (582) described the play's premieres in Spain and in Portugal. From the relative lack of critical interest, it may be assumed that *Lucrèce Borgia* may well be remembered most as the occasion for Hugo's meeting Juliette Drouet.

### Marie Tudor (1833)

Not very popular even in Hugo's lifetime, this prose drama has remained in critical and theatrical oblivion despite a valiant effort by Jean Vilar in 1955 to revive it. Earlier reprises drew the criticism, repeated often since then, that *Marie Tudor* exemplifies an aesthetic firmly rooted in the taste of a bygone era. Brisson (600) first voiced this thought after seeing the 1916 production at the Odéon. The 1938 revival at the Arènes de Lutèce received similar criticisms. Vilar's production with Maria Casarès in the title role at the Festival d'Avignon, in Paris, and in New York was more favorably welcomed by Beigbeder (596), Descotes (602), and Bracker (599). Descotes pointed out, however, that Vilar had to change the play so much for modern audiences that even Hugo would not have recognized it. Duvignaud (606) called the play "inutile" ("useless") and said movies fill this need of the masses for melodrama much better.

The centenary of *Marie Tudor* in 1933 drew little comment. Du Bos (605) printed a letter from Sainte-Beuve to Victor Pavie after the premiere in which he told that Juliette Drouet was so poor in her role as Jane that she lost the part to Ida Ferrier. The entire process of composition and production was fully recounted by Schneider (613). He judged the play inferior to other Hugo dramas only because it was in prose, and he qualified as minor masterpieces the Jew's song and that of Fabiani.

The picture of England in *Marie Tudor* and sources of the play have been examined more than any other apsects. Hill (611) found the portrait of Mary Tudor completely distorted. Dringenberg (603) agreed that England and the English are portrayed rather unrealistically in the drama. *Favras*, an 1831 play by Merville and Sauvage, as well as Dumas père's *Christine*, were identified by Fitch (609) as important literary sources for the play. The most comprehensive investigation of Hugo's claimed historical sources is that of Blanchard (597), who acquitted Hugo of the accusation of plagiarism but agreed that he padded his list of consulted sources and used the few he did study only for local color and not for historical fact.

One separate edition of *Marie Tudor* with critical apparatus was published in 1961. The French text is preceded by a solid introduction by Palmer (32), who presents the play's history through colorful anecdotes and offers good sections on its sources and themes. Büchner's translation is discussed by Furness (578) and Bell (573).

### Angelo, tyran de Padoue (1835)

Hugo has been accused of having written plays solely as vehicles for his main actors and actresses. Nowhere is that possibility more visible than in *Angelo, tyran de Padoue*. The great acting duel between Mlle. Mars and Marie Dorval apparently was the reason for the play's initial success, according to Lyonnet (222) and Descotes (130). The 1850 reprise featured Rachel in her debut in a role from a *drame romantique*. It is quite fitting, then, that the significant event in *Angelo*'s fate in the twentieth century was Sarah Bernhardt's revival of the play in her own theatre in 1905 with herself in the role of the actress La Tisbé.

All critics reviewing this revival had only praise for the divine Sarah, but the play did not fare so well. Doumic (622), Faguet (623), and Hérold (624) excoriated this ridiculous "mélo à la Pixérécourt." The eminent Faguet offered the most intelligent and perceptive article on the place of *Angelo* in Hugo's dramatic career and in the literature of a newly industrialized society. Another apsect of the production commented upon is Bernhardt's reinsertion of the Homodei death scene on stage. Sardou (629) believed it should have been left out because Hugo himself took it out for the 1835 premiere.

In 1909 Pavie (505) offered an interesting glimpse, through unpublished letters of 1835 contemporaries, of the competition between *Angelo* and Vigny's *Chatterton*. Patin (627) came across additional unpublished letters in an original edition of the play, the most interesting of which are from Marie Dorval to Hugo about her role.

The centenary produced only two articles. Ambrière (616) preferred to recount the acting battle rather than analyze "le pire drame de Victor Hugo" ("the worst drama of Victor Hugo"). In answer to Ambrière's question about Auguste Jouhaud, P. V. S. (628) furnished details about this author of one of the many parodies of *Angelo*.

No study has been undertaken uniquely on the sources of this play. A few previously mentioned works do treat the matter in summary fashion. Crump (620) outlined the literary sources Hugo probably used. Cheek (111) showed that historical inaccuracies abound in the play. The prose style of the play was considered by Brun (97). Borer's 1978 article (618) analyzed the play's structure, based on "figures géométriques." No single annotated edition or translation seems to have been published in this century.

## La Esmeralda (1836)

In the 1830s Hugo was asked several times by composers to join with them in making an opera of his *Notre-Dame de Paris*. It was only for his daughter's friend, Louise Bertin, that Hugo agreed to write a libretto. The opera, *La Esmeralda*, was a failure when performed in 1836.

The centenary year 1936 produced a general article by Croze (631) on *La Esmeralda*'s history and a longer study by Tiersot (633). Tiersot concluded that Hugo was at least partially to blame for the opera's weaknesses.

Yet other operas have been drawn from Hugo's libretto, as indicated in 1937 by J. G. P. (632), who published a previously unpublished letter from Hugo to Paul de Saint-Victor, thanking him for his kind words about *Notre-Dame de Paris* in a review article on Lebeau's *La Esmeralda*, an operatic adaptation from Hugo's libretto.

It is ironic that Hugo did such a poor job in actually composing for an opera when a commonplace in criticism of Hugo's theatre is that it belongs more to and succeeds better in the realm of opera than in that of drama.

## Ruy Blas (1838)

Second only to *Hernani* in critical popularity as measured by the number of revivals, editions, studies, and critical comments, *Ruy Blas* has been most appreciated for its lyrical beauty and excellent comic figure, don César de Bazan. The most important revivals of *Ruy Blas* in this century were the 1938 centenary performances at the Comédie-Française, Jean

Vilar's production in 1954 at the Théâtre National Populaire, and the 1960 revival staged by Raymond Rouleau. Like *Hernani*, *Ruy Blas* still seems to attract directors for revivals. The 1974 reprise by José Valverde at the Théâtre Gérard Philipe was gratefully welcomed by the primarily youthful audience and by Gamarra (667), who proclaimed the production proof that Romanticism is not dead.

Critics have offered mixed opinions in their reviews of these and other productions of *Ruy Blas*. The 809th performance of the play in 1960 inspired Mme. Chevalley to edit a monograph (654) as a tribute to the play's enduring popularity. She wrote three articles on famous actors who have played in *Ruy Blas* (652), on ten parodies of the play from 1838 to 1904 (653), and on the play's fortune at France's foremost national theatre (655). Also included was an intelligent analysis of the play by Hugo scholar Barrère (637), who considered *Ruy Blas* Hugo's most human, least rhetorical, and therefore most successful play. Bauër (640) repeated his favorable article for the 1938 centenary reprise and said that his views had not changed over the years. In the same volume Maurois (693) described events involving Juliette Drouet's role in the play.

Jean Cocteau's 1948 film adaptation of *Ruy Blas* (656, 657) was, indeed, a new creation rather than a faithful version of Hugo's original. Charensol (651) pointed out this transformation and indicated that the project, though a failure, was still "un beau, un magnifique spectacle."

In addition, *Ruy Blas* has enjoyed quite a few intriguing productions abroad this century. In 1933 Brian Hooker's adaptation was first performed in Pittsfield, Massachusetts, with Walter Hampden in the title role. Apparently the production was well received (704), as was Robert Edmond Jones's 1938 production of the same adaptation in Central City, Colorado (668). In 1957 Andrew Szekely staged J. D. Cooper's adaptation at the Royal Playhouse, but Brooks Atkinson judged the result harshly (634). In May of 1979, the Comédie-Française performed *Ruy Blas* to celebrate the Romantic Epoch Festival at the Kennedy Center in Washington, D.C. Saal (705) found the performance appropriate and energetic, while Lardner (681) described it as "vivid" but difficult for non-francophones dependent upon portable radios and earphones for a simultaneous translation.

Besides comments on the centennial reprise, 1938 produced two articles evaluating *Ruy Blas* as Hugo's best play. Henriot (670) offered details of literary history surrounding the play and examined a purported source, Latouche's *La Reine d'Espagne*, only to conclude that Hugo's "merveille de théâtre" did not owe much to its predecessor. Le duc de la Force (678) suggested the influence of Hugo's play on Coppée's *Severo Torelli* and Paul Meurice's *Struensée*.

The date of Paul Souchon's interesting compilation (713) of Juliette Drouet's unpublished letters to Hugo before, during, and after the composition and first performances of *Ruy Blas* was also 1938. Simon had previously published letters (711) from Anténor Joly to Hugo on the founding of the Théâtre de la Renaissance, where *Ruy Blas* was to be the first production, as well as Hugo's clever contract for the play's initial run. Bart (638) indicated through some unpublished verse that Hugo was not above poking fun at contemporary hostile critics in the play itself.

The most interesting and important area of criticism since 1900 has dealt with the sources and genesis of the play. This intriguing dimension of *Ruy Blas* has drawn speculation from many outstanding scholars. Prototypes from real life have often been suggested. In 1902, Labadie-Lagrave (677) cited Fernando de Valenzuela. Lyonnet (688) referred to the passage in *Victor Hugo raconté* that named Rousseau's *Confessions* as the major inspiration, then suggested Struensée, Catherine of Sweden's doctor, as model for Ruy Blas. Escholier (665) would have Ruy Blas's passion for the queen a disguised version of Hugo's own platonic love for Hélène de Mecklembourg, Duchess of Orleans. Manuel Godoy was identified by Dauzat (660) and Charles Lassailly (683) as the "real" Ruy Blas.

The pattern of literary sources suggested over the decades is even more fascinating. Dumesnil (662) and Marion (691) offered Maurice de Pompigny's *Barogo* trilogy as the origin of the play's great comic character, don César de Bazan, and his act (IV). In 1913 Rigal's excellent article appeared (702), a classic on sources and composition, which identified three prime sources —Bulwer-Lytton's *Lady of Lyon*, Gaillardet's *Struensée*, and Mme. d'Aulnoy's *Mémoires de la cour d'Espagne*. Two years later Lanson (680) indicated a French novel, *Angelica Kauffman* of Léon de Wailly, that could replace Bulwer-Lytton's play as a source. Through daughter Adèle's Jersey diary, Lancaster (679) suggested as the original point of departure for the play an imagined scene in which a minister of state at the height of his powers suddenly sees himself ordered about like a lackey by an unknown man. In 1918 Simon (710) published Hugo's own list of twelve works he claimed to have used. Henriot (673) examined how Hugo adapted Mme. d'Aulnoy's *Mémoires* which, Henriot claimed, she had plagiarized from those of the French ambassador to Spain. *La Reine d'Espagne* of Latouche was rejected by Henriot as an important influence on Hugo (672). In reviewing all possible sources for *Ruy Blas*, Ludwig (687) showed how typical the play was of Hugo and of French Romanticism. By comparing variants, Moore (694) determined just when Hugo discovered and used Wailly's novel. Levaillant first offered a survey for the interested reader of all previous scholarship on the question of sources (684), then traced the development of Maglia-don César from 1833 on through his transformation into Ruy Blas's double and beyond (685). In an article that compared similar treatments of the same theme, Showalter (708) hinted that Hugo may have known the Perourou legend or borrowed his basic plot idea from

Diderot's story of Mme. de la Pommeraye in *Jacques le fataliste*. Rejecting the use of sources alone as inadequate, Ubersfeld-Maille (715) preferred to examine two "schémas internes" to clarify the play's genesis and Hugo's process of composition.

Other aspects of *Ruy Blas* have also attracted comment. Character studies of the hero and his nemesis were offered by Bruner (98, 645, 646). In Ley-Deutsch's study (218) on Hugo's beggar, Spanish historical and literary models were sought for Zafari-César.

Humor in the play itself seems to have encouraged humorous reactions to it. Praviel (699) printed Jules de Rességuier's three witty versions of the king's dry letter to his queen in the play, all of which Rességuier sent to Hugo. Cam (648) discussed the many immediate parodies of the play, due, he claimed, to its improbability. Picard (696) quoted Zola's review of the 1879 reprise—then Abraham Dreyfus's amusing rewriting of *Ruy Blas* in Zola's style.

Odd moments in the play's history have not gone unnoticed. In 1913 a plot summary was circulated to the audience with the program, and Bainville (635) wondered what had happened to the intelligence of the general public. In rereading *Ruy Blas*, Régnier was inspired to compose a series of poems on various moments in the play (700, 701). When *Ruy Blas* was put on the "programme scolaire," Vandérem (717) approved this mark of scholastic acceptance. In the 150th year from Hugo's birth, 1952, Bruyelle (647) and Vier (718) explained why they loved this play, the best of Hugo's plays in their opinion.

The 1960s and 1970s saw a number of editions of *Ruy Blas* as well as several articles on it. Warning (720) treated Hugo's theatre, as represented by *Ruy Blas*, as a failure, dead today because of Hugo's poor theory and weak dramaturgy. Falk asserted (452) that, in contrast to Hernani, Ruy Blas recognized in himself the "unconscious and involuntary" effects of love. Florenne's most urbane apology for *Ruy Blas* (666) served well also as the introduction to the 1969 Livre de Poche edition of the play. An *explication de texte* by Maillet (690) of Ruy Blas's confession to Don César of his love for the queen stressed Hugo's "art" and "artifice." Vandegans (716) saw some influence of *Ruy Blas* in Ghelderode's *Escurial*. An appreciation of *Ruy Blas*'s new colloquial style and "noteworthy range of metaphor and imaginative diction" was offered by Houston (674). The grotesque of the play was examined by Lyons (689), and act IV was seen, not as the often criticized "hors-d'oeuvre," but as an integral foreshadowing of the play's denouement.

American, English, and French scholastic editions of *Ruy Blas* abounded from 1900 through the 1960s. The American texts (46, 47, 49) stressed poetic beauty and literary history, as did the English editions (48, 55). There were several French scholastic editions (51, 52, 54, 56, 57). Maurice Levaillant's excellent "édition classique" (50), with variants, sketches, and documents, was superseded only by Ubersfeld-Maille's two-volume definitive critical edition (58). The Livre de Poche volume, including *Hernani* (25), is quite satisfactory for the general reader. Strona's 1970 article (714) discussed principal editions of the play from 1869-1891.

Unfortunately, neither the poetry nor the dramaturgy of *Ruy Blas* seemed to translate well. Crosland's stilted 1887 verse translation was brought out with new introductions in 1901 (60) and again in 1964 (64). In 1931 Hooker offered a better verse translation (61) that was designed for performance, but it, too, lacked excellence. Beerbohm (642) reviewed a 1904 performance of Davidson's early version, *A Queen's Romance*, but complained about the loss he experienced in hearing the play in English. Shipley (527), however, did mention relatively successful performances of *Ruy Blas* in England and America. In 1936 a commented Russian version (62) appeared.

## Les Jumeaux (1839)

Most intriguing about this play is the fact that Hugo interrupted his composition in the third act and never returned to finish the work. Faguet (344) was the first twentieth-century critic to argue that the play deserved to be published. He also saw in it an example of Hugo's puzzling manner of composition. Without an outline Hugo managed here to produce a well-organized work with almost no corrections in the manuscript.

The publication of *Les Jumeaux*, with *Amy Robsart* and *Torquemada* in volume 4 of the Imprimerie Nationale edition of the dramas in 1933, produced most of the little criticism there is on this play. Henriot (181) talked about the play's genesis and approved of Hugo's unfinished attempt to dramatize the popular legend of "le masque de fer" ("the iron mask"). In a second article (723), Henriot sought an explanation for Hugo's leaving the play incomplete. He suggested that it was because Hugo realized that Vigny had already treated the subject fully in "La Prison" (1821), a poem on which Hugo had written an article. Levaillant (725) offered possible endings for *Les Jumeaux* and judged the poetry in the finished portion to be so good that he felt that the play, had it been completed, would have been among Hugo's finest. A year later, Berret (721) offered another suggestion as to why Hugo never finished the play; Berret said Hugo borrowed his plot and characters from an 1831 melodrama of Arnould and Fournier, *L'Homme au masque de fer*. More recently, Kirton (724) argued that Hugo's attitudes and political views were changing and becoming less radical in 1839, and that consequently "he had outgrown the facility of his early dramatic technique" and needed to find a larger framework to hold his new ideas.

In *Le Roi et le bouffon* (317) of 1974, Annie Ubersfeld-Maille devotes an important section to *Les Jumeaux*. Her thorough investigation of all details of the work makes it the best treatment thus far. She isolates themes in *Les Jumeaux* based on Hugo's unfortunate relationship with his mad brother, Eugène, and amply demonstrates the play's position as a transition between *Ruy Blas* and *Les Burgraves*. Her contention that it is essentially an antitragedy is interesting, but much more important is her demonstration of similarities between it and Calderón's *La vida es sueño*. Until a critical edition is established, this analysis and the text of the Imprimerie Nationale edition will have to suffice.

## *Les Burgraves* (1843)

The high points of the disappointing fortune of this play in the twentieth century include two reprises at the Comédie-Française—in 1902 to celebrate the centenary of Hugo's birth and in 1927 to mark the centenary of Romanticism—and the publication in 1962 of a very comprehensive study of the play's manuscripts and sources. In both performances *Les Burgraves* was chosen for revival only after *Cromwell*, the first choice, proved too unwieldy for actual stage performance.

Reviews of the 1902 performance were generally unfavorable. Flat (744) and Lemaire (751) stressed that the play's melodramatic plot betrayed Hugo's epic vision. Larroumet (750) asserted that the 1843 public was right to reject this mass of improbabilities, no better today than at its premiere. Some stalwart defenders like Hérold (747) pointed to the epic grandeur of the play. Jules Claretie, director of the Théâtre-Français in 1902, chose *Les Burgraves* for the special tribute to Hugo, and he offered details of literary history surrounding the play (737). An unusual note was added to the centennial celebration by the grandson of Ponsard (761), who assured us of the long, friendly relationship between Hugo and the author of the triumphant *Lucrèce* (1843).

Aderer was stirred by the 1902 revival to offer three interesting articles on *Les Burgraves*. He first wrote an intriguing account of the play's composition and premiere (727), in which he blames a cabal for the play's failure and offers colorful descriptions of the event from accounts by Gautier, the author of *Victor Hugo raconté*, and Léon Chevrau. Next, Aderer (726) analyzed one of the many parodies that immediately plagued *Les Burgraves*, Duvert and Lauzanne's *Les Barbus graves*. Finally, Aderer (728) printed the prologue that Hugo had cut out from the play before the premiere and judged it to be quite as good as the verses in the final form of the play.

Other revivals of *Les Burgraves* that have encouraged both positive and negative opinions took place in 1913, 1927, and 1935. Antoine Vitez's highly experimental production in 1977-1978 in Paris and London is representative of recent attempts to make Hugo's plays transform an audience into a "peuple" ("community") in accordance with Hugo's goals. Critics praised Vitez for the boldness of his efforts (730, 766, 772, 773) and yet often found the play still unplayable.

Hugo's attempt to create epic drama has received more attention than the passing remarks indicated above. Rigal (763) devoted a chapter to *Les Burgraves* in his book on Hugo as an epic poet. He agrees that the play announces the excellent epic poetry of the later exile period, as in *La Légende des siècles*, but he characterizes as unsuccessful the generic mixture in *Les Burgraves*. According to another critic, Carrère (736), the epic proportions of the play are good, but the drama is bad.

Allied to the question of epic qualities in *Les Burgraves* has been the problem of sources and genesis. Hugo claimed Aeschylus's trilogy as his major inspiration, but most scholars seem to find only a superficial link. Berret (733) stressed Hugo's dependence on Scott's *Ivanhoe*, particulary in the creation of Guanhumara. In a solid article on the Romantic themes in the work, Baldensperger (732) outlined Hugo's Germanic sources, especially for the idea of fatality. In his classic study of the play's sources, Giraud (745) enumerated Schiller, Grillparzer, and Kohlraush, as well as Hugo himself. By concentrating on the figure of Barberousse, Vianey (774) found an excellent presentation of the legendary, if not the historical, figure. Wolff (777) emphasized the identical inspiration for both *Le Rhin* and *Les Burgraves* in Hugo's 1838 trip to the Rhineland. Lemercier's *Clovis* was pointed out by Moreau (757) and Thiessé's *Le Tribunal secret* by Debidour (740) as important influences on the melodramatic plot of Hugo's drama. In his introduction to the play in his chronological edition of the *Oeuvres complètes*, Massin (754) reviewed sources and genesis, concentrating upon Hugo's search in 1843 for a new dramatic aesthetic. In her book on the medievalism of Hugo, Ward (776) singled out the motif of pardon and redemption as the political idea forming the heart of the play.

Unfortunately, the centenary of *Les Burgraves* occurred during World War II, and this most Germanic of Hugo's plays drew little attention at that time. It is of interest that the two 1943 works on *Les Burgraves* tried to link Hugo's conception of art as expressed in the play with that of Wagner. Cru (738) signaled the Germanic inspiration in the play, while Lugli (752) characterized it as "un'opera di pura poesia." Previously, Weil (326) had painstakingly refuted the thesis that Hugo's *Hernani* and *Les Burgraves* influenced Wagner, but the claim still persisted.

No critical edition of *Les Burgraves* is available. Eve (2) brought out a scholastic edition in England that is, however, rather weak in its introductory material. In 1962 Russell's comprehensive study (764) of the play's manuscripts, unpublished material, sources, parodies, and fortune furnished everything for a critical edition except the text itself.

Mention should be made also of Léo Sachs's 1924 musical adaptation of *Les Burgraves*, described by Messager (756). An interesting curiosity of literary relations, furthermore, was revealed by Regard (762) in 1951 when he published two letters by François Buloz about *Les Burgraves*. In the second, Buloz mentioned that Alfred de Musset had found Hugo's play "admirable."

### *Le Théâtre en liberté* (1886) and Other Plays from the Period of Exile—General Criticism

Many people are under the impression that Hugo renounced the theatre entirely after the failure of *Les Burgraves* in 1843. Hugo's armchair theatre of the exile period deserves to be more widely known. It is comprised of *Le Théâtre en liberté (La Forêt mouillée, La Grand-mère, Mangeront-ils?,* and *L'Epée)*, published posthumously in 1886; *Torquemada*, published in 1882; *Mille Francs de récompense*, published in 1934; *L'Intervention*, appearing in 1950; *Le Prologue mystique*, brought out in 1954; and *Les Deux Trouvailles de Gallus (Esca* and *Margarita)*, forming *le livre dramatique* of *Les Quatre Vents de l'esprit* of 1881. A few other dramatized scenes, published in collections of poetry, and many plans, projects, and fragments date from the exile period as well. Several of the plays mentioned above have had a successful history of stage presentation in this century, but extensive critical studies are lacking.

In 1920 Truffier (785) attempted a *critique d'ensemble* that indicated the characteristics of the earlier *drames romantiques* which reappear in the *Théâtre en liberté*. Schwab (784) located a text of the *Théâtre en liberté* with comments in the margin by Pierre Louÿs, who was intrigued by Hugo's theme of "life is a stage" and by his "métamorphoses de l'image." In 1953 Jamati (780) identified in *L'Epée* the same tone and theme as those in *Les Châtiments*, stating that the play rightfully belonged with that volume. Barrère (778) linked parts of the *Théâtre en liberté* with other Hugo creations dating from 1859. It is unfortunate that recent comprehensive studies on Hugo's theatre have left aside the *Théâtre en liberté*. Gaudon (154) offered some interesting observations on *Mille Francs de récompense*, but did not include a systematic analysis of these later plays. The diverse plays of the exile period, then, will furnish important, relatively untouched material to the interested scholar who wishes to examine the continuity of Hugo's dramatic inspiration and conceptions.

### *Le Prologue mystique* (1854)

In 1954 Levaillant first published this strange prose dialogue between two stars in his *Crise mystique de Victor Hugo* (216). It seems to be connected to the unfinished play *Shakespeare*, dictated by the turning table.

## Mille Francs de récompense (1866)

Little has been written about this play, deliberately called a melodrama by Hugo. It has, however, enjoyed some success on the stage. Its premiere was staged by Hubert Gignoux with the Comédie de l'Est at the Théâtre Municipal de Metz in April of 1961. Cézan's article (790) featured an interview with Gignoux and indicated that the play was well received by the public. Because he did not appreciate Gignoux's parody of the traditional melodrama in the play, Dumur (791) preferred to focus upon the extraordinary protagonist, Glapieu. Later in 1961, Christian Cassadesus presented the play at the Théâtre de l'Ambigu. To celebrate the occasion, Marrey (796) and L'Avant-scène offered the play's full text, excellent photos of the production, and a sample of press reviews, almost all of which were quite favorable.

The 1966 reprise, by Marcel Maréchal at the Théâtre des Célestins in Lyon, was also well received. Butheau (789) interviewed Maréchal, who intended to introduce a Brechtian note into his production. A televised production by Gignoux and the Comédie de l'Est in 1967 elicited a favorable review from Saurel (798).

Critical study and analysis of the play has centered, for the most part, upon Glapieu. The first publication of Mille Francs de récompense in the edition of the Imprimerie Nationale in 1934 encouraged Maurice Levaillant to offer to the general public a sample—act I, scene 1 (792)—and a brief presentation of the play's history (795). Levaillant said it was merely Les Misérables adapted to the stage. Later he published a longer article (794), which included more details of composition and inspiration and in which he found that "Glapieu est un Jean Valjean qui se souviendrait d'avoir été Don César" ("Glapieu is a Jean Valjean who remembers having been Don César"). Ley-Deutsch (218) traced this evolution of the character Maglia into Glapieu in a chapter of her book on Hugo's beggar. A two-volume critical edition of the play was done by Jacques Tephany (34) as a doctoral thesis in 1970, but it does not seem to be widely available. There is no study as yet of Hugo's dramaturgy in the play, one of only two he sets in a modern scene, or of the place of Mille Francs within his dramatic works as a whole.

## L'Intervention (1866)

Guillemin (800) published this brief play in 1950. Like Mille Francs de récompense, it is set in a "modern" time. In his commentary, Guillemin signals the "fantaisie" of the play, Hugo's "arrière-pensée politique," and personal demons visible in the drama.

In May of 1978 Ewa Lewinson, Antoine Vitez's assistant, and her drama students chose to stage *L'Intervention* at the Théâtre de la Cité Internationale. This "intelligent" experimental production succeeded in breaking through the text's melodramatic logic, according to Attoun (799).

## *Mangeront-ils?* (1867)

*Mangeront-ils?* had its premiere in Brussels at the Théâtre du Parc in March of 1907; yet not until its Paris premiere in March of 1919 at the Comédie-Française did it seem to attract much interest among the French. Brisson (801) liked the production very much and praised Hugo's knowledge of men and vision for mankind. Vandérem (810), however, found the brilliantly mounted production more dated than *Ruy Blas*, despite the fact that it was enthusiastically received by the audience.

Various revivals of *Mangeront-ils?* have been followed by mixed reviews. In 1952, Christian Tsingos was interviewed by Carlier (802) on his choice of Hugo's play for the Théâtre Gaîté-Montparnasse. Reviewer Kemp (806) explained that he had to leave at intermission because the play was so bad. The 1957 reprise at the Théâtre du Tertre was greeted by praise from Lalou (807). Christ (803) admired the director and troupe that staged the play at the Alliance-Française in 1968, but detested the play itself. Gautier (805) offered a very favorable review of the same production, seeing a hint of Shakespeare in Hugo's effort.

Criticism based on a study of the play, as opposed to reviews of performances, is sparse. In 1965, Riffaterre (808) examined parody and the juxtaposition of philosophy and slapstick in this "comédie symboliste." A fine critical edition was published in 1970 by Journet and Robert (31). It contains variants, notes, and a painstaking introduction on the play's composition and history.

## *Les Deux Trouvailles de Gallus* (1869)

Perhaps Hugo never really intended this play for performance since he inserted it into his volume of poetry, *Les Quatre Vents de l'esprit*, as the *livre dramatique*. Yet its premiere at the Comédie-Française in 1923 was welcomed by many reviewers with favorable articles. Allem (811) and Doumic (814) alluded to some weaknesses and Romantic paraphernalia in the play, but admitted that the splendid verses outshone the flaws. The premiere induced Max and Alex Fischer (815) to look up the fables from La Fontaine and Phaedrus which inspired Hugo—the fables on the cock which, while looking for grain (Esca), found a pearl (Margarita). They found the sources far superior to Hugo's version.

Gustave Simon (818) published, in honor of the premiere, a history of the play's composition and publication, some unpublished material, and a list of those, like Catulle Mendès, who have long wished to see the play mounted. Other than an Italian adaptation discussed by Domenico (813) in 1911, there appears to have been little else done on this intriguing work.

## *Torquemada* (1882)

Hugo has created one of his most memorable characters in the Grand Inquisitor, yet relatively few studies of *Torquemada* have emerged in the twentieth century. In 1933, upon the publication of *Torquemada* in the edition of the Imprimerie Nationale, Henriot (181) offered the opinion that Torquemada "a beaucoup vieilli" ("has aged much"). By focusing on Torquemada as the bad and implying that Hugo saw himself as embodying the good, Cassou (823) concluded that this is the most metaphysical of Hugo's plays, the one he lived all his life.

In 1942 Mécréant (824) investigated all of Hugo's sources for the play and found his details quite well documented, particularly from Llorente's history of the Spanish Inquisition. Furthermore, he suggested that the origin of the play lay in Voltaire. Zumthor (826) linked *Torquemada* with *La Fin de Satan* in Hugo's inspiration. In a recent article, Peyret (825) has tried to show similarities and differences in the techniques and visions of Hugo and Brecht.

### Plans, Projects, Sketches, Fragments

The edition of the Imprimerie Nationale (41) is equipped with a manuscript *reliquat* for most works. It is still useful, but has been criticized for being arbitrary and incomplete. The Pauvert edition (44) of the complete dramatic and critical works augments and improves upon the Imprimerie Nationale edition, upon which it is based. Fragments, plans, projects, and some variants are offered by Purnal, Thierry, and Mélèze (63). However, the most comprehensive edition in this respect is the chronological one of Massin (43), which includes a "portefeuille dramatique" for each major period of Hugo's life. Mme. Ubersfeld-Maille's introduction to the final "portefeuille dramatique" (316) is quite good, especially on the themes and characters that remain constant in Hugo's dramatic vision.

# ANNOTATED
# BIBLIOGRAPHY

# Editions and Translations

1. Hugo, Victor-Marie. <u>Amy Robsart</u>. Translated by Ethel and Evelyn Blair. Boston: Christopher Publishing House, n.d. [c 1933]. Pp. x+141.

> Publisher's note and foreward present basic information on Soumet/ Hugo collaboration, Foucher/Hugo problem and historical Amy. "No claim to dramatic merit is made for the play--Hugo himself realized and admitted that it had little. But great interest attaches to it as a literary curiosity. . . ." Translation somewhat stiff.

2. _____. <u>Les Burgraves</u>. Edited by H. W. Eve. Cambridge: The University Press, n.d. [1904]. Pp. xi+168.

> Introduction contains standard biographical information and literary history. Section on historical background and sources of play good. French text followed by notes on French Alexandrine and helpful explanatory notes. Eve does not stress epic qualities of play, but rather the process of composition: "The general conceptions animating the poet, and his deliberate choice of a <u>milieu</u> raised above ordinary life, are brought out in the preface, which deserves careful study, not only for the beauty of its style, but for the light it throws on the methods of a master of his craft." Scholastic edition.

3. _____. <u>Cromwell</u>. Chronologie et introduction par Annie Ubersfeld. Paris: Garnier-Flammarion, 1968. Pp. 512.

> Fine scholarly edition with full text of <u>Preface</u>, play, notes from original edition. Sensitive analysis of neglected play and its resounding preface included in detailed introduction on sources, genesis, history of work: "Le drame lui-même est infiniment plus brillant et plus riche qu'on ne l'imagine d'ordinaire et la critique actuelle s'efforce de lui rendre la justice qu'il mérite, en montrant dans Cromwell, non seulement l'annonce de tout le

théâtre de Hugo, mais déjà beaucoup des thèmes organizateurs de
l'oeuvre et de la pensée hugolienne."
a) Hunt. French Studies 24 (1970): 406-07.

4. Hugo, Victor-Marie. Les Deux Trouvailles de Gallus. Edition
critique de Johne J. Janc. Thèse, 3e cycle, littérature française,
Université de Paris III, 1977.

5. _____. Hernani. Introduction et notes par H. Gaillard de
Champris. Paris: J. de Gigord, n.d. [19--]. Pp. 134.

Same format as Classiques Larousse. Introductory material sketches
brief, ordinary literary history. French text has a few scenes
eliminated, notably those where semi-comic figure don Ricardo
appears. In Appendix are various critical opinions on the play.
Gaillard de Champris cites play's strengths and weaknesses.
Concludes: "Aujourd'hui encore, Hernani survit aux caprices de
l'opinion, non seulement comme souvenir typique d'une époque,
mais comme exemplaire d'un genre maintenant dépassé et même comme
une manière de chef-d'oeuvre en soi." (Problem apparent in dating
this edition. National Union Catalogue pre-'56 Imprints list it
as 19--. Only copy in U.S. at Univ. of Cal. at Berkeley listed
as 1900 edition. However, "jugements" section at end contains
comments from 1930 articles. Copy itself has no publication date.)

6. _____. Hernani. With explanatory notes by the late Gustave
Masson. London: Dulau & Co., 1902. Pp. iv+115.

This and the "new and revised edition" of 1933 are merely
reprintings of the original nineteenth-century Masson edition,
one of first available printed in England [1878?]. It is a
scholastic edition with complete French text preface and text.
Brief introduction composed largely of quoted article by Paul
Foucher.

7. _____. Hernani. With introduction, notes and vocabulary by
James D. Bruner. New York: American Book Co., 1906. Pp. 264.

School text. Introduction contains sections on theory of Romantic
drama, French versification, première of Hernani, its plot and its
characters. Scanty bibliography. No detailed, comprehensive
evaluation of work. Bruner does offer, however, this interesting
critical comment: "With Hugo, as with Aristotle and Poe, plot is
supreme, and this predominance of the interest of plot is characteristic of Romanticism, which is concerned with the federation or
harmony of stories, the 'amalgamation of drama and romance.' Hugo's
success in Hernani (and Ruy Blas) is assured because he has blended
great poetry with perfection of plot."

8. _____. Hernani. Edited by C. Kemshead. Oxford: Clarendon
Press [1906]. Pp. xvi+106.

Another school edition. Introduction presents literary history of
French drama from beginnings to 1830, facts of Hernani's composition
and performance, characterization and biographical sketch. Notes
and bibliography both skimpy. Kemshead rates Hernani as excellent

despite its historical inaccuracies and weak psychology: "But these blemishes do not prevent the play from being full of beauties of the first order, and Hernani, whatever its defects, will always remain one of Hugo's masterpieces, since in portions of the tragedy the lyric powers of the poet have risen to very great heights."

9. Hugo, Victor-Marie. Hernani. Edited by H. A. Perry. London: Longmans, 1910. Pp. xiv+125.

Of little value. Perfunctory introductory material covers scantily Hugo's life, play's history, Charles V's position in 1519 and the Alexandrine. French text followed by a few mundane notes.

10. _____. Hernani. Reconstitution intégrale, minutieuse et fidèle du manuscrit, exécutée par Daniel Jacomet. In-folio en feuilles, fac-similé dans un emboîtage parcheminé, édition de 300 exemplaires. Paris: A. Michel, 1927. Pp. 58 f°.

Exact reproduction of original manuscript of Hernani.

11. _____. Hernani. Revised edition with introduction, notes, exercises and vocabulary by John E. Matze and D. S. Blondheim. Boston: D. C. Heath & Co., n.d. [c 1929]. Pp. xxiv+263.

Updating of 1891 scholastic edition. Standard literary history and anecdotes. Full notes accompany text. This judgment of play offered: "As regards the plot of the play, it is improbable to the point of absurdity. . . . The characters are no less open to criticism than the plot. . . . Hugo's verse is infinitely better than his history. . . . Nevertheless, the play does have a deceptive atmosphere of truth and reality."

12. _____. Hernani. Annotation and glossary by Paul Vrijdaghs and Walter Ripman. London: J. M. Dent & Sons, n.d. [1929]. Pp. xxi+141.

Scholastic edition. Perfunctory introduction. Editors echo moralistic objections of earlier critics: "Un jugement porté sur cette oeuvre, si marquante dans l'évolution littéraire, serait incomplet, s'il ne relevait ce qu'il y a d'immoral dans le fait que l'auteur y excuse--et même glorifie--le manque absolu de respect pour la vie humaine, en nous montrant des personnages aux nobles et généreux sentiments commettant des meutres et des suicides."

13. _____. Hernani. Edition classique avec des extraits de la Préface de Cromwell. Notices et notes critiques de Maurice Levaillant. Paris: Delagrave, 1933. Pp. 182.

Thorough, scholarly edition. Literary history and theory, play's sources, performance, manuscript, and editions all treated. Appendix contains Gautier's, Victor Pavie's and Viennet's versions of the bataille and première and Gautier's article in the Moniteur on the 1867 reprise.

14.  Hugo, Victor-Marie.  Hernani.  With introduction, notes and
vocabulary by D. O. Evans.  London:  Nelson & Sons, n.d. [1936].  Pp.
vii+283.

   Very good scholastic edition.  Extensive introduction provides
   background of literary history and anecdotes.  Bibliography has
   critical comments.  Fine notes accompanying French text include
   variants, several of which were "hitherto unnoticed."  In evaluation
   of Hugo's dramas, Evans judges Cromwell "superior, as historical
   drama, to Hernani."  Yet Hernani is selected as "the most successful
   drama written in France in the nineteenth century, judged by its
   stage history. . . . We prize Hernani for its poetry, its sublimity
   of thought and feeling, its imaginative charm. . . . It has the
   spiritual values and the formal perfections of great literature
   and of great art."

15.  _____.  Hernani.  Notice de Georges Rency.  2 vols.
Brussels:  Editions Labor, 1941.  Pp. xxiii+140.

16.  _____.  Hernani.  Avec des notices biographique, historique
et littéraire, des notes explicatives, des jugements, un questionnaire,
des sujets de devoirs et une bibliographie par Pierre Richard.  Paris:
Collection des Classiques Larousse, 1941.  Pp. 164.

   Standard scholastic text with succinct, comprehensive presentation
   of background information.  For revised edition, see (23).

17.  _____.  Hernani.  Texte établi et annoté par Charles Beuchat.
Lausanne:  Payot, 1945.  Pp. 157.

18.  _____.  Hernani.  Texte de l'édition définitive.  Commenté
par G.-G. Baardman.  Amsterdam:  J.-M. Meulenhoff, 1946.  Pp. xv+151.

19.  _____.  Hernani.  Avec une chronologie, une notice
littéraire et des notes explicatives par Philippe van Tieghem.  Paris:
Hachette, n.d. [1950].  Pp. 143.

   Scholastic edition.  Introduction includes an outline of Hugo's
   life, a brief historical sketch of play's première, a listing of
   its iconoclastic characteristics, and excerpts from the Préface
   de Cromwell.  Editor concludes:  "Le succès d'Hernani tient surtout,
   aujourd'hui à l'éclat de la poésie, à l'éloquence des tirades, à
   cette richesse et à cette musique des mots, aussi capables, suivant
   les situations, de développer largement un thème oratoire, que de
   se plier à toutes les inflexions d'un amour inquiet, tendre ou
   passionné."

20.  _____.  Hernani.  In Le Drame romantique, pp. 133-274.  N.p.
[Paris]:  Club des libraires de France, n.d. [1957].

   Hernani included with Dumas' La Tour de Nesle and Nerval's Léo
   Burckart to represent best French Romantic drama.  "Avertissement"
   claims:  "Nous avons choisi Hernani parce qu'elle est le type
   même de la pièce de jeunesse. . . . Chez Hugo c'est la conquête,
   amoureuse ou ambitieuse."  Nerval's play, however, "pourrait bien
   être le plus authentique chef-d'oeuvre que l'époque romantique
   nous ait cédé."

21. Hugo, Victor-Marie. Hernani. Introduction et notes par Fernand Letessier. Rome: A. Signorelli, 1961. Pp. 200.

Satisfactory edition. Preliminary note summarily presents life and works of Hugo and editions of Hernani. Introduction offers literary history, value of work, its destiny, and a good section on composition and sources. French text followed by index of proper names in play and appendix on "bataille" containing Victor Pavie's letter on the event, Gautier's account and appropriate excerpt from Viennet's Mémoires. Letessier adopts a generous attitude in evaluating play: "Dans ce drame, jeté à la face des partisans d'un classicisme moribond, admettons que l'auteur commit de propos délibéré certains excès. Mais au lieu de souligner avec mesquinerie des insuffisances partielles, laissons-nous prendre par la puissance globale de l'émotion et de la tendresse, de la générosité et de l'art qui caractérisent une grande oeuvre."

22. _____. Hernani. Avec une biographie chronologique, une notice sur la crise du théâtre de la Révolution à 1830, une analyse méthodique par Alexandre Beaujour. N.p. [Paris]: Bordas, n.d. [1963]. Pp. 192.

Scholastic edition (Les Petits Classiques Bordas). Literary history, outline of drama, Hugo's life and times adequately treated. Bibliography too brief. Play's text accompanied by questions and comments. Best section is final chapter on "Hernani et la critique," reviewing opinions from contemporary press through Valéry, Gide and Colette.

23. _____. Hernani. Avec une notice biographique, des notes par Pierre Richard. Nouvelle édition revue par Gérard Sablayrolles. Nouveaux Classiques Larousse. Paris: Larousse, 1964. Pp. 192.

New, revised scholastic edition of (16). Bibliography too brief. Notes and introduction provide basic information on play succinctly. Editor finds that Hernani deserves its important place in theatrical history: "L'examen objectif de la pièce, malgré la réele défaveur où elle est tombée, . . . révèle son importance dans l'histoire de l'esthétique théâtrale tout entière; elle constitue un remarquable effort d'adaptation du théâtre à des conditions sociales nouvelles, à une forme nouvelle de sensibilité, paradoxalement aussi une résurgence du baroque éternel, que notre époque connaît si bien et doit goûter. . . ."

24. _____. Hernani. Edited by Herbert F. Collins. London: Macmillan, 1968. Pp. lvii+196.

School edition, companion volume to his 1966 edition of Ruy Blas. Standard literary history followed by character sketches and good chapters on Hernani's classical traits and play's sources. Complete French text of preface, play, author's notes, based on 1889 definitive Hetzel edition. Collins signals Hernani's final act as its redeeming feature: "Hugo's stagecraft as revealed in Hernani is much inferior to his brilliant handling of the complicated plot of Ruy Blas (1838). . . . The fifth act makes amends. It

will always remain the most enduring part of the play. . . . Yet,
despite much irrational happening in his play, Hugo has succeeded
in imparting to this fifth act the tragic poignancy of ill-starred
love."

25. Hugo, Victor-Marie. Hernani. Ruy Blas. Suivi de la bataille
d'Hernani racontée par ses témoins. Edition établie sur les textes et
manuscrits originaux, annotée et présentée par Yves Florenne. Le Livre
de poche classique, no. 2434. Paris: Le Livre de Poche, 1969. Pp. 640.

 Handy edition. Florenne's introduction same as his article (666).
 Texts of plays taken from original manuscripts. Each preceded
 by explanation of its genesis, history. Appendix contains pertinent
 documents, such as correspondence, accounts of the bataille
 d'Hernani, contemporary press reaction, notes and variants.

26. _____. Hernani. Translated, with notes by Frederick L.
Slous and Camilla Crosland. With a brief introduction by James
Kendrick. New York: Translation Publishing Co., n.d. [c 1924].
Pp. xvii+148.

 Poor edition. Translation is outdated 1887 version in blank verse.
 Simplistic introduction. Kendrick's view on Hugo's often criticized
 characterization: "Hugo has a remarkable power of characterization.
 Each of the persons portrayed in Hernani are [sic] distinct
 individuals and maintain their individuality throughout the play."

27. _____. Hernani. Dramat w pieciu aktach. Przetozyĺa
Karolina Wagrowska, oprac. Lidia Topatýnska. Wroctaw: Zaktad im.
Ossolińskich, n.d. [1953]. Pp. lxxix+167.

 Polish translation.

28. _____. Hernani. In Teatro francese. Edited by Italo
Siciliano. 3 vols. Vol. 3: Da Victor Hugo a Ionesco. N.p. [Milano]:
Nuova Accademia Editrice, n.d. [1959]. (Hugo, pp. 7-88.)

 Italian translation contained in this anthology. Introduction
 offers succinct literary history, character analyses and critical
 opinions: "Il poeta delle luci e delle ombre ha fatto anche del
 teatro uno di quei suoi amati mostri ai quali carenze ed eccessi
 impediscono di raggiungere il miracolo. Luci ed ombre anche in
 quelli che sono considerati i suoi capolavori, in Hernani e in
 Ruy Blas."

29. _____. Hernani. Translated by Linda Asher. In The Laurel
Masterpieces of Continental Drama. Vol. 2: The Romantic Influence.
Edited by Norris Houghton. New York: n.p. n.d. [Dell Publishing Co.,
1963]. Pp. 281-379.

 Acceptable translation. Volume for general reader.

30. _____. Hernani. Drama. Mit 5 Zeichnungen von Rolf Münzer.
Ubertragen von Heidrun Beltz. Nachwort von Dieter Tauchmann. Leipzig:
Insel-Verlag, 1968. Pp. 150.

German verse translation.  In introduction on the bataille
d'Hernani, Tauchmann evaluates the play:  "Das war der Sieg, 'das
Austerlitz der französischen Romantick' (Albert Thibaudet), und
die Frage, ob Hernani wirklich nicht mehr ist als ein in
wunderbaren Versen geschriebener melodramatischer Reisser, wie oft
und sicher auch zu Recht gesagt worden ist, tritt zurück angesichts
der faszinierenden Unmittelbarkeit seiner Zeitgeschichtlichen
Wirkung:  Noch ehe das Volk von Paris in den 'trois glorieuses'--
den drei bedeutsamen Julitagen des Jahres 1830--die überlebenden
Gerwatten des Ancien Régime vom Schauplatz der Geschichte jagte,
waren sie auf der Bühne der Comédie-Française bereits geschlagen."

31.  Hugo, Victor-Marie.  Mangeront-ils?  Edition critique par René
Journet et Guy Robert.  Cahiers Victor Hugo, publiés avec le concours
du Centre National de la Recherche Scientifique.  Paris:  Flammarion,
1970.  Pp. 272.

Following their method adopted for previous critical edition of
Dieu, these scholars carefully present the "cinq couches successives"
uncovered in variants of manuscript and offer their version of the
work's genesis as well as history of its publication, performance
and press reception.  Introductory essay good on composition,
sources and characters.  Of play's main character, they suggest:
"Aïrolo est comme l'achèvement dans le domaine poétique de
plusieurs créations antérieures du poète. . . . Aïrolo est aussi
le frère du gueux dont Hugo a multiplié les silhouettes dans les
fragments qu'on rattache au Théâtre en Liberté."  Suggest also
interesting link with another play from period of exile:  "Mille
francs de récompense peut-être considéré comme une première
version prosaïqie (et encore  maladroite sous bien des aspects)
de Mangeront-ils?  Authors outline "une interprétation idéale" of
the play they would like to see performed.  Appendices give long
variants, sketches, good notes on text and variants.  One helpful
index gives complete listing of images, another of all proper names.
a) Franceschetti.  Studi Francesi 14 (1970):  570-71.
b) Pia.  Carrefour, 20 janv. 1971, pp. 14-15.
c) Seebacher.  French Studies 26 (1972):  337-38.

32.  _____.  Marie Tudor.  Edited with an introduction and notes
by R. E. Palmer.  London:  Hutchinson Educational, n.d. [1961].
Pp. 174.

Scholastic edition.  Introduction good on English sources of play
and its themes.  Palmer concludes:  "It is doubtful whether
Marie Tudor justified the claim to be true nineteenth-century drama,
but by its directness of language, simplicity of plot, and force
of emotion, it captured an audience.  There are faults in the
play. . . . Yet it continues to appeal; the almost unbearable
suspense of the final scenes and the memorable portrayal of the
queen show that 'admirable toute-puissance du poète' which is
characteristic of Hugo."
a) Baldick.  Modern Language Review 58 (Jan. 1963):  156-57.

33. Hugo, Victor-Marie. <u>Marion de Lorme</u>. Edited with introduction, notes and vocabulary by Maxwell A. Smith and Mary Ruth Smith. New York: Appleton-Century Co., 1934. Pp. xxiv+258.

    First annotated edition in English of this play. School edition with basic information given in introduction. Good notes. Play's text in French.

34. _____. <u>Mille Francs de récompense</u>. 2 vols. Edition critique par Jacques Tephany. Thèse, 3e cycle, Lettres, Université de Paris, 1970. Pp. 556.

35. _____. <u>Morceaux choisis de Victor Hugo</u>. <u>Théâtre</u>. Avec études et analyses par Hippolyte Parigot. Paris: Delagrave, 1900. Pp. 453.

    Contains well chosen excerpts from <u>Cromwell</u> through <u>Les Burgraves</u> and from six plays of the exile period. Introductions to each work concise and quite informative. In the <u>avant-propos</u> Parigot highly praises the poet: "On peut discuter sur la technique du drame de Victor Hugo. Mais toute la critique s'accorda toujours à saluer et admirer l'éblouissante forme dont le poète a revêtu ses conceptions dramatiques. . . . [Hugo] inonde la scène de la plus belle musique qui ait chanté sur la scène tragique, depuis Bérénice, Phèdre et Athalie. . . . Victor Hugo dramaturge est un étonnant visionnaire." 1936 edition same as 1900.

36. _____. <u>L'Oeuvre de Victor Hugo</u>. <u>Poésie</u>. <u>Prose</u>. <u>Théâtre</u>. Edition classique par Maurice Levaillant. Paris: Delagrave, 1931. Pp. viii+717.

    Solid one-volume chronological anthology with good notes. <u>Hernani</u>, <u>Ruy Blas</u> and <u>Les Burgraves</u> only plays excerpted. Each work situated well with comments on literary history, variants, "décor" and summary bibliography at end. 1936 and 1959 editions essentially same on plays with brief survey in introduction of new works on Hugo published since previous edition.
    a) Maynial. <u>Quinzaine Critique</u>, 10 févr. 1931.

37. _____. <u>Oeuvres</u>. 24 vols. Avant-propos et notes de Jeanlouis Cornuz. Illustrations de Jean Monod. Lausanne: Editions Rencontre, 1960-1967. (Hugo's theatre, vols. 13-18.)

    Attractive, leather-bound, relatively inexpensive edition for general public. Introduction to each volume discusses generally all plays contained in that volume. Presentation gives facts of Hugo's life at time of plays' composition, lots of anecdotes and quotations from contemporary reviewers. His broad theme is: "Il faut redécouvrir Hugo!"

38. _____. <u>Oeuvres choisies</u>. 3 vols. Paris: Hachette, n.d. [c 1950]. (Hugo's theatre, vol. 2.)

39. Hugo, Victor-Marie. Oeuvres choisies. 2 vols. Disposées
d'après l'ordre chronologique, avec une biographie, des notes
critiques, grammaticales, historiques et des illustrations documen-
taires, par Pierre Moreau et Jean Boudout. Paris: Hatier, 1950.
Pp. 1064, 1060.

Solid, compact Hugo anthology. All plays Cromwell through Les
Burgraves and one play from Le Théâtre en liberté excerpted.
Selections well made and accompanied by excellent introductions
and notes. Very interesting suggestions on influence of Hugo's
plays. Editors not kind to the Hugo of the Théâtre en liberté:
"Nous sommes aujourd'hui un peu blasés (depuis Rostand) sur ce
genre d'acrobatie scénique, et plus difficiles (depuis Giraudoux)
en matière de fantaisies et de symboles." Ruy Blas is selected
as the most significant play of Hugo: "Il ne semble plus douteux
que Ruy Blas soit destiné à représenter à l'avenir un genre qui
a pris définitivement sa place dans l'évolution de notre théâtre."

40. _____. Oeuvres choisies illustrées. Par Léopold-Lacour.
Préface de Gustave Simon. 2 vols. Paris: Larousse, n.d. [1912].
Pp. 558, 540.

Vol. 1 verse, vol. 2 prose. Anthology of excerpts for general
public. Neither biography nor "jugements" particularly useful.
Bibliography sufficient for time. Vol. 1 contains excerpts from
all verse dramas, Cromwell through Le Théâtre en liberté, including,
Les Jumeaux and Torquemada; vol. 2 has excerpts from Hugo's three
prose plays of the 1830's. Each excerpt is encased in explanatory
text recounting circumstances of composition and performances and
a plot résumé. Illustrations good but not numerous for plays.

41. _____. Oeuvres complètes. Edittées par Paul Meurice,
Gustave Simon et Cécile Daubray. Edition dite "de l'Imprimerie
Nationale." 45 vols. Paris: Ollendorf-Albin Michel, 1901-1952.
(Hugo's theatre, vols. 40-45.)

An excellent edition. Amounts to a critical edition because each
volume contains "une notice historique, . . . dessins de Victor
Hugo commentant le texte, . . . des revues de la critique à
diverses époques, des notes bibliographiques et iconographiques,"
and a manuscript reliquat. Some errors and omissions. Yet
surpassed only, perhaps, by the Massin chronological edition (43).

42. _____. Oeuvres complètes. Préface de Michel Braspart.
Edition illustrée. Givors: A. Martel, 1948-1955. (Hugo's theatre,
vols. 4, 12, 13, 16, 17, 30.)

Edition for general public with minimum amount of information on
composition, performance, critical reception, merit of plays in
each volume.

43. _____. Oeuvres complètes. Edition chronologique publiée
sous la direction de Jean Massin. Avec la collaboration d'Eliette
Vasseur. 18 vols. Paris: Le Club français du livre, 1967-1970.

Perhaps the best edition of Hugo's complete works, certainly the
most comprehensive to date. Chronological arrangement permits a
view of Hugo's literary development and progress not otherwise
possible. Each work has solid introduction by specialist. Useful
reliquat for each period and genre included in volumes. "Documents
divers" also offered where appropriate, as well as notes, outlines,
inédits. Some general essays on Hugo's characters, Hugo and music,
Hugo and Baudelaire add extra dimension to this impressive display
of talent and detailed work. See also Duchet (355), Massin (754),
Mauron (229), Ubersfeld-Maille (316).
a) Abraham. Europe, No. 458 (juin 1967), pp. 237-40.
b) Bellour. Lettres Françaises, 11 déc. 1968, pp. 3-5.
c) Gaugeard. Lettres Françaises, 30 mars 1967, pp. 4-5.

44. Hugo, Victor-Marie. Oeuvres dramatiques complètes. Oeuvres
critiques complètes. Réunies et présentées par Francis Bouvet. Paris:
J.-J. Pauvert, n.d. [c 1963]. Pp. xiv+713.

Excellent edition uniting in same volume Hugo's theories, as
expressed in critical works, and his practice, as evinced in
dramas. "Avertissement" situates theatre in his works as whole:
"L'oeuvre dramatique de Hugo, tout irrégulière qu'elle soit, dans
la qualité comme--du moins en apparence--dans le temps, n'en est
pas moins caractéristique de son génie: le lecteur reconnaîtra
sans peine le poète et le romancier dans l'auteur dramatique. . . ."
Bibliography of original editions helpful, as is list of date and
place of each play's première. Selections from manuscripts
reproduce Hugo's handwriting and illustrations. Texts from
Le Château du diable through Comédies cassées followed by reliquat
and "Plans et projets." Type and format easy to read, but volume
very heavy.

45. _____. Préface de Cromwell. Hernani. Edited with introduction and notes by John R. Effinger, Jr. Chicago: Scott, Foresmann
Co., 1900. Pp. 261.

Edition designed for use by American students. Introduction
presents much biographical material and literary history but
little critical comment. Bibliography weak and notes on text few.
Effinger evaluates Hugo thus: "As a dramatist, he was the head
and leader of the revolt against the classic tradition, but can
not be called a man of exceptional talent and ability in this
line of work although . . . his plays have remained in public
favor."

46. _____. Ruy Blas. Edited with explanatory notes for the use
of students by R. A. Michaels. New York: H. Holt & Co., n.d. [1900].
Pp. iv+117.

47. _____. Ruy Blas. Edited with introduction and notes by
Kenneth McKenzie. New York: H. Holt & Co., 1909. Pp. xxvii+223.
(Publishing information for 1926 edition same except for year and
pp. 258.)

Valuable edition of play for English-speaking students of that
time. Good bibliography, updated in 1926 edition. Solid literary

history given as background in introduction. Sources, plot,
character sketches, history of performances included also in
introduction. Notes full, reliable. McKenzie feels that three or
four of Hugo's plays deserve study for historical importance,
artistic achievement and dramatic power. He assesses Ruy Blas's
lasting value thus: "Out of the many elements Victor Hugo has
constructed a complex work of art,--a play of great poetic beauty,
with scenes and characters that remain in the memory."
a) Brush. MLN 25 (April 1910): 123-25.

48. Hugo, Victor-Marie. Ruy Blas. Edited by H. L. Hutton. Oxford:
Clarendon Press, n.d. [1919]. Pp. 316.

Scholastic edition. Good historical notes and bibliography on
sources, weaker on criticism of play. Introduction compares
Ruy Blas and Hernani in light of theories from Préface to Cromwell
and offers a scene-by-scene plot analysis. Hutton agrees with
all critics from Jules Janin to Emile Faguet who praise play's
language. Also finds play's ending outstanding: "If we accept
the romantic form, we cannot hesitate to admire the simplicity, the
concentrated power of this final act."
a) Lancaster. MLN 35 (Jan. 1920): 34-36.

49. _____. Ruy Blas. With introduction, notes, exercises and
vocabulary by Olin H. Moore. Boston: D. C. Heath & Co., n.d.
[c 1933]. Pp. xxvi+253.

Edition for American students. Introduction succinct, adequate,
not brilliant. Notes fairly good on French text. Appendix contains
original manuscript variants without comment. Moore evaluates
Hugo's play: "In Ruy Blas we find the same brilliant qualities of
style which had distinguished Hernani: dazzling antithesis, and
stirring lyricism. Ruy Blas equals Hernani also in another
Romantic quality, melancholy, which according to Hugo was one of
the greatest contributions of Christianity to human thought. As
for local color, that prime essential of Romanticism, Ruy Blas
is distinctly superior to Hernani.

50. _____. Ruy Blas. Edition classique avec des extraits de
la Préface de Cromwell. Notices et notes critiques de Maurice
Levaillant. Paris: Delagrave, 1934. Pp. 228.

Excellent edition for programme de l'enseignement secondaire.
Introductory material contains very detailed information on history
of drame romantique, quotations from the Préface de Cromwell,
complete analysis of Ruy Blas. Stresses connection of play with
Hernani and investigates its success on stage and in the press as
well as its manuscript variants, brouillons, sources, and related
fragments. Companion "édition classique" to his Hernani (13).
In introduction Levaillant singles out examples in Ruy Blas of
Hugo's dramatic power: "Les vers sont dignes du tableau: plus
souples, plus colorés, plus variés de coupes et d'effets que ceux
d'Hernani, ils marquent l'apogée du style dramatique de Victor
Hugo. Au début du troisième acte ils s'élèvent jusqu'au ton épique
dans l'apostrophe de Ruy Blas aux ministres."

51. Hugo, Victor-Marie. Ruy Blas. Avec une chronologie, une notice littéraire et des notes explicatives par Philippe van Tieghem. Paris: Hachette, n.d. [c 1950]. Pp. 143.

52. _____. Ruy Blas. Avec une biographie chronologique de V. Hugo, une notice sur le théâtre romantique par René Laparra. N.p. [Paris]: Bordas, 1963. Pp. 192.

Employs familiar format of Petits Classiques Bordas editions. Biographical and literary background information in concise, schematic form. Bibliography contains only nine items. Complete preface, text of play and 1838 note all fully commented. "Etude" at end scholastic aid. Review of play's première, important reprises and critical reception good.

53. _____. Ruy Blas. Édition par Fernand Letessier. Rome: A. Signorelli, 1963.

Companion volume to his 1961 edition of Hernani (21). Format same: literary history and biography followed by play's genesis and fortune.

54. _____. Ruy Blas. Nouvelle édition. Avec une notice biographique, des notes explicatives par Gérard Sablayrolles. Nouveaux Classiques Larousse, no. 22. Paris: Larousse, n.d. [1965]. Pp. 206.

School edition with basic biographical facts, literary history and analysis of plot, characters and style. Text accompanied by adequate notes, questions, pictures and followed by "jugements" on play and suggested theme topics. Sablayrolles sees Ruy Blas as mark of Hugo's political evolution: "Cette prise de position va rejoindre le souci, que Hugo affirme de plus en plus, d'atteindre un public populaire, d'écrire des pièces de théâtre qui s'adressent à la foule et cherchent à l'élever. Elle nous permet de comprendre le sens profond du drame romantique de bien y voir une rupture avec la littérature aristocratique, une tentative peut-être prématurée d'un art populaire qui trouvera son épanouissement dans le roman Les Misérables." 1971 edition essentially unchanged.

55. _____. Ruy Blas. Edited by Herbert F. Collins. London: Macmillan, 1966. Pp. xxxviii+192.

Fairly good school edition. Adequately presents literary history and anlysis of Ruy Blas in introduction. Graph shows number of performances of play at Comédie-Française from 1838 to 1860. Complete French text based on definitive edition of Hetzel complemented by Collins' good notes. On lasting value of play, Collins states: "An actual happening in life, certain identified history source books and occasional echoes from earlier plays, all contributed to the genesis of Ruy Blas, but the work still lives as the original creation of a very great poet."

56. _____. Ruy Blas. Présenté par Francis Lafon. Avant-propos de J.-B. Barrère. Paris: Didier, 1966. Pp. 176.

Avant-propos of this school edition same as Barrère's 1960 article (637). Collection of critical opinions from Gustave Planche through Gaudon and Rouleau of interest in this edition, as is section on genesis of the Romantic hero. Good outline and notes accompany the text. Appendix contains brief chapter on Spain and French literature, theatrical and critical vocabulary, brief bibliography.

57. Hugo, Victor-Marie. Ruy Blas. Texte présenté et annoté par Pierre Moreau. Nouveaux Classiques Hatier, 600. Paris: Hatier, 1966. Pp. 176.

58. _____. Ruy Blas. Edition critique établie par Anne Ubersfeld. 2 vols. Annales littéraires de l'Université de Besançon, vols. 121 et 131. Paris: Les Belles Lettres, 1971-1972. Pp. 361, 212.

Sound critical edition. Vol. 1 contains editor's previously published study (715) on play's genesis, "Notes pour une étude littéraire" on various aspects of the play including its "signification," history of its composition, performance, critical reaction, and a presentation of manuscript and variants. Text offered with variants at bottom. Notes at end thorough. Vol. 2 composed of various "documents," like "brouillons," rehearsal notes, appropriate letters, quotations from historical texts, description of Palianti's scenery. Excellent bibliography. Bibliographical notices and lexicon also useful.
a) Barrère. RBPH 51 (1973): 412-13.
b) Franceschetti. Studi Francesi 16 (1972): 510-11.

59. _____. Ruy Blas. Avec un tableau de concordances chronologiques, une notice littéraire, des notes explicatives, des questionnaires et une lecture thématique, établis par Jacqueline Morini et Yves Hucher. Paris: Hachette, 1976.

60. _____. Ruy Blas. In Great Plays (French and German). Translated by Mrs. Newton Crosland. With biographical notes and a critical introduction by Brander Matthews. New York: Appleton & Co., 1901. Pp. xiii+504.

Old nineteenth-century verse translation by Mrs. Newton Crosland. Matthew's good but sweeping general history of theatre offers these words on Hugo, whose contribution he sees largely as a negative destruction of classical code: "In the prose plays the melodramatic skeleton is a little too barely displayed, but it is hidden in the verse plays where the splendid lyric fervour of the poet helps to cloak and conceal the artifices of the mere playwright. Hernani and Ruy Blas still hold their own in the French theatre."

61. _____. Ruy Blas. Modernized in English verse by Brian Hooker. With an introduction by Clayton Hamilton. New York: H. Holt & Co., n.d. [c 1931]. Pp. xxvii+164.

Verse translation adequate. Hooker explains changes he made in adapting play for English-speaking audience and for Walter Hampden in main rôle. Hamilton remarks in introduction. "The plays of

Victor Hugo are either too lyrical or too mechanical, too theatrical or too poetic. . . . The main merit of Ruy Blas as a dramatic composition is the fact that its four leading characters . . . are contrasted in such a manner as to complement each other, so that, between them, they cover the entire gamut of theatrical emotion."

62. Hugo, Victor-Marie. Ruy Blas. Preveo u Stixovima Andreja Mili evi, predgovor napisao Svetislav Petrovi. Beograd. (Stampari a Gregori a), 1936. Pp. xvii & 134 p.

Russian translation.

63. _____. Théâtre complet. Préface par Roland Purnal. Notices et notes par J.-J. Thierry et Josette Mélèze. Bibliothèque de la Pléiade, no. 66. 2 vols. Paris: Gallimard, 1963-1964. Pp. xxviii+1805, 1932.

This compact set, although basically sound, contains errors and omissions in its critical apparatus. Vol. 1 includes text of verse dramas through Ruy Blas and preface evaluating Hugo's works in context of history of French Romantic theatre. Says: "Le meilleur de son théâtre n'est autre chose qu'un magasin de morceaux de bravoure dont le lyrisme fait tous les frais. Sorti du livre, le théâtre de Hugo est donc contraint d'y rentrer." Notices and notes usually helpful, offering succinct history of plays' composition and performance and some variants. Vol. 2 presents text of remaining verse drames, then prose drames, lyrical theatre (La Esmeralda), Le Théâtre en liberté, modern theatre (Mille Francs de récompense and L'Intervention) and fragments. Appendix lists Hugo's dramatic projects, plans, sketches and his speech on freedom of theatre. Notices and notes for plays in this volume follow. Bibliography only of editions is incomplete. Arrangement of plays interesting.
a) Franceschetti. Studi Francesi 9 (1965):  375-76.
b) Gaudon. Modern Language Review 61 (1966):  520-21.

64. _____. Three Plays: Hernani, The King Amuses Himself, Ruy Blas. Edited with an introduction by Helen A. Gaubert. New York: Washington Square Press, n.d. [1964]. Pp. xiv+338.

Translations are old nineteenth-century versions by Crosland and Slous. Introduction superficial and somewhat inaccurate. Interpretation too political: "The plays, in fact, are Romantic dramatizations of [Hugo's] political philosophy." Finds plays still valuable: "A great deal of enjoyment and interest remains for English-speaking audiences and readers of Hernani, The King Amuses Himself and Ruy Blas. They cannot help being carried away instinctively by the overpowering passions of love and vengeance (albeit somewhat melodramatic) of the heroic and the villainous characters." No notes or separate introduction to each play.

# General Criticism

65. Affron, Charles. A Stage for Poets: Studies in the Theatre of Hugo and Musset. Princeton, N.J.: Princeton University Press, 1971. Pp. xii+254.

Argues strongly that drame romantique is a mixed genre whose center is lyric. Claims, therefore, that plays of Hugo and Musset should not be evaluated according to criteria for strictly dramatic theatre: "It is absurd to expect Hugo to write a play structured like Phèdre or to conceive of character as Shakespeare does in Hamlet. He searches for harmony and metaphor rather than the measure of the five-act classical tragedy and the imitation of psychological complexity." Series of interesting essays on Hernani, Les Burgraves, Torquemada and Mangeront-ils? as Hugo's best examples of lyric theatre. Ruy Blas not included because it is more dramatic and less poetic. Treats Mangeront-ils? too much as Hugo's parody of himself. Extensive plot summaries and prosaic, demeaning translations unnecessary.
a) Franceschetti. Studi Francesi 18 (1974): 177.
b) Howarth. Modern Language Review 69 (1974): 880-81.
c) Mall. MLN 88 (1973): 917-19.
d) Shaw. French Studies 29 (1975): 99-101.
e) Sices. French Review 45 (May 1972): 1192-93.
f) Van Erde. Studies in Romanticism 11 (1972): 253-56.
g) Ward. Romanic Review 66 (1975): 155.

66. Albouy, Pierre. La Création mythologique chez Victor Hugo. Paris: J. Corti, 1963. Pp. 517. (Albouy gives a synopsis in L'Information Littéraire 17 [1965]: 193-95. Hugo's theatre, pp. 181-82, 267.)

Relatively little on theatre per se, but valuable perceptions offered on importance of myth in Hugo's development: "Au plus nuancé de ses personnages, qui est le héros de son premier drame, s'oppose le plus invraisemblable de tous ses personnages, le héros de son dernier drame, Torquemada. De Cromwell à Torquemada, l'itinéraire va du psychologique au mythique. . . . Ruy Blas est

le chef-d'oeuvre et le point d'aboutissement du théâtre hugolien. Les Burgraves, en 1842, marquent le début d'une époque nouvelle, qu'illustreront les chefs-d'oeuvre de l'exil. . . . Déjà, en effet, Les Burgraves, plutôt que du symbolisme dramatique, relèvent du mythe. . . ."
a) Barrère. La Revue des Sciences Humanines, n.s. no. 117 (1965), pp. 149-52.
b) Franceschetti. Studi Francesi 10 (1966):  106-10.
c) Journet. La Revue d'Histoire Littéraire de la France 65 (1965): 521-23.
d) Piatier. Le Monde, 23 mai 1964, p. 13.

67.  Allevy, Marie-Antoinette. La Mise-en-scène en France dans la première motié du dix-neuvième siècle. Paris:  E. Droz, 1938. (Hugo, pp. 121-26.)

Indicates Hugo's innovations in technical aspects of play production. With advent of Hugo's Hernani, "désormais le poète, le décorateur, le machiniste, le costumier, le metteur en scène ne faisaient qu'un. . . . Le drame romantique avait réduit la mission de l'auteur tragique du côté de l'art pour l'étendre du côté du métier."

68.  Amico, Silvio d'. Storia del teatro drammatico. 2 vols.  Milan: Garzanti, 1960.  (Hugo, II, 54-58.  Fifth edition of 1968 has four volumes.  Hugo's theatre, III, 109-15.)

Hugo characterized as an unsuccessful dramatic poet:  "All' autore difetta il senso dell'intrigo, dell'azione del procedere per sintesi.  Dove vuol essere misterioso, riesce ingenuamente romanzesco, o puerile.  Il ricchissimo temperamento dello scrittore, la sua prodigiosa vena oratoria, le sue enormi qualità di creatore di contrasti e d'immagini, fecero di lui, nei suoi grandi momenti, un rètore fecondo, un lirico ispirato, un prosatore di straordinaria ricchezza:  ma non riuscirono a farne un poeta drammatico."  1968 edition contains same opinions in amplified form.

69.  Antoine, André. Mes Souvenirs sur le Théâtre-Libre.  Paris: Fayard, 1921.  Pp. 324.  (Hugo's influence, pp. 23-24.)

Antoine, in looking for correct name for his new theatre, searching more for epigraph than title, remembers thinking:  "Il y en a une qui serait excellente:  'Le Théâtre en liberté,' emprunté à Hugo, mais je ne sais quoi nous gêne, cela nous semble bien romantique. Et, comme nous tournons autour de cette idée, Byl s'écrie tout à coup en remuant son pernod:  'Alors, le Théâtre Libre,' et je sens tout de suite que c'est vraiment cela que nous cherchions."

70.  Armade, Francisque d'. Le Théâtre français des origines à nos jours.  Extraits et analyses, notices biographiques.  Paris:  Delagrave, n.d. [1909?].  (Hugo, pp. 161-91.)

With perhaps unintentional irony, Armade calls Hernani "la pièce classique de Victor Hugo."  Cites the verbal brilliance and epic grandeur of Les Burgraves, "[qui] sont, avec Torquemada, la plus superbe vision de Hugo.  Il y a prodigué les richesses

éblouissantes de son génie lyrique et surtout épique." Excerpts
from plays mentioned above and from Ruy Blas. Closes with regret
that it is Hugo the poet, not the dramatist, who draws applause.

71. Ascoli, Georges. Le Théâtre romantique. 5 fascicules. Paris:
Centre de documentation universitaire. Tournier & Constans, n.d.
[1936?]. Pp. 186.

Reproduction of course lectures. Treats fully Amy Robsart,
Cromwell, Hernani and the Théâtre en liberté; last chapter especially
good. Calls Ruy Blas the masterpiece of the works performed.
Observes that, in the Théâtre en liberté, Hugo is looking for "la
liberté scénique" in a mixture of reality and fantasy, and chooses
Les Deux Trouvailles de Gallus as the best play in group: "Ici
plus de symboles ni de contrastes factices; mais la vie simple et
familière avec la grâce de la fantaisie."

72. Ayer, Charles. "Foreign Drama on the English and American Stage:
French Drama." University of Colorado Studies, 6, 4 (1909): 287-97.

Author claims that although Ruy Blas was "well known to American
playgoers" with Edwin Booth and Salvini in the title rôle,
"strangely enough the Hernani of Victor Hugo seems to have had no
career on the American stage." Ayer seems to be unfamiliar with
Zanthe, a pirated version of Kenney's translation of Hernani.
Ruy Blas is called "Hugo's dramatic masterpiece." Hugo's plays
had much more success on the English stage; but, Ayer summarizes,
"the romantic drama of Victor Hugo seems not to have held its own
very well, even in Paris." Other irritating errors (e.g., 1827
as date of Hernani's première).

73. Bach, Max. "Saint-Beuve critique du théâtre de son temps." PMLA
81 (Dec. 1966): 563-74.

From letters and articles, Bach gleans great critic's views on
Musset and Hugo. Sainte-Beuve never appreciated Musset and became
disenchanted with Hugo for professional and personal reasons. He
never wrote the promised "article d'ensemble" on Hugo's theatre,
and at the time of Ruy Blas, he even tried to hurt new play's
success by praising a competing play. Bach asks: "L'évidente
amertume de Sainte-Beuve n'est-elle pas la conséquence de toutes
les déceptions que Victor Hugo et surtout le théâtre hugolien lui
ont causées?" And he continues: "Pendant un certain temps il
avait cru fermement que le théâtre était le genre le plus important
de l'art moderne et il n'avait pas hésité à prédire la naissance
du drame nouveau. Il fut déçu et se croit trahi" (by Hernani).
See also Sainte-Beuve (273).

74. Barrère, Jean-Bertrand. "Etat présent des recherches sur Victor
Hugo." Cahiers de l'Association Internationale des Etudes Françaises,
no. 19 (mars 1967), pp. 169-76.

Author brings up to date his 1961 article (78) on Hugo scholarship.
Nothing new on the theatre.

75. Barrère, Jean-Bertrand.  La Fantaisie de Victor Hugo.  3 vols.
Paris:  J. Corti, 1949-60.

Excellent treatment of this previously neglected aspect of Hugo's
inspiration.  Barrère's massive study opens new era in Hugo
scholarship.  Volume 1 has brief sections on plays through 1851
and examines "le sorcier et son apprenti" in Amy Robsart, the
buffoons in Cromwell, don César in Ruy Blas, and the use of masks
and costumes.  Volume 2, on works from 1852 to 1885, presents
exact details of composition, the "sensibilité" expressed and a
careful analysis of plays in the Théâtre en liberté:  "Hugo . . .
désirait s'affranchir des contraintes de la convention, de la
logique et peut-être même du réel pour accorder à l'imagination
toute sa liberté de conception et d'expression."  Finds Hugo
generally successful here, but "un peu moins que dans la poésie."
Volume 3 on "thèmes et motifs" collects quotations from Hugo's
works to illustrate his "fantaisie."  Not much from dramas except
from the Théâtre en liberté.
a) Amer.  La Nouvelle Revue Française 18 (1961):  132-35.
b) Franceschetti.  Studi Francesi 5 (1961):  501-04.
c) Gaudon.  Modern Language Review 58 (1963):  438-41.
d) Hunt.  French Studies 6 (Jan. 1952):  81-83; 16 (1962):  74-77.
e) Moreau.  La Revue d'Histoire Littéraire de la France 54 (1954):
   234-36; 62 (1962):  440-44.
f) Savey-Casard.  La Revue de Littérature Comparée 36 (1962):
   457-63.

76. _____.  Hugo, l'homme et l'oeuvre.  Paris:  Boivin, 1952.
Pp. 256.  (Slightly revised as Hugo.  Connaissance des lettres,
no. 35.  Paris:  Hatier, 1967.  Pp. 288.)

Excellent, clear, concise study of all Hugo's writings.  Offers
new thoughts and fresh perceptions on plays.  Notes, for example,
the growing importance of women and rôle of le peuple in dramas
from Lucrèce Borgia on.  Identifies distinctive characteristic
of Cromwell as "l'excès" and sees in Amy Robsart the birth of some
of Hugo's "personnages-types du théâtre."  Especially good comments
on Le Théâtre en liberté, which is inherently an échec because
Hugo cannot decide between the two meanings of its title.

77. _____.  "Le Lustre et la rampe.  Petite note sur la
conception de la scène selon Victor Hugo."  La Revue d'Histoire du
Théâtre 1, 4 (1948-49):  282-86.

Barrère places Hugo in intermediate position on questions of
realistic dramaturgy, useful art versus pure art, and theatre for
elite versus popular theatre.  By making theatre closer to life,
"Hugo espérait ramener ainsi au bon théâtre le public qui courait
au mélodrame. . . ."  At the same time, however, Hugo opposed too
realistic a dramatic technique, such as the use of natural overhead
lights, because "la réalité crue de la représentation serait en
désaccord avec la réalité poétique de la pièce, que le drame
n'était pas la vie même, mais la vie transfigurée en art. . . ."

78. Barrère, Jean-Bertrand. "Vingt Ans de recherche sur Victor Hugo." L'Information Littéraire 13 (sept.-oct. 1961): 139-45.

A fine état présent. In discussing work on Hugo as a playwright, Barrère mentions only Gaudon's book (154). Summarizes: "Malgré la reprise de Ruy Blas et la 'première' de Mille Francs de récompense, faisant suite aux récentes représentations de Marie Tudor et de Mangeront-ils?, le théâtre de Hugo ne semble pas avoir exercé d'attrait sur les chercheurs: il offre pourtant encore beaucoup à trouver."

79. Bassan, Fernande. "Alexandre Dumas père et le théâtre romantique." French Review 47 (March 1974): 767-72.

In this attempt to rehabilitate Dumas' romantic theatre, editor of his théâtre complet unfairly minimizes importance of Hugo's theatre: "Le triomphe du drame romantique a été remporté par Dumas, le 10 février 1829, avec Henri III et sa cour, sur la scène du Théâtre-Français, . . ." Also accuses Hugo of taking Marie Tudor and Lucrece Borgia from various Dumas characters. Furthermore, supports Dumas in his belief that "le style trop soigné de Hugo empêche le public de se laisser aller à son émotion."

80. Baudouin, Charles. Psychanalyse de Victor Hugo. Geneva: Editions du Mont-Blanc, 1943. Pp. 255. (New edition has same title. Paris: Colin, 1972. Pp. 304.)

Very responsible investigation of Hugo's complexes as discovered in biographies and examined in his works. Much attention focused on Les Burgraves and Torquemada: "Il est d'ailleurs remarquable que le genre dramatique paraisse se prêter tout particulièrement à l'expression des conflits oedipiens." Themes of fatalité and redemptive power of love also play large role in dramatic works. Analysis shows well how fully Hugo was working on archetypal, mythic level. 1972 edition essentially same. See also Hugi (189).

81. Bayet, Christiane, ed. Victor Hugo s'amuse. Anas, jeux de mots, calembours. Illustrations d'Henri Monnier. Paris: Editions Atlas, 1955. Pp. 186.

Most examples given from Le Théâtre en liberté, as one would suspect. However, both Cromwell and Mille Francs de récompense also contain quite a few indications of Hugo's humor.

82. Beauplan, Robert de. "Exposition du théâtre romantique au musée Victor Hugo." Illustration, année 79 (25 juin 1921): 605-06. (Also in L'Illustre Théâtre 4 [10 janv. 1957]: 42-45.)

Exposition in Hugo museum mounted by Raymond Escholier and composed of portraits, manuscripts, posters, costume models, paintings, tributes to authors, actors, painters and composers of the epoch. Beauplan says his impression is that this period, not so far away in time, is like another world: "De toutes ces choses mortes, une mélancolie se dégage. Elles évoquent la beauté, la grâce, l'amour, l'enthousiasme, la jeunesse, le sourire et aussi, parfois, des drames intimes, des chagrins, des misères, des rivalités, des déceptions."

83. Bédier, Joseph and Paul Hazard. Histoire de la littérature française illustrée. 2 vols. Paris: Larousse, n.d. [1923-1924]. (Hugo's theatre, II, 200.)

Fondness and admiration expressed for Hugo's theatre: "L'ampleur de la composition, la fougue du dessin, l'éclat du coloris, la poésie des figures, peuvent bien compenser dans le théâtre de Hugo, des anachronismes et des erreurs. . . . Louons Victor Hugo d'avoir cherché plus loin que les apparences, et d'avoir donné une valeur symbolique aux âmes de ses héros. . . . Lyrique, épique, dramatique: il semble que ce théâtre relève de tous les modes de la poésie à la fois." Opposite view expressed, however, in 1948 revised edition by Martino and Fuchs (148).

84. Bellessort, André. "Victor Hugo. II: Le Théâtre." La Revue Hebdomadaire, 2 févr. 1929, pp. 22-50. (Also in his Victor Hugo. Essai sur son oeuvre, pp. 35-69. Paris: Perrin, 1930.)

Chronological examination of plays. Bellessort considers Hugo's theatre to be today only "une des moins bonnes parties de son oeuvre, presque un poids mort." Much attention to theories in prefaces and to flaws of plays. Selects Ruy Blas without enthusiasm as best play.

85. Bentley, Eric. The Modern Theatre: A Study of Dramatists and the Drama. London: R. Hale, n.d. [1948]. (Hugo, p. 47.)

Negative view of Hugo's plays expressed: "It is depressing to note that French Romantic Drama is a portentous failure, that Hernani is a schoolmaster's classic far inferior to anything of Schiller's (not to compare it with Shakespeare, as Matthew Arnold did), and that the plays of the French Romanticists succeeded best, when they succeeded at all, on the operatic stage for which God, if not always their authors, intended them."

86. Bérence, Fred. "Admirable et détestable Hugo." In his Grandeur spirituelle du XIXe siècle, II, 177-200. Paris: Colombe, 1959.

Hugo's reputation and appeal will be sustained by his lyric poetry, not by his plays. "Quant à son théâtre, ramassis de lieux communs, de situations rocambolesques, de sentiments faussement nobles, avec, de temps à autre, des cris de protestation, des éclats de passion, des murmures lyriques, il est acceptable lorsque Ruy Blas est joué par Gérard Philipe. A condition, toutefois, de ne pas voir le même acteur jouer Lorenzaccio dix jours après! . . . Le Roi s'amuse ressemble à une gageure et je n'en parlerais pas s'il ne résummait le 'détestable' Hugo. . . ."

87. Bergeaud, Jean. "Hugo, Victor." In his Je choisis . . . mon théâtre, pp. 335-36. Paris: Editions Odilis, n.d. [1956].

In this alphabetical listing of world's dramatists, commented by Bergeaud, Hugo's plays are termed worthy of consideration only

"comme un moment de l'histoire du théâtre." Plays' faults are
detailed, then overall judgment rendered: "Seul Ruy Blas pour
ses qualités musicales paraît encore capable d'enthousiasmer
une salle lorsqu'il trouve pour l'interpréter les 'ténors'
indispensables."

88. Berret, Paul. "Le Théâtre." In his Victor Hugo, pp. 274-325.
Paris: Garnier Frères, 1927. (Title and publishing information same
for 1939 edition.)

A generally favorable appreciation of Hugo's plays. Calls
Ruy Blas Hugo's "chef-d'oeuvre de composition dramatique."
Despite Hernani's weak characterization, il "nous montre ce que
peut l'art,--et l'art tel que l'a entendu Victor Hugo,--pour
l'exaltation de l'émotion." In Les Burgraves, Berret singles out
"la grandeur épique" and "l'émotion lyrique des sentiments."
Finds that Torquemada "fait horreur," yet "des visions épiques
séduisent . . . ça et là." Of the Théâtre en liberté, excluding
L'Epée, Berret offers praise: "Tout le reste est plein de grâce,
d'esprit délicat ou de rire énorme, . . . et rien n'est plus
éloigné, cette fois, des banalités du mélodrame." 1939 edition
expresses same opinions.

89. Bersaucourt, Albert de. "Le Théâtre de Victor Hugo et la parodie."
Le Mercure de France 81 (sept. 1909): 20-42, 254-76. (Also in his
Les Pamphlets contre Victor Hugo, pp. 280-384. Paris: Mercure de
France, n.d. [1912].)

After an enumeration of many of Hugo's contemporary enemies whose
favorite means of revenge was the parodie, Bersaucourt offers a
complete list of all known parodies, play by play. Hernani and
Les Burgraves both drew six, Marion de Lorme two, Torquemada one,
the rest three each. There follows an analysis of a few parodies
and their general traits. See also Blanchard (92) and Travers
(310).

90. Bertaut, Jules. "Le Théâtre romantique." In his Victor Hugo,
pp. 47-74. Paris: Louis-Michaud, n.d. [1909].

Historical re-creation of period 1829-1843 by means of dramatized
scenes. Rather flat. No real literary criticism.

91. Biré, Edmond. "Le Centenaire de Victor Hugo." Le Correspondant,
n.s. 170 (10 févr. 1902): 432-48. (Also in his Biographies
contemporaines. XIXe siècle, pp. 265-92. Lyon: E. Vitte, 1905.)

This noted detractor of Hugo continues his criticisms. Still
doubts if Hugo had much talent in dramatic art. Objects to
invraisemblance in all of Hugo's plays and to licentiousness in
Le Roi s'amuse and prose plays. Signals Hernani as Hugo's best
drama and as second best Les Burgraves, in which Hugo was another
Aeschylus without the public's realizing it.

92. Blanchard, M. Andre. "Le Théâtre de Victor Hugo et la Parodie."
Mémoires de l'Académie d'Amiens, sér. 4, t. 50 (1903): 99-163.

(Also Le Théâtre de Victor Hugo et la Parodie. Amiens: A. Picard, 1903. Pp. 68.)

Quite informative chronological presentation of myriad parodies following each of Hugo's acted dramas. Not all described in detail. Extensive quotations given from best ones. Parody at that time a well developed genre; but these examples, Blanchard concludes, are "de valeur inégale." Emphasizes that, true or false, they are based on literary judgment built around what authors see as faults in plays. Hugo's greatest weakness is that "l'auteur manquait d'invention dramatique." Aderer's analysis of Les Barbus graves (726) appears in appendix. See also Bersaucourt (89) and Travers (310).
a) Faguet. Journal des Débats, août 1906.

93. Boer, Joseph P. C. de. Victor Hugo et l'enfant. Wassenaar (Holland): Dieben, 1933. (Hugo's theatre, pp. 91-100.)

Examination of moral function of the child, whose innocence redeems guilty parents, in Le Roi s'amuse, Lucrèce Borgia and Les Burgraves. In all three dramas, Boer remarks, "l'enfant paraît surtout comme contraste à la méchanceté de ses parents, méchanceté que son innocence, sa pureté sont destinées à résorber par l'effet de l'amour paternel ou maternel."

94. Borne, Etienne. "Gloses sur Victor Hugo." Terre Humaine, année 2, no. 21 (sept. 1952): 51-57.

Attempt to re-evaluate and elevate Hugo's position as dramatist. Defends Hugo's invraisemblance, antitheses and lack of psychology, often by comparing his plays to those of Claudel. Says in fifty years Hernani and Ruy Blas will still be performed: "On plaiderait donc volontiers pour une révision du procès de Hugo dramaturge. . . . Que ce théâtre hugolien fasse toujours question, que la célèbre bataille se continue encore, c'est peut-être la preuve d'une vie qui n'est seulement une survie."

95. Bourgeois, Rene et Jean Mallion. Le Théâtre au XIXe siècle. Paris: Masson, 1971. Pp. 245. (Hugo, pp. 36-46; 60-76; 110-116.)

Anthology includes excerpts from Cromwell to illustrate new Shakespearian form attempted in drame romantique and from Les Burgraves as example of new epic drama. "Je suis une force qui va" speech comprises section demonstrating violence of passions and destiny as commonplaces of drame romantique. Explantory material connecting excerpts offers some interesting ideas: "Le théâtre de Hugo, c'est un monde analogue peut-être à celui de La Comédie humaine: les personnages s'y retrouvent de pièce en pièce, sous des noms et des visages différents. . . . Hernani est, selon Hugo, une 'porte presque moresque à la cathédrale gothique' que constitue son théâtre."

96. Bowley, Victor. "English Versions of Victor Hugo's Plays." French Quarterly 10 (juin 1928): 86-98. (Also in Adam International Review, 19, 229-230 [1952]: 8-15.)

Quite intriguing indication of Hugo's good fortune in England
through melodramatic adaptations of his plays. Often objectionable
scenes cut out and happy ending substituted. Except for John
Davidson's A Queen's Romance from Ruy Blas, however, literary
quality of the versions is poor from lack of "poetic insight,"
in Bowley's opinion. Concludes with list of English plays based
on those of Hugo. Ruy Blas and Angelo furnished six, Hernani five
(Les Misérables nine!). Taken from author's M.A. thesis in 1927
at University of London.

97. Brun, Auguste. Deux Proses de théâtre; drame romantique, comédies
et proverbes. Annales de la Faculté des Lettres, Aix-en-Provence,
n.s., no. 6. Gap: **Editions** Orphrys, 1954. (Hugo, pp. 43-52.)

Important study on attempts to renovate theatrical language during
Romantic period through prose. Examines Hugo's doctrines on
question, then analyzes his prose plays. Hugo applies prose style
of novels to theatre: "La phrase de Hugo est un combiné permanent
de tous ces moyens rhétoriques. Et l'on remarquera que par son
souci d'élaborer une prose théâtrale qui ait la même puissance
expressive que le vers, il atteint à une vigueur qui est celle
de l'alexandrin tragique de Corneille." Finds that Hugo's new
"style à effets," though successful at times, today is exhausted.
Real innovator, Brun suggests, is Musset, who pulls prose back to
classical mesure.

98. Bruner, James D. Studies in Victor Hugo's Dramatic Characters.
With an introduction by Richard G. Moulton. Boston: Ginn & Co.,
1908. Pp. 171.

First two chapters appeared previously (422, 645). In preface to
this book, Bruner calls his method "sympathetic induction." In
practice it displays the limitations of a highly subjective
criticism which leads to some conclusions of doubtful validity.
Yet Bruner does go to the heart of one problem of Hugo's theatre--
characterization. Chapter on don Salluste in Ruy Blas cites his
one redeeming quality as "intellectuality." In section on
Lucrezia Borgia, Bruner calls her "one of Hugo's dramatic
impossibilities . . . an abstract idea rather than a concrete
individual."

99. Brunetière, Ferdinand. "Le Théâtre de Victor Hugo." In his
Victor Hugo, II, 96-121. Paris: Hachette et Cie, 1902. (Also in
Annales politiques et littéraires, année 23 [5, 12 févr. 1905]: 88-89,
104-06.)

A sensitive and coherent analysis of Hugo's theatre (except for the
unexplained omission of Le Théâtre en liberté). Brunetière calls
Hugo's drama "une oeuvre de circonstance . . . volontaire et
réfléchie." Its most striking characteristic is its artificiality
in subject and method. Essentially a series of lyric digressions,
each play is unified only through the use of local color. The
echoes of contemporary events and Hugo's personal preoccupations
are two further distractions. Brunetière concludes: "Tel qu'Hugo
l'avait réalisé, le drame romantique ne pouvait guère réussir á
la scène."

62   *ANNOTATED BIBLIOGRAPHY*

100.  Butor, Michel.  "Le Théâtre de Victor Hugo."  La Nouvelle Revue
Française, 12 (nov., déc. 1964):  862-78, 1073-81; 13 (janv. 1965):
105-13.  (Also as "La Voix qui sort de l'ombre et le poison qui
transpire à travers les murs," in his Répertoire III, pp. 185-213.
Paris:  Editions de minuit, 1968.)

Re-examines some of Hugo's much criticized dramatic techniques--
asides, gestures, portraits, poison, objects with dramatic
function (le cor)--and finds in them an attempt by Hugo to free
himself from conventions of Racinian psychological theatre and to
forge a new way for future dramatists.  Calls Hugo "le précurseur
de toutes nos tentatives de théâtre total."  Suggests that Hugo,
subconsciously perhaps, wanted failure of Les Burgraves to "mettre
dans leur tort les théâtres de son temps, et par ricochet leur
public. . . . Il réalise ainsi une sorte de démonstration des
insuffisances techniques du théâtre de son temps, invitant à un
nouveau théâtre lequel ne doit pouvoir advenir que dans une
nouvelle société."  Intelligent re-evaluation.

101.  Calogero, Giorgio.  Victor Hugo nel terzo cinquantenario della
sua nascita.  Rome:  Tip. Scuola Salesiana del libro, 1952.  Pp. 16.
(Hugo's theatre, pp. 6-7.)

Another summing up of Hugo's life and works:  "Come drammaturgo,
V. H. si può gloriare di due tra i maggiori successi del tempo,
Hernani e Ruy Blas, di cui il secondo appare oggi alquanto
illeggibile per l'assurdità dell'intreccio, ma ambedue sono
tutt'altro che privi di originalità e di bellezza."

102.  Carlson, Marvin.  "French Stage Composition from Hugo to Zola."
Educational Theatre Journal 23 (1971):  363-78.

Finds Hugo to be break between old stage composition in tradition
of Molière and new.  Some innovative techniques of staging in later
productions, but Hernani remains most experimental:  "Hernani
utilized the stage space in a far more fluid and flexible manner."
Angelo uses furniture "in an unusually informal way" so that
furniture itself participates in development of action.

103.  _____.  The French Stage in the Nineteenth Century.
Metuchen, N.J.:  Scarecrow Press, 1972.  Pp. 326.  (Hugo's theatre,
pp. 4-5, 57-65, 89-145.)

In this history of the theatre, little attention is paid to
dramatic literature from literary point of view, but a wealth of
information is offered on Hugo's premières, details of staging,
directing, rehearsals.  Introduction stresses Hugo's debt to
mélodrame in making it respectable under the name of drame
romantique.  It is of interest that Hugo was the last important
dramatist of the nineteenth century to create major works at the
conservative Comédie-Française, and that even he left after the
success of Hernani for the more congenial boulevard theatres.
a) Lowin.  French Review 47 (1973):  426-27.
b) Smith.  NCTR 1 (Autumn 1973):  131-32.

104.  Carter, Jeannette.  "The Women Characters of Victor Hugo's
Dramatic Works."  M.A. thesis, University of West Virginia, 1901.
Pp. 39.

105.  Castex, Pierre et P. Surer.  "Victor Hugo."  In their Manuel des
études littéraires françaises, Vol. 5, pp. 65-98.  Paris:  Hachette,
n.d. [1951].

> Standard literary history, for most part.  Chooses as Hugo's
> dramatic masterpiece Ruy Blas.  "En alliant ainsi le 'grotesque'
> au 'sublime,' l'écrivain illustre mieux qu'il ne l'avait fait
> dans Hernani le principe du mélange des tons, formulé dans la
> Préface de Cromwell."  On the Théâtre en liberté:  "Quelques-unes
> de ces fantaisies ont pu être représentées; leur fraîcheur, leur
> esprit, ne sont pas indignes d'un génie qui, jusque dans ses
> jeux, révèle les ressources infinies de son invention poétique."
> In explication de texte of the "Je suis une force qui va" speech
> in Hernani, authors state:  "Cette tirade offre peu de valeur
> dramatique et psychologique. . . . Mais elle possède une grande
> valeur poétique."

106.  Cellier, Léon.  "Le Renouveau des études hugoliennes."  Les
Nouvelles Littéraires, 8 janv. 1973, p. 13.

> Surveys recent work being done on Hugo.  Underestimates attraction
> of plays:  "Le théâtre de Hugo manifestement a perdu de son
> attrait."  See Leuilliot (215).

107.  Chahine, Samia.  La Dramaturgie de Victor Hugo.  (1816-1843).
Paris:  A.-G. Nizet, 1971.  Pp. 365.

> Originally author's thesis.  Comprehensive study of produced plays'
> characters, time, place, mise en scène, structural and technical
> aspects and analysis of original characteristics of Hugo's theatre.
> First section situates Hugo's work in "climat de l'époque" with
> attention to influence of mélodrame and drame romantique.  Good
> section on central position of theatre in Hugo's life and
> inspiration.  Lengthy examination of dramatic procedures at times
> tedious but does uncover Hugo's constant, masterful techniques,
> which Chahine defines generally as "une recherche de la trans-
> parence."  Stresses Hugo's attraction to symbolic characters,
> language, objects and his rôle as director.  Refuses to believe
> Hugo's theatre "un échec," rather points to plays' success at
> original performances and often in reprises.  Says recent new
> criticism "ajoute une nouvelle dimension à cette oeuvre et en
> révèle le côté moderne, voire actuel."

108.  Chancerel, Léon.  "Victor Hugo, metteur en scène, décorateur et
costumier."  La Revue d'Histoire du Théâtre, 4, 3 (1952):  232.

> Review of Bibliothèque Nationale's exposition (249).  Chancerel
> refers to previous studies on Hugo as director by Glachant frères
> (163) and Allevy (67), and stresses Hugo's originality.
> Accompanying photo shows Hugo's pen and ink sketch for Act II of
> Les Jumeaux.

109. Charvet, Patrick. A Literary History of France. Vol. 4: The Nineteenth Century, 1789-1870. London: Benn, 1967. (Hugo's theatre, pp. 155-57.)

Balanced, traditional evaluation of Hugo's theatre: "Hernani and all Hugo's plays are improvisations, and even to the best of them similar criticisms apply: historical objections where important historical figures are involved . . . with a strong admixture of personal and contemporary politics, . . . psychology and plot improbabilities. . . . [Yet] audiences can be brought to overlook the niceties of psychological mechanisms or plot structure if they be moved by broad human effects. . . . And what better way of inducing it . . . than the rhythms and rich sensuous imagery of Hugo's poetry?"

110. Chatel, Nicole, Madeleine Oeuvrard, Aline Alquier, Christian Colombani et al., eds. Hugo. Textes sur Hugo. Paris: Paris-Match, 1970. Pp. 136. (Theatre, pp. 38-42, 81-82, 124.)

For general public. Stresses Hugo's political position. Lavish color and black and white illustrations. Brief anthology includes one scene from Hernani. Chapter on "L'Oeuvre" praises Cromwell for its "pénétration psychologique" and "vigueur satirique," Hernani for "la beauté des vers" and "le pathétique de quelques scènes," Ruy Blas for its "savant mélange de poésie, de fantaisie et de satire." Some irritating inaccuracies. Good chapter on Hugo's characters and fine section on Verdi and Hugo in "Victor Hugo dans son siècle."

111. Cheek, Atlas Lawrence. "The Prose Plays of Victor Hugo in Relation to Historical Fact." M.A. thesis, University of North Carolina, 1937. Pp. 112.

Claims that Hugo "does not adhere to history as his numerous notes and prefaces seem to infer" in his prose plays. History merely "a spring-board into philosophical and moral convictions, which, in a disguise as weak as some analogies in the Préface de Cromwell, the author wishes to force upon the rest of the world."

112. Chevalley, Sylvie. "Les Documents et la vie." Comédie-Française 31 (sept. 1974): 30.

113. _____. "Géographie du répertoire." Comédie-Française 31 (sept. 1974): 32.

114. Chiaromonte, Nicola. "Victor Hugo e il cinema." Il Mondo, 16 febbr. 1965, p. 15.

Finds theatre weakest part of Hugo's work because it has fewer exciting images and is full of theatrical conventions and coups de théâtre. Says Hugo wanted to "offrire al popolo riunito degli esempi grandiosi e terribili di comportamento umano attraverso non già e non tanto la parola o la trama, ma un seguito d'immagini in movimento: un'azione, nel senso più immediato trascinante e irreflesso della parola. In altri termini, i drammi di Hugo volevano essere cinematografo." Asserts that W. D. Griffith would have been

perfect director for Hugo's "teatro barocco." See also
Fernández-Cuenca (141).

115. Ciana, Albert. Victor Hugo. Ouvrage orné de nombreux autographes.
Geneva: Editions Helvética, 1941. Pp. 147.

A sort of psychoanalysis of Hugo through chronological study of his
handwriting in manuscripts. Early plays receive much attention.
Many examples of changing handwriting provided. Some conclusions
interesting, if of questionable significance. Illustration of
technique: "L'écriture de Cromwell est encore fine, mais déjà
depouillée, plus ramassée et plus ferme qu'on ne l'a jamais encore
vue; il est d'évidence que la marche à la simplification
s'accélère."

116. Claudon, Francis. "Giacomo Meyerbeer et Victor Hugo: dramaturgies
comparées." In Regards sur l'opéra, pp. 101-111. Publications de
l'Université de Rouen. Centre d'art esthétique et littérature.
[n.p.] Presses Universitaires, 1976.

117. Clément-Janin, Noël. "Le Théâtre de Victor Hugo." In his Drames
et comédies romantiques, pp. 7-56. Paris: Le Goupy, 1928.

Appreciative survey of Hugo's dramatic efforts. Contains many
anecdotes and critical clichés. Author prefers Ruy Blas to all
other Hugo plays but identifies Musset as a deeper, more lasting
dramatist. Hugo's greatest contribution to French drama is "ce
droit au mélange du pathétique et du comique, que Hugo appelait
'la vie' et qu'il ne réalisa que sur le plan du 'plus que la vie,'
par l'extraordinaire, le surhumain et parfois l'exagéré, au bruit
de bronze, de cristal et d'or de son vers puissant comme la tempête,
délicat comme un chant d'oiseau."

118. Cluzel, Etienne. "Victor Hugo et la Comédie-Française en 1838."
Bulletin du Bibliophile, no. 6 (1956), pp. 307-10.

Anecdote in Revue de Paris of epoch recounts Hugo's successful
suit against Comédie-Française to have Hernani, Marion de Lorme and
Angelo performed, according to contract, despite their weak box
office receipts. A few months later Hugo returns to the theatre's
director 20,400 francs awarded to him in court, indicating his
basic generosity, according to Cluzel. Adds: "Un tel déclin
n'était-il pas annonciateur de l'échec sévère que devaient subir
Les Burgraves quelques années plus tard?"

119. Coeuroy, André. "Richard Wagner s'est-il inspiré de Victor Hugo
dans Lohengrin?" La Revue Musicale, année 4 (1er avril 1923): 278-79.

Influence of Hugo on Wagner suggested by Le Breton (211) supported
by Coeuroy with extensive comparisons. Says Wagner probably saw
Hernani performed in 1841 reprise. See also Weil (326).

120. Constans, Charles. Victor Hugo poète de l'amour. Béziers:
J. Rodriquez Imp., 1931. (Hugo's theatre, pp. 109-29.)

Devotes entire chapter to theme of love and poésie d'amour in verse dramas. Asserts plays' action in large part sustained, propelled by passion of love, which also produces excellent lyrical quality of dramas. Finds all levels of love in Hugo's theatre from François I's amour canaille and don César's amour léger to most poignant culmination of amour-passion in Act V of Hernani.

121. Cordié, Carlo. "Il Teatro di Victor Hugo. La lira e la scena." Il Mondo, 13 ott. 1964, pp. 9-10.

Sums up position of Hugo's plays in 1960s: "Il teatro di Victor Hugo è poco letto," not even in France. Finds even Ruy Blas and Marie Tudor "opere più lette e citate per stima che per convinzione," and rates operas from Angelo and Le Roi s'amuse better than originals. Considers the Théâtre complet, edited by Thierry and Mélèze (63), excellent for seeing sources and contrasting with other dramatic works of period. Concludes: "Certo una volta di più spicca, di opera in opera . . . il genio oratorio e formale del poeta, quel suo abbandonnarsi alla parola e al gesto con insuperabile abilità. Attore e spettatore del suo teatro, Victor Hugo non finisce di stupirci. E, anche sulla scena, 'toute la lyre' è sua."

122. Cryer, Constance. "Theme and Variation: A Study of Victor Hugo's Theater." Ph.D. dissertation, Yale University, 1965. Pp. 309. (Abstract in Dissertation Abstracts 26, 8 [Feb. 1966]: 4654-55.)

Thematic study of four major leitmotifs in Hugo's theatre: the trap, the mask, death and liberty.

123. Dabrowski, S. "Wictor Hugo na scenach polskich." Pamietnik Teatralny (Warsaw) 4 (1952).

124. Dale, R. C. "Chatterton Is the Essential Romantic Drama." L'Esprit Créateur 5 (Fall 1965): 131-37.

Argues unconvincingly that "thematically . . . Chatterton is an intricate realization of Hugo's theory, and in terms of plot, its point-by-point rejection of melodrama's données makes it the first genuine anti-melodrama" and that "Vigny's character Thomas Chatterton is the first complete Romantic realization of Hugo's mind-body theory of the grotesque." Dale claims that, through his use of dramatic irony to convince audience of the hero's superiority and "his rejection of materialism, Vigny performed the first genuine division of the Romantic hero into his grotesque-sublime components." A weak case presented to support the thesis.

125. Dédéyan, Charles. Victor Hugo et l'Allemagne. 2 vols. Paris: Lettres modernes, 1964-1965. Pp. 265, 308.

Sound study of German sources of Hugo's inspiration. Traces in detail evolution of influence of Germany on Hugo's work from pre-occupation with sentimental, fantastic and diabolical to concern with deeper problems, such as struggle between Good and Evil or Faustian motif. Vol. 1 (1802-1830) has chapters on plays, Cromwell, Amy Robsart, Marion de Lorme and Hernani. Vol. 2

(1830-1848) treats plays by examining specific influence of Goethe
and Schiller from Le Roi s'amuse to culmination in Les Burgraves.
a) Bourgeois. Books Abroad 40 (1966): 292-93.
b) Franceschetti. Studi Francesi 11 (1967): 105-09.
c) Georgel. Les Lettres Romanes 20 (1966): 183-88; 21 (1967):
   183-85.
d) Imbert. La Rivista di Letterature moderne e Comparate 18
   (1965): 153-54.
e) Monchoux. La Revue d'Histoire Littéraire de la France 65
   (1965): 709-11.

126. Deffoux, Léon. Le Pastiche littéraire. Paris: Delagrave, 1932.
(Hugo's theatre, pp. 77-92.)

Suggests it was because of Hugo's personality that he bore the
brunt of pastiches and parodies in the Romantic period. Examples
given from Harnali and Le Moine Bleu (1885). The latter is a
pastiche of Ruy Blas and Marion de Lorme, fruit of collaboration of
Nina de Villard, Jean Richepin and Germain Nouveau.

127. Degenhardt, Ernest. Die Metapher in den Dramen Victor Hugos.
2 vols. Wiesbaden: K. Schwab, 1899-1900. Pp. 35, 39.

Originally an inaugural dissertation. Vol. 1 examines plays
through 1830, and Vol. 2 Le Roi s'amuse through Les Burgraves and
Torquemada. As there is no attempt to discover the overall patterns
of Hugo's metaphors, this study is not very helpful.

128. Delaunay, Christian. "Le Théâtre de Victor Hugo." L'Evénement,
année 100 (1er mars 1952): 3.

Very laudatory article by dedicated Hugophile on Hugo's plays,
especially Ruy Blas, Les Burgraves and L'Epée. Investigates
problems of staging Hugo for modern audience. Shows Hugo's desire
to "faire de la pensée le pain de la foule." Finds Les Burgraves
"le plus grand de tout le théâtre français" and states: "le vers
de Victor Hugo est avec celui de Molière, le plus beau vers du
théâtre que nous connaissions."

129. Dereeper, Arlette. "L'Idée démocratique dans le théâtre de
Victor Hugo." Mémoires pour le diplôme d'études supérieures, Université
de Paris, 1962. Pp. 128.

130. Descotes, Maurice. Le Drame romantique et ses grands créateurs
(1827-1839). Paris: Presses universitaires de France, 1955. (Hugo,
pp. 119-35, 215-23, 241-58, 284-99, 318-27.)

Massive thesis on details of actual theatrical productions of
various drames romantiques. Amy Robsart, Hernani, Marion de Lorme,
Le Roi s'amuse, Lucrèce Borgia, Marie Tudor, Angelo, tyran de Padoue
and Ruy Blas all receive attention with emphasis on theatres,
actors and actresses and audiences. Conclusion stresses that
accurate evaluation of Romantic dramas must take into consideration
personalities of actors creating rôles, from Mlle Mars and Joanny to
Marie Dorval and Frédérick Lemaître, as major vehicle for plays'
impact.

131. Descotes, Maurice. "Le Théâtre romantique. Hugo ou le théâtre d'interprètes." In Littérature française, II, 69-72. Edition par Antoine Adam, Georges Lerminier et Edouard Morot-Sir. [Paris]: Larousse, n.d. [1968].

Hugo's theatre survives only through its form and because of its place in literary history. Descotes claims that "on joue toujours Hernani et Ruy Blas. Mais on ne prend plus guère au sérieux l'ensemble de ce théâtre, sinon pour en étudier les intentions politiques et sociales; . . . ce théâtre fut servi à la création, et ne peut plus être désormais sauvé que par des interprètes exceptionnels." Calls Hugo a "médiocre homme de théâtre, au sens artisanal du mot."

132. Doumic, René. "L'Oeuvre du romantisme au théâtre." La Revue des Deux Mondes, sér. 5, 8 (15 avril 1902): 923-34.

There is no "théâtre romantique," only a "période romantique," Doumic claims. No lasting new genre was produced, a fact evinced by the 1843 and 1902 failures of Les Burgraves. Hugo's plays vacillate between tragedy and mélodrame but merit praise for their couleur. Hugo's verbal power and epic genius are developed to their highest point in Les Burgraves, which, according to Doumic, "sont . . . un des plus beaux poèmes qu'il y ait dans notre littérature."

133. Draper, F. W. M. The Rise and Fall of the French Romantic Drama; With Special Reference to the Influence of Shakespeare, Scott and Byron. London: Constable, 1923. Pp. 303.

Good study, best in English until Howarth's (187). First four chapters trace background and English influence; fifth on theories and Cromwell; sixth, seventh, eighth on major plays, Henri III et sa cour through Ruy Blas; ninth very good treatment of heroes, Hernani as prototype; tenth on political side of Romantic drama; final chapter on why it a failure. Hugo also consistent failure as playwright: "He was never a dramatist. He fell into absurdity after absurdity, culminating in 1843 in the Burgraves. . . . The whole play is ridiculous, long-winded and improbable. . . . But it still draws, and the continued popularity of the play shows how fond the French are of tirades." Underestimates Hugo's contributions to style and form of drama and his plays' lyric qualities.

134. Dubech, Lucien. Histoire générale illustrée du théâtre. Avec la collaboration de Jacques de Montibrial et de Madeleine Horn-Marval. 5 vols. Paris: Librairie de France, n.d. [1931-35?]. (Hugo, V, 68-81.)

In this witty evaluation, Dubech chooses Marion de Lorme as "le drame d'Hugo . . . [qui] est le meilleur et le moins extravagant" and Act IV of Ruy Blas as Hugo's "chef-d'oeuvre dramatique." Voices common thought that Hugo's lyric power and Dumas's dramatic flair together might have produced extraordinary plays; then has second thoughts: "Non, c'eût été insuffisant encore. Même si l'on imagine, si l'on rêve une pièce construite par Dumas et écrite par Hugo, il lui manquera encore l'essentiel: la vérité."

135. Dupuy, Ernest. La Jeunesse des romantiques: Victor Hugo, Alfred de Vigny. Paris: Société française d'imprimerie et de librairie ancienne, Librairie Lecène, Oudin & Cie, 1905. (Hugo's theatre, pp. 70-81.)

Chapter on Cromwell, Amy Robsart and Hernani contains anecdotes and details of composition, performance, reception. Letters printed to show Talma interested in playing rôle of Cromwell and that Hugo introduced into Hernani some of the very phrases and verses he had written ten years previously to his fiancée Adèle. Concludes of Hernani: "Dans cette oeuvre, qui marque une date aussi heureuse, aussi lumineuse que le Cid, Victor Hugo avait mis l'ardeur, la poésie et la vertu de sa jeunesse."

136. Dussane, Madame. "Le Théâtre de Victor Hugo: Drame de jadis et poésie de toujours." Bulletin de l'Institut Français en Espagne, no. 67 (juin-sept. 1953), pp. 111-13.

Genial personal view of Hugo's major plays. Stresses Hugo's "préoccupations personnelles, passionnelles et même pratiques" in drames and says that 1843 brought to full light "l'incompatibilité foncière entre la manière fastueuse de Hugo et les nécessités imprescriptibles du théâtre." Closes by stating that we are still basically Romantic [in 1953] and can learn from Hugo's "prodigieuse santé, . . . athlétisme verbal et mental, . . . et cette richesse généreuse."

137. Dzakula, Branko. "La Fortune de Victor Hugo en Croatie." Annales de l'Institut Français de Zagreb, ts. 10-11, nos. 28-29 (1946-1947): 123-231. (Also published separately. Same title. Zagreb: Institut français, 1949. Pp. 116.)

Hugo was known first in Croatia as a dramatic author, largely through German translations. Lucrèce Borgia his only real success in Zagreb, but other plays were popular elsewhere in the area. During second half of the nineteenth century, Hugo was almost totally forgotten as a dramatist. In 1930 Lucrèce Borgia put on at the Théâtre de Zagreb to commemorate centenary of Romanticism.

138. Eggli, Edmond. Schiller et le romantisme français. 2 vols. Paris: Gamber, 1927. (Hugo's theatre, I, 339-408; II, 318-92 and passim.)

Vol. I indicates influence of Schiller on Hugo's dramatic theories. Vol. II examines Hugo's "emprunts" from Schiller's plays. Eggli considers Hugo's debt to Schiller very large, but he does acknowledge that Hugo adapts these borrowings with "le plus de personnalité et d'originalité." Lack of an index for these huge tomes renders them much less useful.

139. Evans, David O. "L'Odéon et le drame romantique." La Revue d'Histoire Littéraire de la France 34 (1927): 85-92.

Very intriguing article in which Evans argues that "la fermeture de l'Odéon [en 1832] doit être considérée comme une cause qui explique le rude destin du drame romantique." Until 1838, the

drame romantique remained without a theatre: "Il dut vivre
dangereusement sur des théâtres nullement faits pour initier
laborieusement et couteusement le public à une dramaturgie nouvelle."
Evans attributes to this lack of a sympathetic stage the failure of
Cromwell: "Le commercialisme forcéné des théâtres de Paris, joint
à l'apathie de la première scène suscitée, encouragée par la
fermeture du second Théâtre-Français, explique suffisamment l'échec
de Cromwell. Entre l'inanition de la plupart des scènes et
l'hostilité de l'autre, le débouché essentiel manqua. . . ."

140.  Evans, David O.  Le Théâtre pendant la période romantique (1827-
1848).  Paris:  Les Presses Universitaires de France, 1925.  Pp. 95.

Solid study of development of theatre during Romantic period and of
social and economic forces impinging upon it.  Chapter 5, pp. 41-48,
describes "ideal" Romantic drama never attained and real innovations
accomplished; for Hugo this means introduction of couleur locale
that eventually produces true drame historique.  In chapter 6,
pp. 49-59, Evans tries to identify the origins of the Romantic
drama and concludes, as did Rigal (265), that "le drame romantique,
loin de faire brèche avec le passé littéraire de France, en sort
tant directement, qu'indirectement."  Chapter 7, pp. 60-70, on the
drame historique contains the statement that "le théâtre de Victor
Hugo n'est donc pas un drame historique:  c'est tout entier un
drame de pensée."  At end of book, Evans stresses the commercializa-
tion of the theatres that did not give place to young talents:
"Sachons enfin que le théâtre romantique, tel qu'il a existé (il
n'a pu exister que fragmentairement), est le produit d'une lutte
implacable contre l'esprit matérialiste de l'ère industrielle qui
naît."

141.  Fernández-Cuenca, D. Carlos.  "Victor Hugo et le cinéma."
Bulletin de l'Institut Français en Espagne, no. 67 (juin-sept. 1953),
pp. 143-48.

Sees Hugo as "né pour le septième art" and one of authors most
adapted for movies.  List of thirty films, made in last fifty years,
based on Hugo's works follows; includes four versions of Marie
Tudor and three of Le Roi s'amuse.  See also Chiaromonte (114).

142.  Fiocco, Achille.  Teatro universale dalle origini ai giorni
nostri.  Vol. 2:  Dal classicismo al romanticismo.  Bologna:  Capelli,
1967.  (Hugo, pp. 211-15.)

Judges Hugo's problem in theatrical works as failure to transcend
melodrama:  "Hugo riunisce in sé tutti i generi; ma soprattutto
suona in lui quel melodramma, che intendeva combattere. . . . Il
teatro vittorhugiano non toccò il bersaglio, al contrario, sembrò
recare argomenti agli oppositori, col volgere del tempo; lo stesso
Hugo se ne convinse e passò ad altro."

143.  Fourcassié, Jean.  Une Ville à l'époque romantique: Toulouse.
Paris:  Plon, 1953.  (Hugo's theatre, pp. 174-83.)

Toulouse too conservative in 1830s politically, economically and
socially to appreciate Hugo's drames.  Town had nostalgia for

"vieilles disciplines classiques" and so rejected Hugo's "shocking" immorality and <u>invraisemblances</u>. Lively account, though, of resistance to Hugo's plays includes story of a duel over an 1833 performance of <u>Lucrèce Borgia</u> in which a political liberal was killed, and a story of <u>Hernani</u>'s delayed première in Toulouse in 1843. See also Thomas (535).

144. Franceschetti, Giancarlo. "La Fortuna di Hugo nel melodramma italiano dell'ottocento." In <u>Contributi dell'Istituto di Filologia Moderna</u>, serie francese 2 (1961), pp. 168-251. Milan: Società Vita e Pensiero, 1961.

Excellent study of nineteenth-century Italian musical adaptations of Hugo's works. Bibliographical footnotes and review of previous research very useful. Separate sections devoted to versions of <u>Hernani</u>, <u>Marion de Lorme</u>, <u>Le Roi s'amuse</u>, <u>Lucrèce Borgia</u>, <u>Marie Tudor</u>, <u>Angelo</u>, <u>La Esmeralda</u>, <u>Ruy Blas</u> and <u>Les Burgraves</u>. Judges Felice Romani and Boito as best adapters of Hugo and agrees with common view that Hugo's plays are better in musical form than in the original: "E con ciò ritorniamo all'acquisizione, . . . che il teatro hugoliano, consistendo non già in drammi tragici, quali erano le intenzioni del dramaturgo, ma bensì in melodrammi lirici, non fu profanato, ma anzi valorizzato dal melodramma italiano, in virtù della musica che in pari tempo ne coprì alcuni difetti."

145. _____. "Studi hughiani in Italia nel decennio 1951-1960." In <u>Contributi dell'Istituto di Filologia Moderna</u>, serie francese 3 (1964), pp. 454-522. Milan: Società Vita e Pensiero, 1964.

New <u>inédits</u> since 1951 have sparked renewed interest in Hugo in Italy, especially in "Hugo mage" of exile, author of "l'oeuvre de fantôme." This scholarly, exhaustive essay reviews Italian research on Hugo and contrasts it with what has been done in France and, to lesser extent, elsewhere. Offers evidence of high quality of Italian scholarship and a plea for it to be considered seriously by French scholars. Says it evident to "la critica non influenzabile che la vocazione teatrale di Hugo fu un fallimento."

146. Franchetti, Augusto. "Victor Hugo e il melodramma italiano." <u>Marzocco</u>, 26 febbr. 1902.

Very brief article claiming Hugo wrong to despise operas based on his dramatic works. The basic theatricality and lyricism of his plays make them perfect for operatic form, which hides their weaknesses of plot and characterization. Hugo should be glad that "le note dell'<u>Ernani</u> e del <u>Rigoletto</u>, non ostante la mediocrità dei libretti, sono degne interpreti dei sentimenti del Poeta . . . [e]ne prolungarono la vita. . . ."

147. Froment-Guieysse, Georges. <u>Victor Hugo</u>. 2 vols. Paris: Editions de l'Empire français, 1948. (Hugo's theatre, I, 115-29, 179-205.)

Chapter 4 of first part on <u>Cromwell</u> quite informative. Chapter 3 of second part offers a few striking remarks about the rest of Hugo's theatre. Suggests that Hugo's <u>Irtamène</u> is a translation from Ausonius and finds Torquemada "un drame à la façon de Calderón, noir, lugubre, fantastique, . . . la plus psychologique de toutes ses pièces." Overall consideration of Hugo's dramas: "A part deux pièces qui demeureront, Hernani et Ruy Blas, peut-être une troisième, Marion de Lorme, et de larges fragments des Burgraves, le reste de son oeuvre théâtrale rentrera dans l'ombre.  Son influence sur le développement du théâtre contemporain n'en aura pas moins été considérable et cela sera dû à Cromwell et à sa retentissante préface."

148.  Fuchs, Max.  "Le Théâtre romantique."  In La Littérature française, II, 234-48.  Publiée sous la direction de Joseph Bédier et Paul Hazard. Nouvelle édition refondue et augmentée sous la direction de Pierre Martino.  Paris:  Larousse, n.d. [1948-1949].

Total revision of the opinion expressed by Bédier and Hazard in 1923 (83):  "Tous les drames de Hugo sont aussi romanesques, aussi dénués de vraisemblance qu'il est possible d'être; on retrouve dans tous le même bric-à-brac lugubre."  Ruy Blas and Hernani still performed, Fuchs believes, because of "la supériorité de la forme, . . . la grandeur et la générosité."  Judges Les Burgraves unworthy of its décor and its failure a "défaite méritée."  Musset chosen as best dramatist of Romantic period.

149.  Fucilla, Joseph.  "Menéndez Pelayo and Victor Hugo."  Hispania 39 (Sept. 1956):  275-80.

Over eighty pages of the last volume of the great Spanish critic's unfinished Historia de las ideas estéticas en España (1891) are devoted to Hugo.  His theatre does not fare well despite kind words for epic qualities of Les Burgraves:  "'Su teatro está muerto, muerto sin remisión.'"  His plays' one redeeming quality is that they were written in a "'nuevo alejandrino . . . la más positiva conquista, quizá lo único en el teatro que hará que se recuerden sus dramas, con los cuales modestamente pretendió eclipsar a Corneille y a Racine, y ponerse al nivel de Shakespeare y de Schiller.'"

150.  Fucini, Catone.  Il Teatro di Victor Hugo.  Genoa:  Tip. Artigianelli, 1925.  Pp. 63.

151.  Gabbert, Thomas A.  "Notes on the Popularity of the Dramas of Victor Hugo in Spain during the Years 1835-1845."  Hispanic Review 4 (April 1936):  176-78.

Corrects misstatements he finds in articles of Parker and Peers (251, 250).  From theatrical announcements and a private diary, he charts the number of performances of Hugo's "popular prose melodramas" in Spain from 1835-1845.

152.  Galletti, Alfredo.  L'Opera di Vittor Hugo nella letteratura italiana.  Giornale storico della letteratura italiana, supplemento, no. 7.  Turin:  E. Loescher, 1904.  Pp. 181.

Solid investigation of reciprocal influence of Hugo and Italy. Especially good sections on Manzoni's influence (pp. 19-24) and on

popular and critical reception of plays in Italy (pp. 77-126).
According to Galletti, "tra il 1828 e il 1851 V. Hugo, più che come
lirico o romanziere, fu ammirato, vituperato, discusso in Italia
come poeta drammatico." After 1843, however, his plays enjoyed
less success and survived principally as operas: "E il melodramma
musicale trovò materia eccellente nei drammi di Vittor Hugo, così
poco addatti al teatro di prosa." Unfortunately, this long essay
with no chapter divisions and index only of people's names is very
difficult to use.

153. Gaudon, Jean. "Hugo." In Enciclopedia dello Spettacolo, VI,
428-34. 10 vols. Fondata da Silvio D'Amico. Rome: Le Maschere,
1954-63.

Complete, compact information on all Hugo's dramatic attempts,
including fragments. Selects Hernani and Ruy Blas as best dramas
and says he has to set aside judgment of Le Théâtre en liberté
because Hugo makes no attempt to confront staging problems, so that
those plays belong to the history of poetry. Describes recent
attempts by various directors to highlight popular side of Hugo's
dramas, especially at festivals. Good bibliography.

154. _____. Victor Hugo dramaturge. Paris: L'Arche, 1955.
Pp. 158.

Sound presentation of basic information about place of theatre in
Hugo's life with intriguing personal views on plays. Identifies
Hugo's aim: "Seul de tous les romantiques français, Hugo conçoit
un projet inouï: redonner au théâtre une vie nouvelle en trans-
formant le fait historique en fait littéraire." Finds, however,
this attempt to create popular theatre through use of historical
moments and a dramaturgy of "transparence" ultimately a failure:
"Hugo n'a pas réussi à faire du gigantesque politique, un
gigantesque littéraire, il n'a pas réussi à fonder un théâtre qui
soit figuré de l'histoire. . . . En se faisant complices des forces
obscures, les héros vont retrouver un peu de leur épaisseur
psychologique: le signe historique redevient destin individuel.
Dans cette aventure, la 'moira' n'a gagné qu'une généralité sans
grandeur." Attention paid to Hugo's use of masks, his revolutionary
rhetoric, and his own role in designing scenery, costumes and acting
styles. Les Burgraves cited as his weakest play, Mille Francs de
récompense and Ruy Blas among his best. Forty-four pages of well
chosen quotations from various Hugo texts illustrate Gaudon's
points. Short bibliography, no index.
a) Temple-Patterson. Modern Language Review 52 (Jan. 1957):
   118-19.
b) Hunt. French Studies 11 (Jan. 1957): 68-69.

155. Gély, Claude. Hugo et sa fortune littéraire. Bordeaux: G.
Ducros, 1970. Pp. 196.

Very fine panorama of critical thought on Hugo and his works from
1817 to 1970. This comprehensive study with illustrative details
and examples in appendix shows trends and high and low points of
Hugo criticism, yet does not become bogged down with too many names
and titles. A great amount of information clearly presented and

evaluated. Fascinating survey of Hugo's continuing appeal. Puts
criticism on theatre in proper perspective with that of all of
Hugo's works. A more complete index including separate titles of
Hugo's works would have made valuable study even more readily useful.
See also Pendell (256) and Hervier (182).
a) Franceschetti. Studi Francesi 15 (1971): 569.
b) Lyons. French Review 46 (1972): 162-63.

156. George, Albert. "Early American Criticism of Victor Hugo."
French Review 11 (Feb. 1938): 287-93.

Though comment in the United States on Hugo is sparse from 1827-
1852, it is largely negative and based on moral principles:
"America found its chief interest in Hugo's drama, and next in his
novels, while his poetry ran a poor third. . . . American Babbitts,
slaves to the economic, sociological, and philosophical back-
grounds, disparagingly admitted Hugo to be France's greatest
writer."

157. Ghazi, Djenat Mohamed Khaled. "Les Thèmes du mal dans le théâtre
de Victor Hugo." Ph.D. dissertation, University of Illinois, 1975.
DAI 35 (1975): 7305A.

158. Ghéon, Henri. "D'Hernani au Théâtre Libre." In his L'Art du
théâtre, pp. 41-60. Montréal: Editions Serge, n.d. [1944].

From talk given to Jacques Copeau's students, actors and friends at
Le Vieux Colombier. Has harsh words for Hugo's theatre: "Hugo
invente un artifice bien plus grave, funeste à la vérité même. . . .
Il était incapable de sortir de lui-même et de créer des
personnages. . . . Humainement parlant, je ne sais rien de plus
abstrait que sa pensée sous le débordement magnifique de
l'ornement. . . . Théâtre populaire? Si l'on veut, mais dans le
plus mauvais sens du mot; un théâtre où l'auteur ne collabore avec
la foule qu'en la flattant, qu'en l'aveuglant et qu'en rusant avec
sa bonne volonté."

159. Giardini, Cesare. Victor Hugo. Milan: Periodici Mondadori,
1969. Pp. 135.

Entertaining, succinct biography of Hugo with lavish illustrations.
For general Italian reader. No literary criticism, but basic
information on theatre presented in chapters on battle of Hernani,
Hugo as head of Romantics, his obsession with the theatre. English
translation by Diana Snell as The Life and Times of Victor Hugo.
London: Hamlyn, 1969. Pp. 75.

160. Gide, André. "Préface." To his Anthologie de la poésie
française, pp. vii-li. Paris: Gallimard, 1949. (Hugo's theatre, p.
xxxii.)

Author of the famous "Hugo, hélas!" elaborates his view of Hugo's
dramatic works: "Pourtant je ne puis me tenir de juger les
ressorts de ses drames aussi sévèrement, plus sévèrement encore,
que je ne faisais autrefois. La psychologie de ses héros reste à
nos yeux aussi conventionnelle et arbitraire qu'il se doit pour

les effets de contraste scénique qui seuls lui importent, pour le
saisissement qu'il en escompte et qui, trop prévus et factices,
manquent leur but auprès de ceux qui répugnent à couper dans cette
flagrante duperie."

161. Ginisty, Paul. France d'antan: le théâtre romantique. Paris:
A. Morancé, n.d. [c 1922]. (Hugo, pp. 16-28, 34-47.)

Beautiful, sturdy set of separate planches, nineteen of which are
devoted to Hugo, accompanies rather succinct and ordinary text of
literary history and anecdotes. Good chapter, pp. 34-36, on
parodies of Romantic dramas. Last chapter, pp. 37-47, presents
material on outstanding actors of period, like Frédérick Lemaitre
and Marie Dorval.

162. Girault, Madeleine. "Victor Hugo et la justice." Effort
Claréiste, année 7 (mai 1935): 52-54.

Brief résumé of Hugo's lawsuits. Hugo lost first one against the
Théâtre Français over Le Roi s'amuse for "des motifs d'ordre
politique." Won second suit to have reprises of Angelo, Hernani
and Marion Delorme put on as in contract.

163. Glachant, Paul et Victor. Un Laboratoire dramaturgique. Essai
critique sur le théâtre de Victor Hugo. 2 vols. Vol. 1: Les Drames
en vers. Vol. 2: Les Drames en prose. Paris: Hachette, 1902-1903.
Pp. 403, 516.

Still useful work on genesis of plays with painstaking study of
manuscripts and textual variants. Out of date in only a few
details. Minute description of manuscripts, their history, sources
of plays, method of composition, résumé of critical opinion, authors'
own opinion all offered. Appendix to vol. 1 has very interesting
article on Hugo and music, followed by list of all operas based on
his works. Ruy Blas, they find, is Hugo's dramatic masterpiece.
Conclude that, in general, Hugo's manuscript corrections produced
a less melodramatic work in better taste.
a) Audiat. Polybiblion, sér. 2, t. 57 (1903): 241-42.
b) Biré. Univers, 24 juin 1903.
c) Marsan. RHLF 10 (1903): 519-22.
d) Rigal. Revue des Langues Romanes, sér. 5, t. 6 (1903): 537-39.

164. Grant, Elliott M. The Career of Victor Hugo. Harvard Studies in
Romance Languages, vol. 21. Cambridge: Harvard University Press, 1945.
(Hugo's theatre, pp. 44-64, 108-22, 329-30.)

Solid biographical approach. Chapter 3 discusses plays from Amy
Robsart through success of Hernani, chapter 4 through Les Burgraves.
Slight treatment of the Théâtre en liberté and Torquemada in later
chapter. Grant chooses Ruy Blas as Hugo's best play and evaluates
Hugo as dramatist thus: "While he possessed genuine dramatic
sense, while he revealed a capacity for situation, for dialogue,
for staging, he was nevertheless essentially a poet gone astray in
the theater. . . . But, of course, Hugo's great weakness throughout
his theater lies in his presentation of human character." Credits

Hugo with breaking down rigidity of traditional theatre and formulating concept of the "useful theatre."

165. Grant, Elliott M. Victor Hugo: A Select and Critical
Bibliography. U.N.C. Studies in the Romance Languages and Literatures,
no. 67. Chapel Hill, N.C.: University of North Carolina Press, 1967.
(Hugo's theatre, pp. 77-82.)

Brief, intelligent comments on selected studies. Forty entries
specifically on theatre.

166. Grant, Richard B. The Perilous Quest: Image, Myth and Prophecy
in the Narratives of Victor Hugo. Durham, N.C.: Duke University Press,
1968. (Hugo's theatre, pp. 28-45, 73-121, 239-40.)

This excellent study analyzes long prose fiction, major plays and
La Légende des siècles and La Fin de Satan with theme of the "heroic
quest" as focal point. Examines images of rise and descent in plays
through Les Burgraves and finds same pattern as in novels. "A hero
must turn downward if he is to have any hope of rising to a great
height." Only Hernani and Ruy Blas of "high quality" in coherent
use of principle motifs. Fine examination of Act IV of Ruy Blas,
"in which the most central motifs of Hugo's previous work are
brilliantly parodied." Concludes: "From Cromwell to Les Burgraves,
he wrestled with the problem of adapting fatality to the stage."
Grant sees Les Burgraves as Hugo's first mature effort to move beyond
imagery into myth. Sound bibliography and index make volume even
more useful.
a) Bassan. French Review 43 (Dec. 1969): 345-46.
b) James. French Studies 24 (1970): 189-90.

167. Gregh, Fernand. "Le Théâtre." In his L'Oeuvre de Victor Hugo,
pp. 152-83. Paris: Flammarion, 1933.

Although Gregh still admires Musset's theatre more than Hugo's for
being more accessible to today's public, he revises his negative
opinion expressed in 1902 (168). Ruy Blas he cites as Hugo's real
masterpiece. In Le Théâtre en liberté Hugo is closest to
Shakespeare. New reading causes Gregh to stress the plays' beauties
even while recognizing weaknesses: "Mais il reste que de tout le
répertoire du XVIIIe et du XIXe siècles, le théâtre en vers de Hugo
est le seul qui tienne encore la scène avec celui des trois grands
classiques du XVIIe. . . ."

168. _____. "Victor Hugo." La Revue de Paris, 1$^{er}$ avril 1902,
pp. 569-89. (Also in his Étude sur Victor Hugo, pp. 162-64. Paris:
E. Fasquelle, 1905.)

Gregh's opinion quoted by Glachant brothers (163) to summarize
current critical opinion of Hugo's theatre: "Les drames en vers de
Victor Hugo sont des mélodrames écrits par un poète de génie. . . .
Ce qu'il y a de bon dans ses drames, c'est le décor, le pittoresque,
l'extérieur; l'intérieur lui échappe. . . . Hernani est supérieur à
toutes les autres pièces de Hugo, même à Ruy Blas. . . ." Yet
later on Gregh revises his opinion of Hugo as dramatist.

169. Grimanelli, A. "Les Innovations, la vérité, l'intérêt dans le
théâtre de Victor Hugo." Le Journal de l'Université des Annales, année
9, t. 1 (1$^{er}$ fevr. 1915): 247-52.

> Prize-winning school essay on assigned topic. Traces stages of
> opinion on Hugo's theatre and its contributions to literary
> history. Traditional attitudes resumed: "Ces drames, merveil-
> leusement versifiés, ne valent plus, aujourd'hui que par leur
> lyrisme; . . . ce sont de beaux et curieux documents."

170. Gschöpf, L. "Die Dramen Victor Hugos in der operndichtung."
Doctoral dissertation, University of Vienna, 1951.

171. Guex, Jules. Le Théâtre et la société française de 1815 à 1848.
Paris: Librairie Fischbacher, 1900. (Hugo, pp. 35-117.)

> Guex concludes that the characters in French romantic drama are not
> representative of that epoch's society. Through passionate heroes,
> picturesque local color and rapid action, Hugo offers to the
> spectator's imagination the elements his real life lacks. In Hugo's
> dramas especially, "c'est l'amour qui est cette force inéluctable
> et fatale." Guex sees doña Sol as the most romantic of the
> passionate heroines and finds Ruy Blas a good example of the
> "désaccord entre le désir et la volonté, entre le rêve et l'acte."
> Suggests that Vigny and Hugo took their public too seriously in
> considering the drame a lectern or chaire.

172. Guinard. M. "Victor Hugo et les musiciens." Bulletin de
l'Institut Français en Espagne, no. 67 (juin-sept. 1953), pp. 139-40.

> Brief treatment of musical adaptations of Hugo's writings. Declares
> Hugo hostile to Italian opera then in vogue and quite indignant
> at musical piracies of his works in Italy. Mentions Hugo's use of
> music in La Esmeralda and in his drames. Interesting list at end
> of composers inspired by Hugo's plays, poems, novels.

173. Guth, Paul. Histoire de la littérature française. 2 vols.
Paris: Fayard, 1967. (Hugo's theatre, II, 120-36.)

> Highly personal evaluation of Hugo as dramatist: "Il a donc fait,
> au théâtre, du grand, du terrible. Mais il faisait ainsi de
> l'épique, c'est-à-dire du statique, et non du dramatique. Il
> perdait le nerf du théâtre: l'action. . . . Pourtant, au théâtre,
> Hugo avait une sortie de secours, mais il ne l'a pas vue: le
> comique." Says Hugo should have created more characters like don
> César de Bazan.

174. Guyer, Foster. The Titan, Victor Hugo. New York: S. F. Vanni,
n.d. [1955]. (Hugo's theatre, pp. 25-64.)

> Chapter 3, "Dramatic Success," gives plot summaries, for most part,
> in this saccharine popular biography. Brief evaluation of plays:
> "Ruy Blas is Victor Hugo's best and most successful play. . . .
> Les Burgraves . . . contains a large element of melodrama which does
> not fuse with the grandiose epic setting where it shrieks in

disjointed and incongruous conflict with bright ornaments of tender
lyrism; for some of Hugo's best poetry is to be found here."

175. Haedens, Kléber. Une Histoire de la littérature française.
Paris: René Julliard, n.d. [1943]. (Hugo's theatre, pp. 315-20.  New
edition. Paris: B. Grasset, 1970.)

In this unfair judgment of Hugo, Haedens fills several pages with
denigration, almost vilification.  Says Hugo needs to be forgotten
for a century, then rediscovered.  On theatre: "Son théâtre,
construit sur l'indigente pensée qu'il est urgent de marier le
grotesque et le terrible, le bouffon et le sublime, semble avoir
été inventé par un spadassin de mélodrame en délire.  On l'excuse
en disant que les vers sont beaux.  Ce n'est pas vrai.  Hormis
quelques tirades clinquantes qui font encore leur effet, les vers
sont une provocation constante au goût et à la poésie." Same
words in 1970 edition.

176. Halfants, Paul.  La Littérature française au XIXe siècle.  3 vols.
Vol. 1: Le Romantisme (1800-1850).  Brussels: A. Dewit, 1906.
(Hugo's theatre, pp. 186-200.)

Much standard literary history given first.  Halfants then
attempts to explain why Hugo's drames, so full of faults, "aient
eu tant de succès." He enumerates strong dramatic situations
supplying "le frisson de l'horreur et de l'inattendu," exotic
local color, prestigious lyrical style and "le caractère
démocratique" of the plays as reasons for their success.  Finds
Les Burgraves, Hugo's least successful play, chosen for centenary
through "une certaine coquetterie."

177. Hamilton, Clayton. "The Plays of Victor Hugo." Sewanee Review
11 (1903): 169-86.

This study displays a thorough knowledge of Hugo's plays.  However,
Hamilton makes a surprising choice of Hugo's best plays--Marion
Delorme, closely followed by Le Roi s'amuse.  Berates the prose
plays and praises Torquemada.  Sums up the worth of Hugo's plays
thus: "Powerful and captivating they certainly are, and imbued
with many of the prime excellences of dramatic composition; but
they are also marked with numerous shortcomings which prevent them
from being classed with what is greatest in the theater of the
world."

178. Harden, Maximilian [M. H.]. "Theater." Die Zukunft (Berlin) 38
(22 märz 1902): 490-98.

Comparison of Goethe and Hugo: "Victor Hugo schien für das Theater
geschaffen.  Nur wenige Borstellung lebten, mit der Kraft grosser
Bisionen, in seinem Hirn. . . . Das Theater fordert den Schein
lebensfähiger Menschlichkeit and Hugo gab ihm faft immer nur
beredte Schatten."

179. Heimbacher, Hans-Joachim. Victor Hugo und die Ideen der grossen
französischen Revolution.  Romanische Studien, heft 27.  Berlin: E.
Ebering, 1932.  (Hugo's theatre, pp. 180-212.)

Rather dogmatic, somewhat distorted interpretation of Hugo's
revolutionary and social ideas as expressed in his works.
Heimbacher insists: "'Leben ist Revolution, d. h. dauernde
Auflehnung gegen bestehende Widerwärtigkeiten und erkannte Mängel,
Leben ist Liebe, Leben ist Gerechtigkeit, Freiheit und Gleichheit,'
sich schon in schon in seinen Dramen mehr und mehr ausgeprägt hat
und daher der Schlüssel zu allen Werken ist, die er von 1827 ab
geschaffen hat."

180. Henriot, Emile. "Hugophilie ou hugolâtrie?" Le Temps, 1933.
(Also in his Courrier littéraire, XIXe siècle: Les Romantiques, pp.
9-16. Paris: A. Michel, n.d. [c 1953].)

Main point of this discussion is that one does not have to like all
of Hugo's work to like Hugo. Moreover, "son théâtre, évidemment la
partie la moins défendable de son oeuvre, a quelques vertus: c'est
d'abord de très bon théâtre, animé, pittoresque et rebondissant;
d'une splendeur verbale et poétique indéniable et non touchée;
excellent même dans le comique (Ruy Blas, le premier acte de
Marion, le Théâtre en liberté)."

181. _____. "Le 'Théâtre à lire' de Victor Hugo." Le Temps, 31
oct. 1933, p. 3. (Also in his Courrier littéraire, XIXe siècle: Les
Romantiques, pp. 51-58. Paris: A. Michel, n.d. [c 1953].)

Recent publication of Vol. 4 of the Théâtre complet of the
Imprimerie Nationale edition encourages Henriot to give genesis of
and evaluate Torquemada, Amy Robsart and Les Jumeaux. Finds that
"ce n'est toujours pas du meilleur Hugo," but approves of the
unfinished Les Jumeaux. Attributes to the 1882 persecution of the
Jews in Russia Hugo's decision to publish Torquemada "comme une
protestation contre le fanatisme religieux. . . . Torquemada a
beaucoup vieilli dans l'intervalle."

182. Hervier, Marcel, ed. Les Ecrivains français jugés par leurs
contemporains. Vol. 3: Le Dix-neuvième siècle. Paris: Mellottée,
n.d. [1942]. (Hugo's theatre, pp. 128-67, 241.)

Useful compilation of contemporary critical opinion indicated
through numerous, well chosen quotations from press, letters,
documents, and diaries. First chapter on Hugo includes comments on
plays, Cromwell through Les Burgraves; second has small section on
Le Théâtre en liberté. Editor offers literary history of each work
and summarizes trends of criticism. General reaction to Le
Théâtre en liberté is "surprise admirative." On Hugo's theatre as
a whole, Hervier concludes: "Si nos générations acceptent, malgré
des défauts reconnus, d'entendre Hernani et Ruy Blas, c'est d'une
part que leur souffle lyrique et l'éclat du style et des images ne
sont pas sans effet; en outre un pieux respect nous porte à ne pas
bannir de la scène des pièces qui restent une date dans l'histoire
du théâtre."

183. Hervieu, Paul. "L'Oeuvre dramatique de Victor Hugo." Le Figaro,
7 juill. 1914, p. 1.

Speech "aux fêtes de Guernesey" for la Société des Auteurs et
Compositeurs dramatiques, of which Hugo was a charter member and
four times president. Rambling official encomium: "Grace à
l'audace de sa conception théâtrale, Victor Hugo renouvela les
ressources, les moyens, les situations, le langage de leur art,
octroya de la sorte, maintes libertés fécondes. . . ." Marion
Delorme is chosen as "le plus harmonieux" drama while Les
Burgraves is seen as Hugo's "plus grandiose essor."

184.  Hooker, Kenneth W. The Fortunes of Victor Hugo in England.
Columbia University Studies in English and Comparative Literature, no.
134.  New York:  Columbia University Press, 1938.  (Hugo's theatre,
pp. 20-23, 43-66, 97, 236-37.)

Excellent study of English critical reception of Cromwell (chapter
1), Romantic dramas of 1830-1840 (chapter 3) and Les Burgraves
(chapter 5) and of general view from poet's death to 1902 (chapter
12).  Claims that Cromwell "caused the downfall of French
Romanticism in England" and that the bataille d'Hernani was regarded
as "an amusing scene" with no great repercussions in England.
Hugo's prose plays were highly criticized on moral grounds: "By
1838, then, the English were ready to discard French dramas without
even reading them, and were convinced that Hugo could not write a
good play." That last opinion predominated through 1902.

185.  _____, and Victor Bowley.  "A Chronological English
Bibliography on Victor Hugo. List of English Plays Founded on Those of
Victor Hugo." Adam International Review, 19, 229-230 (1952):  26-32.

List same as that at end of Bowley's 1928 article (96). Bibliography almost entirely composed of nineteenth-century studies of
Hugo.  Only nine 1900+ works cited; yet it is still interesting to
see which English authors, such as Swinburne and Arnold, wrote on
Hugo.

186.  Houston, John P.  Victor Hugo.  Twayne's World Authors Series, no.
312.  New York:  Twayne Publishers, Inc., 1974.  (Hugo's theatre,
pp. 42-66, 125-28.)

Good, solid general presentation in English of Hugo's works.
Chapter 3, "Plays through Les Burgraves," treats succinctly but
well Cromwell, Marion de Lorme, Ruy Blas and Les Burgraves.  Houston
finds Hernani "vastly inferior" to Marion de Lorme and to Cromwell,
which he calls "one of Hugo's most remarkable pieces of dramatic
poetry."  Of Ruy Blas states:  "It is for this larger kind of
coherence, as well as for its remarkable style and tightness of plot
that Ruy Blas stands out so in Hugo's dramatic production."
Unfortunately, chooses not to write about Le Théâtre en liberté.
However, does describe Torquemada as "unique in its somber
brilliance."  Fine for non-specialist.
a) Delattre.  Modern Language Journal 60 (1976):  76-77.
b) Nash.  French Review 49 (1976):  619-20.

187. Howarth, William D. <u>Sublime and Grotesque: A Study of French Romantic Drama</u>. London: Harrap Books, 1975. Pp. 448. (Hugo's theatre, pp. 91-201, 225-46, 338-39, 371-72, 401-02.)

Only thorough study in English on French Romantic frama since that of Draper (133) and perhaps best one in any language to date. Well researched and well written. Traces development of Romantic drama from social and literary <u>milieux</u> of France through 1820s and evaluates plays as literature as well as theatrical productions. Emphasizes great, though uneven, range of Hugo's dramatic talent and products. Author obviously loves <u>Hernani</u>. Uses opera as constant metaphor in discussing Hugo's plays. Calls for new productions of <u>drames romantiques</u>, particularly <u>Marion de Lorme</u>. Finds modern interest in performing Hugo's armchair theatre "rather perverse." Very favorable evaluation of Hugo's contributions to renewed vocabulary and innovative style in theatre. <u>Lorenzaccio</u>, however, he considers single best play produced during the period. Appendix contains chronological list of plays (1827-1852), and rôles created by leading actors. Bibliography and index adequate.

188. _____. "Victor Hugo and the 'Failure' of French Romantic Drama." <u>L'Esprit Créateur</u> 16 (Fall 1976): 178-97.

Concise snythesis of material on Hugo from his <u>Sublime and Grotesque</u>. Suggests that the failure of Romantic drama to make appreciable changes on the Paris theatrical scene by 1840 was due largely to the relatively poor contemporary reception of Hugo's plays. An analysis of each play's reception identifies the following factors in Hugo's "failure": financial difficulties; poor casting and selection of theatre; theatrical censorship; bad press reaction (some merited but some politically reactionary); varying quality of plays themselves; use of prose to attract a wider audience.

189. Hugi, Hermann. <u>Les Drames de Victor Hugo expliqués par la psychanalyse</u>. Berne: Buch und Kunstdruckerei, 1930. Pp. 88.

1925 doctoral dissertation at Berne, redone for publication. Reduces all plays to archetypal situation in which "le complexe paternel" dominates. Chapters on "la vierge et la courtisane," Hugo's obsession with fire and psychic origins of his "coups de théâtre" of some interest. One conclusion Hugi reaches bears repeating: "Ce sont les drames où se reflète le mieux la vie inconsciente du poète qui ont toujours aussi le plus de succès."

190. Huszár, Guillaume. <u>L'Influence de l'Espagne sur le théâtre français des XVIIIe et XIXe siècles</u>. Paris: H. Champion, 1912. (Hugo's theatre, pp. 115-61.)

"Victor Hugo et l'Espagne," pp. 115-32, outlines Hugo's general debt to Spain for concepts of honor, fatality, "l'ardeur religieuse" and artistic synthesis as achieved in the <u>comedia</u>. "Les Drames de Victor Hugo, au point de vue de l'influence espagnole," pp. 133-61, examines more closely possible Spanish sources for each play. <u>Cromwell</u>, Huszár suggests, derives from Hugo's "esprit jésuitique." Works of Calderón, Cervantes and Alarcón directly influenced

Angelo, La Esmeralda, Marion de Lorme and Hernani. Furthermore,
Le Roi s'amuse is a "comedia de capa y espada;" Torquemada displays
a Spanish conception of souls and of royal passion; and Ruy Blas
is a "pícaro idéalisé." Very interesting comparisons offered, but
conclusions appear somewhat forced and not totally convincing at
times. See Martinenche (495).

191. Ihrig, Grace P. Heroines in French Drama of the Romantic Period.
1829-1848. New York: Columbia University King's Crown Press, 1950.
Pp. 246. (Hugo's theatre, pp. 41-51, 81-88, 148-57, 171-72.)

Originally doctoral dissertation at Columbia University. In
chapter 3 on "Idealized and Sentimentalized Heroines," Ihrig selects
doña Sol as "the most perfect and best known representative of this
type, . . . the devoted daughter . . . frequently synonymous with
the 'sheltered ingenue' type of heroine," and also analyzes Blanche
of Le Roi s'amuse. Marion de Lorme, Marie de Neuborg and Jane of
Marie Tudor receive consideration in chapter 5 on "Historical
Figures Reincarnated." Chapter 9 presents criticisms of heroines in
contemporary press, largely negative, yet stresses their long vogue
with popular audiences. Concludes: "The beautifully poetized
heroine is one of the major contributions of Hugo, Vigny, and
Musset to the Romantic theatre. A mystical conception of woman as
the perfect, worthy object of man's adoration is embodied in Doña
Sol."

192. Jamati, Paul. "Défense du théâtre de Victor Hugo." Europe, année
30 (févr.-mars 1952): 184-95.

Discovers that "l'oeuvre dramatique de Hugo est d'une importance
primordiale. Tout Victor Hugo en découle. . . . Elle donne la clef
de son évolution." Traces Hugo's "invention" of the drame and
development of his theory of literary, social, political romanticism
in plays' prefaces. Stresses great lyricism in most Hugo plays:
Ruy Blas et Hernani . . . [sont] les plus beaux fleuves lyriques de
tout le théâtre hugolien." Quotes from Act IV of Ruy Blas to show
that Hugo excels in dialogue and comic creation. Finds "le roi de
Mangeront-ils? [une] vague ébauche de Père Ubu. . . ."

193. Jasinski, René. Histoire de la littérature française. 2 vols.
Paris: Boivin & Cie, 1947. (Hugo's theatre, II, 445-47. New edition.
Paris: A. G. Nizet, 1966.)

Rather traditional approach and conventional opinions offered on
Hugo's theatre: "Toutes ces pièces, en prose ou en vers, présentent
de terribles défauts: . . . pauvreté psychologique, . . . action
. . . artificielle. Mais [elles se relèvent] par la magnificence de
la forme. . . . Chaque drame se développe ainsi comme une succession
de poemès superficiellement reliés, mais admirables d'éclat et de
variété. Le moins vieilli semble aujourd'hui Ruy Blas. . . .
Toutes les éclatantes richesses de la mise en oeuvre séduisent
encore le lecteur, plus qu'elles ne se soutiennent peut-être à la
scène." 1966 edition voices same views.

194.  John, S. B.  "Violence and Identity in Romantic Drama."  In
French Literature and Its Background.  Edited by John Cruickshank.
Vol. 4, pp. 132-51.  5 vols.  Oxford:  Oxford University Press, 1969.

   Interesting investigation of responses of Romantic drama to social
   and political pressures of its age in two dominant themes:
   historical violence and quest for identity.  Hugo, too, drawn to
   genuinely popular art form of melodrama to render effectively
   struggle of the individual seeking identity in a changing world.
   Hugo portrays characters in unsettled situations "with graphic power,
   but in such a way as to obliterate understanding of human motive and
   complexity through the mechanisms of gross melodrama, culminating
   too frequently in scenes of gothic horror."  By failing "to work
   out, in imaginative terms, the full implications of those
   ambiguities, both social and moral, with which he surrounds his
   major characters, . . ."  Hugo fails to convince us that "the hero's
   fate is linked with his character in a coherent and organic way."

195.  Josephson, Matthew.  Victor Hugo:  A Realistic Biography of the
Great Romantic.  Garden City, N.Y.:  Doubleday, Doran & Co., 1942.
(Hugo's theatre, pp. 135-36 and passim.)

   Stresses psychoanalytical interpretation of plays; highlights the
   "mother complex" in Marion de Lorme and Lucrèce Borgia, the "rebel
   or Oedipus complex" in Hernani.  In the plays, Josephson suggests,
   "Hugo is essentially and remarkably rich in symbolism rather than
   in reason or logic."

196.  Joussain, André.  "A l'occasion du centenaire du romantisme:
l'humour chez Victor Hugo."  La Revue Philomatique de Bordeaux et du
Sud-Ouest, année 30 (janv.-mars 1927):  25-32.

   Begins by stating that Hugo has more "humour" than "esprit."  In
   the few instances when Hugo allows his humor to overflow, as in
   Act IV of Ruy Blas and in parts of the Théâtre en liberté, "Hugo
   est excellent, parce qu'en réalisant l'énormité dans le comique, il
   se montre vraiment lui-même dans un genre qui n'est pas le sien."
   Contrasts aspiration toward sublime realized in don César's
   successfully comic act with failed humor of Rochester's wit and
   actions in Cromwell.

197.  Jouvet, Louis.  "Victor Hugo et le théâtre."  In his Réflexions
du comédien, pp. 61-78.  Paris:  Librairie théâtrale, 1952.

   This outstanding actor-director opens with an intriguing dialogue à
   la Diderot between himself, anti-Hugo, and a painter friend who
   tells him:  "Pour ta profession, il est le seul maître.  Hugo,
   c'est le théâtral par excellence."  Jouvet tries to appreciate Hugo
   but must conclude that his plays are "de l'opéra."  Finds ultimately
   Hugo's theatre weakest part of his work because it lacks "un sentiment profond"; there is no real suffering in it.  Ruy Blas and
   Hernani remain too transparent, he believes; so characters lose
   their "apparence humaine."

198. Kammel, W. Die Typen der Helden und Heldinnen in den Dramen Victor Hugos. Pr. Abh. D. St. R. Sch. Prag: Kleinseite, 1905.

199. Kirton, W.J.S. "The Contemporary Relevance of Hugo's Dramatic Theories." Trivium 11 (May 1976): 78-89.

Identifies similarities between Hugo's dramatic vision, techniques, and use of grotesque and those of various contemporary dramatists, such as Meyerhold, Peter Brook, Artaud, and especially Ionesco. Sees actual influence of Hugo in plays of Audiberti and Ghelderode. Despite Ionesco's belittling of Hugo, Kirton concludes: "It is obvious that both men are describing an identical vision of life. . . . Hugo constructs his mysticism and finds a way through the doubts while Ionesco insists on the absurdity in order to open our minds to it . . . ."

200. Lacey, Alexander. Pixerécourt and the French Romantic Drama. Toronto: University of Toronto Press, 1928. Pp. 88.

Important, well argued study tracing considerable influence of Pixerécourt's brand of melodrama on Romantic drama with respect to dramatic techniques, plot, characters and "sentimental and sensational elements." Each of Hugo's plays is examined for mélo qualities, pp. 35-59. Hugo's prose plays contain "much more that is purely melodramatic" than the verse plays, but even in the latter "there exists . . . the same tendency to exaggerate the idea of Fate (though in the opposite direction), the same lack of logical development, the same use of accidental and external means, the same lack of connection between character and issues as in melo-drama." In Conclusion, Lacey characterizes Hugo's Romantic drama as "lyrical melodrama masquerading under a cloak of pseudo-philosophical symbolism."

201. Lacretelle, Jacques. de. "Hugo." La Revue (des Deux Mondes), 1er sept. 1967, pp. 6-21. [Also in Victor Hugo, pp. 7-25. Paris: Hachette, 1967.]

Calls Hugo's theatre "une faillite," born old, still far from "le naturel" and "le réalisme." Hernani today is only a symbol of angry youth; Ruy Blas, though "agencé" and amusing, is secondary and not alive, as Musset's theatre is today. But Lacretelle praises Hugo's critical theories and judgments.

202. Lafargue, E.-P. "Carlos s'amuse." Le Rire, 1er mars 1902.

Amusing parody of Hugo's dramas, especially of Hernani and Le Roi s'amuse. Illustrated by Lucien Métivet.

203. Lagarde, André et Laurent Michard. Le Dix-neuvième siècle. Grands auteurs français du programme, t. 5. Paris: Editions Bordas, 1967. (Hugo's theatre, pp. 231-45.)

Scholastic presentation of background, theories, literary history. Analysis of and excerpts from Hernani and Ruy Blas. Summarizes: "Intrigue serrée, péripéties émouvantes, dénouement frappant: ces qualitiés dramatiques caractérisent le génie de Hugo même dans ses

romans et sa poésie; pourtant l'épreuve du théâtre lui est peu
favorable. . . . . Il en est de même des sentiments ardents, romantiques, dessinés avec vigueur, mais qui n'atteignent pas à la profondeur d'analyse de la tragédie cornélienne ou racinienne. . . .
Mais le théâtre de Hugo est transfiguré par la poésie. Sans doute
cette poésie n'est-elle pas proprement dramatique comme celle de
Racine; mais, lyrique ou épique, . . . elle n'en fait pas moins le
charme et la grandeur de ses principaux drames."

204. Lancellotti, Arturo. <u>Victor Hugo</u>. <u>L'Uomo, il poeta, il drammaturgo, il romanziere</u>. Rome: E.R.S., 1957. (Hugo's theatre, pp. 81-
102.)

Superficial discussion of Hugo's theatre. Many anecdotes, little
literary criticism presented. Calls <u>Hernani</u> "un forte dramma" but
believes it should close with Act IV since Act V "guasta tutto."
Emphasizes Hugo as thinker rather than creator: "Possiamo dire che
Victor Hugo tanto nella poesia quanto nel romanzo e sul teatro,
non fece mai della vuota letteratura ma volle sempre portare delle
idee, combattere delle battaglie politiche e sociali, dandoci opere
di pensiero attraverso sentimenti d'elevata bontà."

205. Lanson, Gustave. <u>Esquisse d'une histoire de la tragédie
française</u>. New York: Columbia University Press, 1920. (Hugo's theatre,
pp. 143-45.)

Outline form of lecture series given at Columbia. Begins with
tribute to Hugo: "D'<u>Athalie</u> à <u>Hernani</u>, pas une note pleinement
tragique dans la tragédie française." Hugo, however, Lanson claims,
was so obsessed with the idea of historical drama that he failed to
be concerned with saving or resurrecting true tragedy. Yet Hugo's
epic vision and lyricism at times manage to reach level of tragedy:
"La philosophie morale de Hugo a un caractère mystique (duel du
bien et du mal dans l'âme humaine et dans l'histoire), d'où pourrait
sortir le tragique. . . . Le génie lyrique de V. Hugo lui a fait
parfois rencontrer le tragique. . . ." Lanson cites Act II of
<u>Ruy Blas</u>, V of <u>Marion Delorme</u> and II and V of <u>Hernani</u> as Hugo's
closest approaches to real tragedy.

206. _____. <u>Histoire de la littérature française</u>. Paris:
Hachette, 1903. (Hugo's theatre, pp. 971-89.)

Although published originally in 1894, Lanson's much quoted remark
on <u>Ruy Blas</u> appears in later editions and bears repeating: "La
plus complète inintelligence--le mot n'est pas trop fort--de la
vérité et de la vie y éclate." Out of nine <u>drames</u> from <u>Marion de
Lorme</u> to <u>Les Burgraves</u>, six of the heroes are "Didier refait."
Lanson deplores this poor psychological invention as well as the
staple "trucs du mélodrame" and the childish plots employed. Admits,
though, that "les drames de Victor Hugo ont été sauvés par le lyrisme
du style." In pointing out Hugo's ability to create "un comique
d'imagination," he signals Act IV of <u>Ruy Blas</u> as "un chef-d'oeuvre
de comique énorme et truculent." Nothing on <u>Le Théâtre en liberté</u>.

207. Laplane, Gabriel. "Victor Hugo, génie hispanique." <u>Bulletin de l'Institut Français en Espagne</u>, no. 67 (juin-sept. 1953), pp. 156-61. (Also in Spanish as "Victor Hugo y España." <u>Clavileño</u> 4 [marzo-abril 1953]: 29-34.)

    General article on Hugo's relationship with Spain offers specific comments on Spanish plays <u>Hernani</u> and <u>Ruy Blas</u>, "leyendas poéticas brillantemente escenificadas." Sees influence of Lope and Calderón in background and evaluates Hugo's "españolismo" in plays and elsewhere as authentic. See also Martinenche (495) and Huszár (190).

208. Lasserre, Pierre. <u>Le Romantisme français. Essai sur la révolution dans les sentiments et dans les idées au XIXe siècle</u>. Avec une préface de l'auteur. Paris: Mercure de France, 1907. (Hugo's theatre, pp. 231-48.)

    Strongly anti-Romantic doctoral dissertation revised for publication. Hugo is the perfect example, guilty perpetrator even, of what Lasserre calls "l'emphase au théâtre." He continues: "Ce sont le plus souvent dans le théâtre de Victor Hugo, des inventions d'essence mélodramatique que le génie de l'emphase transfigure en conceptions eschyliennes. . . . Un grand style sur des idées petites, de grands ramages sur de petits moyens, voilà ce qui s'appelle emphase." Lasserre verbally devastates Hugo's théâtre except for don César de Bazan's speech and a few episodes in <u>Marion de Lorme</u> and <u>Le Roi s'amuse</u>. Some validity in Lasserre's basic criticism, but his exaggeration and sarcastic tone detract from effectiveness of argument.

209. Laugé, C. <u>Etudes sur les auteurs du baccalauréat</u>. Lyon: Vitte, n.d. [1935]. (Hugo's theatre, pp. 403-12.)

    Conventional approach: "Victor Hugo n'a réussi que médiocrement dans la poésie dramatique. <u>Le mélange du comique et du tragique</u> aboutit à des plaisanteries d'un goût douteux. . . . En outre, Victor Hugo n'a pu créer des personnages avec une <u>individualité propre</u>, parce qu'il n'a pas su se détacher du 'moi'; . . . il a fait des pièces dramatiques qui nous intéressent surtout par la beauté des passages purement lyriques. . . ."

210. Laus, Lausimar. "O Drama Romântico Segundo Victor Hugo." <u>Minas Gerais, Suplemento Literário</u>, 10 apr. 1976, p. 10.

211. Le Breton, André. <u>Le Théâtre romantique</u>. Paris: Boivin et Cie, n.d. [1922?]. (Hugo's theatre, pp. 56-110 and <u>passim</u>. All except chapter on <u>Ruy Blas</u> published previously in <u>La Revue des Cours et Conférences</u>, sér. 1, 23 [1921-1922]: 99-114, 308-21, 408-26, 631-46, 741-57. Chapter on <u>Ruy Blas</u> published in <u>La Revue Bleue</u>, année 60 [15 sept. 1922]: 569-76.)

    Good general treatment of theatre of Romantic period. Whole body of plays produced author calls "un théâtre de poètes," with Hugo as best poet but weak playwright. Chapters on <u>Hernani</u>, <u>Ruy Blas</u>, <u>Les Burgraves</u> investigate sources, lyric beauties, dramatic weaknesses, special qualities, influence. Judges <u>Ruy Blas</u> to be most successful of Hugo's dramas, "le rêve d'un grand poète." In part on Les Burgraves, Le Breton digresses on possible influence of Hernani and Les Burgraves on Wagner's Lohengrin. See also Weil (326). Le Breton's overall evaluation of Hugo as dramatist: "Dans l'ensemble, le théâtre de Hugo est monotone et artificiel. Les exigences de l'art dramatique l'ont embarrassé, gêné." a) Lafoscade. RHLF 30 (1923): 562-66.

212. Lebreton-Savigny, Monique. Victor Hugo et les Américains (1825-1855). Paris: Klincksieck, 1971. (Hugo's theatre, pp. 39-42, 70-108, 170-217, 303, 310-11, 314-16.)

Exhaustive compilation on relationship, in which Hugo gave more to Americans than he took from them. For reading and for stage presentation, author finds: "Le théâtre de Hugo a été moins traduit qu'adapté." Analyzes in detail each stage adaptation and critical and popular reaction to performances. Opera versions of Hugo's plays extremely popular in U.S. 1833 is the first year a Hugo play is discussed in a newspaper; up to 1862 Hugo was berated for immorality and corruption in his plays. Bibliography lists translations and English versions of Hugo's works and Hugo adaptations played in U.S. 1825-1885. See also George (156).
a) Bassan. Nineteenth Century French Studies 1 (1973): 185-87.
b) Bédé. French Review 46 (1973): 616-17.
c) Bowman. French Studies 29 (1975): 338-39.
d) Franceschetti. Studi Francesi 16 (1972): 511.

213. Lemaître, Henri, Thérèse van der Elst et Roger Pagosse. La Littérature française. Vol. 3: Les Evolutions du XIXe siècle. 4 vols. Paris: Bordas, 1970. (Hugo's theatre, pp. 177-94.)

New interpretations offered of standard literary history. Many quotations and excellent illustrations accompany text. Find Hugo's plays "romantiques" in their good/evil dichotomy and theme of individual versus society. Say that a "tentation lyrique" binds Hugo to Corneille. Attempt to show film possibilities of Cromwell: "Mais c'est sans doute dans Cromwell, ce soumet du théâtre imaginaire, qu'apparait le mieux cette recherche d'une présence multi-dimensionnelle de l'histoire, jointe à un pittoresque toujours présent dans la mise-en-scène et dans le langage. . . . Effective-ment, l'espace scénique est incapable d'embrasser cette totalité de personnages et d'événements qu'entraîne le recours à l'histoire selon toutes ses dimensions: l'espace historique et pittoresque de Hugo, c'est déjà, imaginairement, l'espace cinématographique."

214. Le Roy, Albert. L'Aube du théâtre romantique. Paris: Société française d'imprimerie et de librairie, 1902. Pp. 475.

Treats Cromwell, Amy Robsart, Hernani, and Marion de Lorme of Hugo. Plot summaries, many anecdotes and particular attention to parodies and critical reaction. Disapproves highly of Cromwell--"une oeuvre trop guindée, qui n'est qu'un exercice de rhétorique et n'annonce ni un renouveau théâtral ni la floraison du romantisme." In Hernani, however, Hugo "ressent et nous fait ressentir l'émoi d'un sentiment vrai qui secoue la grandiloquence romantique." Likes the first act of Marion de Lorme. A strangely disconnected series of essays. No index.

215. Leuilliot, Bernard. "Editer Victor Hugo!" Romantisme, no. 6 (1973), pp. 111-23.

Another attempt to highlight trends in Hugo criticism. Mentions "nouvelles interprétations proposées par Anne Ubersfeld" and critical editions or specific studies of Le Roi s'amuse, Ruy Blas, Les Burgraves, Mangeront-ils? Expects "un renouveau d'intérêt pour l'oeuvre du dramaturge."

216. Levaillant, Maurice. La Crise mystique de Victor Hugo. 1843-1856. Paris: J. Corti, 1954. (Hugo's theatre, pp. 140-46, 282.)

Pages indicated above contain first publication of Hugo's Prologue mystique, described as a fore-runner of Le Théâtre en liberté. Book traces development of Hugo's interest in the spiritual and the mystical from Léopoldine's death through Les Contemplations and shows rôle of this dramatic treatment of subject in Hugo's total creation from this period.

217. Levrault, Léon. Le Théâtre des origines à nos jours: le drame, la tragédie, la comédie. Paris: Mellottée, n.d. [1932?]. (Hugo, pp. 87-94.)

Very favorable view of Hugo's theatre. Stresses especially form, lyricism, simplicity. Lists faults of "spectacle" and deliberate abuse of "de violentes émotions. . . . Rien cependant n'est plus varié que le théâtre de Victor Hugo."

218. Ley-Deutsch, Maria. Le Gueux chez Victor Hugo. Bibliothèque de la Fondation Victor Hugo, no. 4. Paris: E. Droz, 1936. (Hugo's theatre, pp. 136-89, 430-66.)

Fifth chapter analyzes character of Zafari-César in Ruy Blas and attempts to identify Spanish historical and literary models and French influences. In chapter eight Ley-Deutsch traces development of Maglia in Hugo's creation from 1830 inédits to culmination in Glapieu of Mille Francs de récompense: "Hugo, avec Glapieu, fait le don le plus absolu de lui-même."

219. Lioure, Michel. Le Drame. Paris: A. Colin, 1963. (Hugo's theatre, pp. 48-50, 143-71, 252-61.)

First part a solid history of genre le drame. Section on Hernani very good. Second part an anthology of theories and criticism including excerpts from prefaces to Cromwell, Marie Tudor, Ruy Blas, and from William Shakespeare. Part 3 an anthology of excerpts from drames; Hugo represented by Le Roi s'amuse and Marie Tudor. Chronology, minimal bibliography and index in "Annexes." 1966 edition exactly same. 1973 edition, entitled Le Drame de Diderot à Ionesco, contains no anthology yet shares same estimation of Hugo's dramatic contributions: "Mais entre les théories énoncées dans les préfaces de Cromwell ou de Marie Tudor et les oeuvres échalonnées entre Hernani et Chantecler, il existe une consternante

disproportion. Loin de réaliser leurs gigantesques ambitions, les
drames de Dumas et de Hugo, se sont enlisés dans le mélodrame. . . .
L'auteur du drame le plus accompli de cette période féconde en
demi-réussites est . . . Musset . . . dans Lorenzaccio, le miracle
d'un drame historique et humain. . . ."

220. Lombard, C. M. "French Romanticism on the American Stage." La
Revue de Littérature Comparée 43 (avril-juin 1969): 161-72.

Both Hugo and Dumas were very popular in America. Kenney's version
of Hernani, presented in 1831-1832 season, is first Hugo production
recorded in the U.S. His plays were popular, especially in New
York and Philadelphia, and enjoyed success also in St. Louis, New
Orleans, Mobile, Charleston. His drames drew much critical attention, largely negative at first because of their violence and
"immorality." But there were some comments on the superiority of
contemporary French drama as early as 1837. After 1870 Hugo's
plays were performed less and less. Lombard attributes the
popularity of the drame romantique to audiences seeking "sensation,
emotionalism, escapism, adventure," not supplied by native dramatic
authors. See also Ayer (72), George (156), and Lebreton-Savigny
(212).

221. Lopatyńska, L. "Wictor Hugo w walce o nowy dramat." Pamietnik
Teatralny (Warsaw) 4 (1952).

222. Lyonnet, Henry. Les Premières de Victor Hugo. Paris: Delagrave,
1930. Pp. 234.

Very informative investigation of first performances of Hugo's
dramas and of plays based on his poems and novels. Although far
from complete on these matters, includes material on the plays'
geneses, sources, press reaction, anecdotes, parodies, and translations and a useful table of Hugo's works performed at the Comédie-
Française from 1830 to 1928. As Hugo's best plays Lyonnet chooses
the two verse dramas in the repertory of the Comédie-Française,
Hernani and Ruy Blas.
a) Varenne. Figaro, 22 févr. 1930, p. 5.

223. Maillard, Lucien. "Soirées littéraires, les Romantiques."
Comédie-Française 25 (janv. 1974): 18-19, 25.

224. Martini, Wolfgang. "Der demokratische Geist Neu-frankreichs im
Drama Victor Hugos." Neueren Sprachen 23 (Jan. 1916): 513-35.

Very negative judgment of Hugo's plays. Martini suggests that
conflict between Hugo's aristocratic sense of self and his democratic ideals could not be reconciled in his dramas; therefore, he
relied so much upon antithesis to present life and truth. Wandering
analysis is made of Hugo's failure in his attempt both to please
and to elevate "the people" with his dramas. Closes with further
criticism that Hugo's egocentric subjectivity hindered his character
portrayal and eventually mired him in melodrama just when he most
thought he had created a true "folk theatre."

225.  Martini, Wolfgang.  "Victor Hugos dramatische Technik nach ihrer historischen und psychologischen Entwicklung."  Zeitschrift für Neufranzösische Sprache und Literatur 27 (1904):  298-348; 28 (1905): 83-168, 223-59.

In the first of two parts to this article, Martini examines Hugo's position in the historical development of the Romantic theatre.  In the more valuable second part, he analyzes in detail Hugo's dramatic technique, emphasizing Hugo's preoccupation with the strange and abnormal.  He concludes:  "Nach alledem, was wir über die Dramen selbst und ihre psychologische Entstehung sagen mussten, gehören sie zu jenen Schöpfungen eines genialen Sonderlings, denen 'eine aufgeregte Zeit williges Ohr leiht.'"

226.  Mason, James F.  The Melodrama in France from the Revolution to the Beginning of the Romantic Drama, 1791-1830.  Baltimore, Md.:  J. H. Furst Co., 1912.  (Hugo's theatre, Chapter 6.)

Originally Ph.D. dissertation at Johns Hopkins, 1911, only first chapter of which published commercially.  In sixth chapter of thesis, Mason traces techniques, plot forms, characters and tone of melodrama appropriated by Romantic dramatists.  For fuller treatment, see Lacey (200).

227.  Maulnier, Thierry.  "L'Enigme Hugo."  Le Livre des Lettres, no. 3 (mars-avril 1944), pp. 463-500.

In overall evaluation of Hugo's worth, finds Hugo not a great dramatist or novelist.  He is not entirely just in his views:  "Le théâtre de Hugo et la Légende des siècles ont perdu, pour toujours sans doute, leur prestige. . . ."

228.  Maurois, André.  Olympio, ou la vie de Victor Hugo.  2 vols. Paris: Hachette, n.d. [c 1954].

Popular biography, which presents in solid fashion and highly readable style basic information without much literary criticism. Evaluates plays thus:  "Les drames de Hugo étaient loin de valoir sa poésie lyrique."

229.  Mauron, Charles.  "Les Personnages de Victor Hugo: étude psycho-critique."  In Victor-Marie Hugo, Oeuvres complètes, II, i-xlii.  Paris: Club français du livre, 1967.

Interesting use of some techniques of la nouvelle critique to examine in Hugo's work the hero, the couple and Anakè or fatality. Points out importance of Les Burgraves:  "Le discernement entre Providence et Fatalité, dans les dénouements de Hugo, paraît accompli avec les Burgraves--décidément un point singulier dans la courbe de l'oeuvre totale."  Works from around 1830 show clearly dynamics of Hugo's plot orientation structured around ideal heroine and fatal hero.  Section called "De Lucrèce Borgia aux Burgraves" investigates movement from plays treating personal destiny of hero--Hernani, Marion de Lorme, Ruy Blas-- to those on family tragedy--Le Roi s'amuse, Lucrèce Borgia, Les Burgraves.  Final portion seeks

biographical explanations for Hugo's underlying preoccupations in
creating characters and situations.

230. Meeüs, Adrien de. Le Romantisme. Paris: A. Fayard, 1948.
(Hugo's theatre, pp. 103-32.)

In this series of essays defining "romantisme" and examining its
various stages, Meeüs stresses Hugo's strong link with traditional
theatre, his tendency to create plays around his "débordement
d'éloquence verbale," and his sacrifice of dramatic quality to
facile, popular victory on stage. Meeüs states: "Le sujet de cet
Hernani qui allait faire triompher le romantisme à la Comédie-
Française, était bien plus traditionnel qu'on n'eût pu le croire à
première vue. . . . Hernani . . . est le thème du Barbier de Séville
de Beaumarchais, complété par le dénouement tragique du Roméo et
Juliette de Shakespeare. . . . Les autres drames de Hugo, comme
Le Roi s'amuse, répètent tous la même histoire essentielle."

231. Merian-Genast, Ernest. "Der Einfluss Shakespeares auf das
französische romantische Drama." In Comparative Literature, II, 649-59.
University of North Carolina Studies in Comparative Literature, no. 24.
2 vols. Chapel Hill, N.C.: University of North Carolina Press, 1959.

Considers Cromwell and Hernani as Hugo's plays with strongest
influence of Shakespeare. Hugo falls short of total Shakespearian
vision, yet does create "homo duplex" in Cromwell and fusion of
tragic, comic, lyric and epic in Hernani. Mentions Marion de Lorme
also as displaying touches of Shakespearian style.

232. Michaux, Dr. Flavien. "A travers les oeuvres de Victor Hugo.
Originales, préoriginales, éditions fictives, etc." Bulletin du
Bibliophile. Series of articles dealing with Hugo's works chronolog-
ically and running successively from 1$^{er}$ mars 1928 to 20 juin 1939.

Examines all editions of works to establish true original, second,
third, etc., editions and identify pseudo-editions. Description of
typographical errors and physical appearance of editions and of
publishing history.

233. Milner, Max. Le Romantisme I. 1820-1843. Collection
"Littérature française," dirigée par Claude Pichois, vol. 12. Paris:
Arthaud, 1968. (Hugo's theatre, pp. 209-18, 271-83.)

Personal views expressed on Hugo's plays. In Milner's opinion, of
all the drames romantiques only Musset's Lorenzaccio and Nerval's
Léo Burckhart can be put on today. Except for Les Burgraves, Hugo's
theatre is too close to melodrama. But in Les Burgraves: "Jamais
sans doute--sauf dans les grands drames de Claudel--l'interférence
entre les conflits de l'individu et les grandes forces qui mènent
l'histoire n'a été représentée avec une telle puissance sur la
scène française que dans ce fragment anticipié de La Légende des
siècles où les grands thèmes hugoliens de la conscience, de la
paternité et de l'expiation s'incarnent dans des figures colossales
comme les acteurs du drame antique et s'animent dans une forteresse-
cachot secouée par les sobresauts d'une civilisation agonisante."

234.  Moraud, Marcel.  "The French Romantic Drama and Its Relations with English Literature."  Rice Institute Pamphlet 15 (April 1928):  75-128.

Series of three lectures delivered at Rice Institute.  First on conflict between French Classical and Shakespearian conception of drama; second on evolution of Romantic drama in Dumas' and Hugo's plays; third on French drama in England, 1815-1840.  Calls Ruy Blas particularly important as "the play in which the comic element blends best with the tragic and lyrical element of the drama."  Also places Hugo "closer to Shakespeare than Dumas" because he "seems to have brought in the poetical element, the local color, the meditations which are lacking in the classical drama."  As a whole, Moraud adds, English critics were harsh and inaccurate in their views on Hugo's plays.

235.  _____.  Le Romantisme français en Angleterre de 1814 à 1848.  Paris:  H. Champion, 1933.  (Hugo's theatre, pp. 210-30, 269-78, 360-77.)

Expansion of last part of Moraud's lecture series at Rice Institute.  Fate of Hugo's plays in England follows general acceptance or rejection of French Romanticism in England.  Interesting comments on Hugo's dramas from Leigh Hunt, Bulwer Lytton, Mrs. Trollope, and critic for the Quarterly Review, most of whom object to the plays' immorality and atrocities.

236.  Moreau, Pierre.  Le Classicisme des romantiques.  Paris:  Plon, n.d. [1932].  (Hugo's theatre, pp. 174-232, 334-51.)

This important study shows Hugo obsessed with the seventeenth century and composing "en classique."  Observes that Hugo's type of drame romantique "est une fusion des traits épars des classiques; et un Hernani, par exemple, contient les éléments d'un Cid et d'une Clémence d'Auguste. . . . Le sort malheureux des Burgraves . . . achevait de montrer qu'il est vain de soumettre les génies romantiques aux conditions d'un art classique."  1952 edition essentially the same.

237.  _____.  Le Romantisme.  Histoire de la littérature française, vol. 8.  Paris:  J. de Gigord, 1932.  (Hugo's theatre, pp. 201-10, 275-80.)

Good presentation of period.  Interesting interpretation of significance of Hernani's triumph:  "A la vérité, la lutte n'était plus seulement entre le romantique et le classique.  Elle commençait obscurément, entre deux romantismes. . . . Surtout, le romantisme avait désigné jusqu'ici un art aristocratique, individualiste, dédaigneux. . . . Maintenant, le romantisme est exposé au grand public et au fracas; il parle au peuple, et bientôt parlera pour le peuple; il va signifier un art populaire, enflammé."  1957 and 1965 editions somewhat rearranged but offer same opinions.

238.  Mrodzinsky, Carl.  Die deutschen Übersetzungen der dramatischen Hauptwerke Victor Hugos.  Halle:  Hendricks, 1915.  Pp. 159.

Dissertation originally. Author intends to show weaknesses of German translations, both in their interpretations of the French and in the quality of their German, then to compare different translations of same drama. Germans began translating and adapting Hugo's plays early; first was 1833 version of Hernani. Mrodzinsky studies translations of only Hernani, Ruy Blas, Le Roi s'amuse and Marion de Lorme.

239. Muner, Mario. Victor Hugo. Brescia: La Scuola, n.d. [1956]. (Hugo's theatre, pp. 288-92.)

Largely a study of Dieu, La Légende des siècles, La Fin de Satan and Les Misérables. Section on "l'isidorismo nel teatro" in last chapter offers interesting comments on importance of Hugo's use of the grotesque: "Vittor Hugo ha raggiunto un eccezionale primato nell' arte del grottesco ed è opportuno rilevare che soprattutto a tale genere di antitesi è dovuta la parte più vigorosa e durevole dei suoi drammi, in modo particolare di Ruy Blas, di Le Roi s'amuse, di Angelo, che sono forse le sue opere teatrali più vive, nonchè di certi momenti di Marion Delorme."

240. Nathan, Jacques. "Il Teatro di Victor Hugo." Il Dramma (Turin), nos. 362-63 (nov.-dic. 1966).

241. Nicoll, Allardyce. World Drama from Aeschylus to Anouilh. New York: Harcourt, Brace, n.d. [1949]. (Hugo's theatre, pp. 470-73.)

On Hugo as dramatist: "In all these plays Hugo reveals his deep understanding of the stage's requirements. . . . That Hugo did not reach Shakespeare's level is due, not so much to a failure on his part to comprehend the true aim of the tragic dramatist as to the fact that his genius was less fortunately suited than Shakespeare's to the condition of his time. . . . Hugo's chief contribution to the stage of his time was an element that we may call vitality."

242. Nicollier, Jean. "Actualité du théâtre de Victor Hugo." La Gazette de Lausanne, 23-24 févr. 1952, pp. 1, 11.

After rereading whole theatre of Hugo, critic concludes: "Tout réfléchi, son oeuvre dramatique n'est pas inactuel, ni quoi qu'on en ait dit, dépourvue d'intelligence. Ruy Blas reconstitue avec un sens très sûr de la psychologie d'un peuple, par exemple, l'atmosphère politique de l'Espagne à l'aube du XVIIIe siècle. . . . En effet, ne découvre-t-on pas dans son théâtre, sous le couvert du lyrisme, ce sentiment de la fatalité si répandu dans le répertoire moderne? . . . Ce théâtre extraordinaire . . . n'est certes pas inactuel dans ses interrogations et sa résonance mais proprement injouable."

243. Nitze, William A. and E. Preston Dargan. History of French Literature. New York: H. Holt & Co., 1922. (Hugo's theatre, pp. 553-59. Third edition has same authors and title. New York: Holt, Rinehart & Winston, 1938.)

Theory and background of Hugo's Romantic drama first presented, then bataille d'Hernani. Hugo's liberation of stage and drame stressed. Hugo's dramatic efforts as a whole thus evaluated: "The Romantic theatre remains inferior to the Classical in harmonious artistic worth. The reason is that Hugo's drama is mostly melodrama. . . . There are scenes, situations and coups de théâtre that are extremely effective; there are tirades that can still sweep an audience off its feet; and always Hugo remains the master of poetic expression, especially in love passages. This is the greatest merit of his work. With Hugo, whatever is not lyrical is melodramatic." Same views in 1938 edition.

244. Oliver, A. Richard. "Romanticism and Opera." Symposium 23 (Fall-Winter 1969): 325-32.

Traces development of mélodrame and drame into opera and their reciprocal influence. Notes that Hugo was aware of dramatic effects of music: "Hugo, tone-deaf and anti-operatic though he was (he was amazed that Verdi could make four people speak at the same time in Rigoletto), realized this too late, as his attempts to shore up his moribund drames with music amply testify. Ironically, in so doing he brought the drame full cycle back to its origin: a play with musical commentary, the mélodrame."

245. Omond, T. S. The Romantic Triumph. London: W. Blackwood & Sons, 1900. (Hugo's theatre, pp. 216-19.)

Standard literary history. Omond focuses upon Hernani as Hugo's masterpiece and stresses the freedom Hugo introduced in language, setting, plot and versification.

246. Oyerbide, Sister M. Albertina. "The Treatment of Religion in the Plays of Victor Hugo." Ph.D. dissertation, St. John's University (Brooklyn), 1954.

247. Panne, Marinus C. van de. Recherches sur les rapports entre le romantisme français et le théâtre hollandais. Amsterdam: H. J. Paris, 1927. (Hugo's theatre, pp. 72-93, 158.)

Deals with translations into Dutch of Hugo's plays. Even Romantic melodrama fared better than Hugo's dramas: "Si la Hollande littéraire a admiré le poète lyrique en Hugo, comme les traductions en témoignent, le dramaturge ne lui plaisait pas. . . . C'est là ce qui explique les dates tardives des traductions de Hugo dramaturge." Play by play analysis of translations follows.

248. Pardo-Bazán, Emilia, Condesa de. La literatura francesa moderna: El romanticismo. Madrid: V. Prieto, n.d. [1910?]. (Hugo's theatre, pp. 181-202.)

Interesting views of this Spanish scholar and novelist presented after brief literary history. She feels Hugo mistakenly thought himself a dramatic author for thirteen years: "La forma de Hugo era espléndida, . . ." but he lacked all other necessary qualities. She accuses Hugo of using same theme in all plays--"la rehabilitación de los seres degradados y la depuración del mal por medio de una sola gota de bien." Chooses as his most perfect play, "su primer [sic] drama, Marion Delorme."

249. Paris. Bibliothèque Nationale. Victor Hugo. Catalogue de l'exposition organisée pour commémorer le cent-cinquantième anniversaire de sa naissance. Paris: Imp. Tournon, 1952.

Among editions, manuscripts, documents, Hugo's drawings on display, are sketches Hugo made for his plays' scenery and costumes, his contracts, stage directions and even little stage models. Catalogue gives pertinent information on the works, including details of premières, pictures of actors, caricatures, and parodies. Illustrates graphically Hugo's visual talents put to use for the theatre.

250. Parker, Adelaide and E. Allison Peers. "The Influence of Victor Hugo on Spanish Drama." Modern Language Review 28 (April 1933): 205-16.

Continuation of the authors' general article on Hugo's popularity in Spain below. Claim that his influence on Spanish drama was as brief as the vogue of his plays; but indirect influence, "through the effect of his work on the popularity of historical drama, may well have been considerable." Article closes with bibliography of translations into Spanish of Hugo's plays from 1834-1863. See also Gabbert (151).

251. _____. "The Vogue of Victor Hugo in Spain." Modern Language Review 27 (Jan. 1932): 36-57.

The 1835 première in Spain of Hugo's Lucrèce Borgia in translation "begins the brief epoch of Hugo's true popularity in Spain, corresponding almost exactly with the brief reign of Romantic drama." 1838 marks the highest point of Hugo's popularity in Spain as dramatist and poet. Authors conclude that "the vogue of the revolutionary Hugoesque drama" yielded rapidly to Spanish Romantics who wanted revival of plays of the Siglo de oro.

252. Partridge, Eric. The French Romantics' Knowledge of English Literature (1820-1848) according to Contemporary French Memoirs, Letters and Periodicals. Paris: Champion, 1924. (Hugo's theatre, pp. 234-38.)

Very interesting treatment of English literary influence in Hugo's plays. In Hernani, Partridge suggests Hugo "copied from Shakespeare the habit of passing over in silence a long break in the events. . . ." Triboulet resembles Caliban, he feels, and Ruy Blas is Shakespearian in its mixture of tragedy and comedy. He closes: "In résumé, therefore, Hugo in his dramas owed much to English literature; especially to Shakespeare and Scott, a little to Byron and Bulwer Lytton; some of his most telling situations derived therefrom. But, though he proclaimed his discipleship to Shakespeare, he very rarely mentioned his debts in particulars, whether to that or to any other writer."

253. Patch, Helen Elizabeth. The Dramatic Criticism of Théophile
Gautier. Bryn Mawr, Pa.: n.p., 1922. (Hugo's theatre, pp. 44-52,
131 ff.)

   1921 Bryn Mawr College Ph.D. dissertation. Very good résumé of
   Gautier's articles and views on Hugo as dramatist. Although
   Gautier disagreed with Hugo's theory of the grotesque, he admired
   especially Hugo's style: "In him, Gautier finds the stylist par
   excellence, the one man of his generation who made literary form
   the supreme interest of his work. . . . It is significant that the
   last words of Gautier's long and faithful career as a critic should
   have been ones of enthusiasm and praise for Hugo."

254. Patterson, Helen Temple. Poetic Genesis: Sébastien Mercier into
Victor Hugo. Studies on Voltaire and the Eighteenth Century, vol. 11.
Geneva: Institut et musée Voltaire, 1960. (Hugo's theatre, pp. 126-
66.)

   Traces Mercier's influence, particularly on Hugo's theories.
   Claims: "It is not proposed to comb Hugo's plays for images and
   expressions reminiscent of Mercier. But they exist. . . . Certain
   characters, scenes, situations and details in Hugo's plays have a
   counterpart in Mercier."

255. Pellissier, Georges. Le Réalisme du romantisme. Paris: Hachette,
1912. (Hugo's theatre, pp. 220-25.)

   In describing the realism of the Romantic drama, Pellissier chooses
   Hugo as the prime example of the drama's novelty, especially of its
   new realistic tone. Agrees that there are a few historical errors
   in Hugo's plays, but sees more "vérité historique des 'moeurs'"
   than certain critics allow: "Au reste, lors même que la couleur du
   drame serait fausse, elle dénoterait cependant un souci des milieux
   et des décors réels qui suffit pour le distinguer de la tragédie.
   Rompant avec les abstractions classiques, il y substitue la
   réalité positive et relative. . . . [Donc] le drame a préparé ce
   nouveau genre de théâtre qui, dans la seconde moitié du XIXe siècle,
   peindra les moeurs et les figures de la société contemporaine."

256. Pendell, William D. Hugo's Acted Dramas and the Contemporary
Press. Johns Hopkins Studies in Romance Literatures and Languages,
extra vol. 23. Baltimore, Md.: Johns Hopkins Press, 1947. Pp. 135.

   Excellent, well researched and analyzed study of press reaction to
   Hugo's performed plays. One chapter each devoted to plays from
   Amy Robsart through Les Burgraves. In conclusion Pendell finds it
   hard to give résumé, as reviews vary from journal to journal according to editorial policy and individual whim. Selects as outstanding
   critic, the hugophile Théophile Gautier. Jules Janin of the Journal
   des Débats and Gustave Planche are seen as those critics most in
   tune with "modern judgment," stressing the plays' weaknesses while
   praising the best parts. Bibliography provides helpful listing by
   play of articles in journals during period covered. Good index.
   a) Hunt. Modern Language Review 44 (Jan. 1949): 125.
   b) Godin. French Studies 4 (Jan. 1950): 85-86.

257. Peyre, Henri. Hugo. N.p. [Paris]: Presses universitaires de
France, 1972. (Hugo's theatre, p. 17 and passim.)

Chooses to stress Hugo's later plays rather than the grands drames
romantiques: "Torquemada (1882) est un drame saisissant et le
Théâtre en liberté, affranchi des contraintes de la représentation,
devance toute une série de tentatives modernes pour redonner au
genre dramatique liberté, fantaisie, vie."
a) Kirton. French Studies 29 (1975): 474-75.

258. Picard, Roger. Le Romantisme social. New York: Brentano, n.d.
[1944]. (Hugo's theatre, pp. 241-46. Also as "Le Théâtre social du
romantisme." Messager de New York 27 [1$^{er}$ janv. 1944]: 12-18.)

Suggests moralizing social theatre of Romanticism had good effect
on social attitudes. Through Hugo's sympathy for "le peuple,"
redemption of the fallen woman and defense of the outlaw, he turned
the theatre toward social preoccupations "au sens idéologique."
Picard finds proof in parodies "qui tournaient en dérision les
prétentions moralisatrices ou propagandistes du drame social des
romantiques."

259. Picon, Gaëton. Littératures françaises, connexes et marginales.
Histoire des littératures, 3. Paris: Gallimard, 1958. (Hugo's theatre,
pp. 1111-18.)

After providing background information on Romantic theatre, Picon
offers fresh views on the échec of Hugo's plays. Suggests that the
theatre of that time was "sans contact avec la société. . . . On
peut dire que le théâtre romantique apporte des possibilites dont
il a été rapidement spolié par d'autres genres." Psychological
complexity is taken over by the novel, lyricism by poetry. Musset's
plays are the masterpieces of Romantic theatre while, among weaker
authors, "Hugo, notamment, ne cesse d'osciller entre l'oeuvre
injouable et le mélodrame indigne de l'oeuvre. Le grand drame
littéraire n'existe qu'à l'état mythique dans la préface de
Cromwell. . . . Et ni Hernani, ni Ruy Blas, ni Les Burgraves n'ont
la beauté de ses grandes oeuvres poétiques ou romanesques. . . . La
meilleure part est sans doute dans ce Théâtre en liberté ecrit après
l'échec des Burgraves. . . ."

260. Piétri, François. "L'Espagne de Victor Hugo." La Revue (des Deux
Mondes). 5-part chronological study of Hugo's works. Hugo's theatre
treated as follows: 22 (15 aout 1951): 601-18; 23 (1$^{er}$ sept. 1951):
58-76; 25 (1$^{er}$ janv. 1952): 57-77; 29 (15 oct. 1952): 657-71.

Attempts to show Hugo not so careless in treatment of Spain as often
charged. Hernani, Ruy Blas and Cromwell especially analyzed for
Spanish details: "C'est dans son théâtre que l'Espagne tient la
place principale et qu'elle est, d'autre part le plus scrupuleuse-
ment traitée." As Hugo matures, he leaves Spain aside, as it was
intimately associated with his youth. Piétri concludes: "Hugo,
quand il touche à l'Espagne, se montre en général beaucoup plus
respectueux de l'histoire qu'il ne l'est de la géographie, et que,
finalement, c'est dans le domaine de la langue qu'il accumule le
maximum de bévues." See also Martinenche (495) and Huszár (190).

261. Primo, Levi. [L'Italico]. "Victor Hugo nel melodramma italiano." Rivista Moderna Politica e Letteraria, n.s. 1 (1902): 109-17.

262. Radulescu, Ion H. Le Théâtre français dans les pays roumains (1826-1852). Paris: Minard, 1965. (Hugo, pp. 430-62, 490.)

Lack of index makes this study difficult to use. Table at end indicates Angelo had one performance in Roumanian area in 1840 and Lucrèce Borgia had one in 1841. Conclusion on rôle of Victor Hugo: "La part faite à Victor Hugo est bien modeste, tant par le nombre d'ouvrages . . . que par leur valeur littéraire; ni les drames en vers du théoricien de l'école romantique . . . ni son meilleur drame en prose (Marie Tudor) n'ont été représenté par les Français."

263. Revel, Bruno. Victor Hugo, 1802-1830: la vittoria romantica. Milan: C. Marzorati, 1955. (Hugo's theatre, pp. 75-137.)

Basically biography and standard literary history. In large section on importance of Hernani in "la vittoria romantica" of 1830, Revel credits Hugo with "la fermentazione lirica implicita nella rivoluzione teatrale dei romantici" and with the artistic glorification of "quella parola 'libertà.'" Yet of Hernani itself, Revel remarks: "La vittoria di Hernani non fosse tanto l'avvento del dramma nuovo, quale era auspicato dal cenacolo romantico quanto una rinnovata e più sfacciata estensione del melodramma, passato in quell' occasione dai teatri popolari a quello di stato, ed innalzato da un poeta al rango di genere letterario. . . ."

264. Richepin, Jean. "Victor Hugo: Cromwell, Hernani; Le Roi s'amuse, Ruy Blas, Les Burgraves; Oeuvres de fantaisie." Le Journal de l'Université des Annales, année 8 (15 janv., 1er févr., 1er juin 1914): 119-42, 181-202, 651-74.

Thirteen-part series, three of which treat Hugo's theatre, explaining his works to general public. Maintains that only poets understand Hugo's theatre and considers unjust "le gros reproche contre les drames de Hugo: ce n'est pas du théâtre, c'est de l'opéra." Plays mentioned above presented in historical context and excerpted. Particularly good section on the Théâtre en liberté. Pleasant lectures aimed at instilling appreciation of works.

265. Rigal, Eugène. "Le Romantisme au théâtre avant les romantiques. Introduction à l'étude du théâtre de Victor Hugo." La Revue d'Histoire Littéraire de la France 22 (juin 1915): 1-31.

Point of departure for this learned study is Pierre Nebout's 1895 book, Le Drame romantique, in which author seeks to break bridge between Romantic theatre and all previous plays. Rigal's thesis counters that it is rather the classical theatre which is the aberration and that the very nature of French literary expression has always been a Romantic tendency towards freedom of form. After definition of drame romantique and enumeration of its characteristics, Rigal seeks forerunners in history of French theatre. Offers wide array of plays from every epoch embodying Romantic traits, from Garnier's Bradamante to Pixérécourt's La Tête de mort. De-emphasizes Hugo's rôle as innovator: "Ainsi le théâtre romantique, loin d'être isolé dans notre histoire littéraire, a été, de points de vue différents et à des degrés divers, annoncé par la plus grande partie de notre théâtre."

266. Ripoll, Roger. "Zola juge de Victor Hugo (1871-1877)." Les Cahiers Naturalistes 46 (1973): 182-204.

Investigates articles Zola wrote on Hugo. 1873 reprises of Marion de Lorme and Marie Tudor occasioned following evaluation of the dramatist: "Seulement, il faut dire la vérité bien haut sur son théâtre qui a déjà fait bien des victimes. Que les jeunes auteurs dramatiques s'adressent ailleurs, à la vérité, à la vie moderne."

267. Ritter, Raymond. "Ugolin, tyran de Pise." In his Radio-Parnasse. A la manière de . . . , pp. 67-104. Paris: A. Michel, n.d. [1933].

Ugolino story made into Hugoesque play. Preface written in unmistakably Hugolian terms.

268. Rousseaux, André. "Le Goût du panache." Le Figaro, 2 avril 1952, p. 1.

Critic had previously written: "Hernani me paraît déchu du rang des chefs-d'oeuvre." Resulting mail from readers overwhelmingly against his position; so he concludes that the younger generation, tired of moral debasement in literature and on stage, are seeking panache, moral grandeur in heroes like Hernani: "Le théâtre romantique, c'est manifeste, garde des partisans qui se sont révélés ardents et pugnaces. . . . Et l'argument qui revenait dans beaucoup d'entre elles [les lettres] était que les héros de Victor Hugo, renforcés par ceux d'Edmond Rostand, répondent aujourd'hui à un besoin d'enthousiasme."

269. Roy, Claude. "Hugo en somme. . . ." La Revue de Paris, année 74 (sept. 1967): 20-33. (Also in Victor Hugo, pp. 273-89. Paris: Hachette, 1967.)

Expresses overwhelming admiration for the many talents of Victor Hugo: "On ne fera croire à personne de sensé qu'un homme ordinaire ait pu être tout ce qu'a été Victor Hugo, c'est-à-dire le plus grand poéte de son siècle et un de ses plus grands dessinateurs, un homme politique et un don Juan, un philosophe et un homme d'affaires, l'auteur dramatique le plus important et le romancier le plus populaire de ceux qui n'étaient pas des feuilletonistes."

270. Rudwin, Maximilien J. Bibliographie de Victor Hugo. Paris: Société "Les Belles Lettres," n.d. [1926]. (Hugo's theatre, p. 24.)

Only nine specific items on Hugo's theatre listed. Summary and incomplete.

271. Ruprecht, Hans-George. "Victor Hugo und die mexikanische Romantik." Arcadia 4 (1969): 43-65.

On Hugo's general influence on Mexican Romantics. That of his
theatre, particularly Angelo and Hernani, was strong: "Doch das
zwei fellos entscheiden Ereignis der Hugo-Rezeption in Mexiko ist
die Aufführung des Dramas Angelo, tirano de Padua im Jahre 1837 in
zwei Theatern der Hauptstadt. . . . Er ist naturlich kein Zufall,
dass ein Jahr nach der Erstaufführung seines drama romántico nun
auch ein Mexikaner mit einem ähnlich angelegten Stück hervortritt."

272. Sacher, Herbert. Die Melodramatik und das romantische Drama in
Frankreich. Leipzig: R. Noske, 1936. (Hugo's theatre, pp. 35-45 and
passim.)

Inaugural dissertation at University of Breslau. Finds many
elements of mélodrame in Hugo's plays, especially lack of psychological development: "Die Betrachtung der Versdramen Victor Hugos
er gibt, dass ihre unglücklichen Augänge sich nicht psychologisch
ergeben, sondern stets das Ergebnis derselben Fatalité sind, welche
den Kern der romantischen Lebenshaltung ausmacht. Diese Fatalité
erreicht ihr Ziel mit Hilfe der bekannten melodramatischen Mittel,
welche die willkürlichen Geschehnisse ermöglichen." For better
study, see Lacey (200).

273. Sainte-Beuve, Charles-Augustin. Mes Poisons. Paris: Plon, 1926.
(Hugo's theatre, pp. 37-38, 45-47.)

Although the great critic penned these witty, often petty judgments
in the 1830s, the secret diary was not published until this century.
These opinions on Hugo as dramatist, reserved for only Sainte-
Beuve's eyes, help explain why he never wrote the overall study of
Hugo's theatre he promised. Example: "Ruy Blas vide de fond en
comble la question de Hugo, si tant est qu'elle restât encore
quelque peu indécise; c'est un certificat d'incurable magnifiquement
armorié, historié, avec de grosses majuscules rouges galonnés d'or,
comme les laquais de sa pièce. . . . Hernani, pour moi, c'a été la
fin de l'Assemblée législative. . . . Hugo dramatique, c'est Caliban
qui pose pour Shakespeare."

274. Sand, Robert. "Victor Hugo et le drame moderne." La Revue de
Belgique, sér. 2, année 34 (15 févr. 1902): 144-51.

Finds the drame romantique a "compromis entre la vie et le lyrisme."
Therefore, it evolved in two directions: its realism into the
drame réaliste and its lyricism into Wagnerian opera. Hugo's works,
essentially lyrical, can be admired only as "manifestations
splendides d'un art du passé. . . . Ses personnages ne sont grands
que par l'étendue de leurs passions et l'élévation de leur
éloquence." They can no longer compete with modern opera or drama.

275. Savey-Casard, Paul. Le Crime et la peine dans l'oeuvre de Victor
Hugo. Paris: Presses universitaires de France, 1956. (Hugo's theatre,
pp. 166-73, 343-44.)

Chapter 2 of second part, "Le Criminel dans le théâtre de Victor
Hugo: le criminel pittoresque," examines Hernani, Ruy Blas, Les
Burgraves, Le Théâtre en liberté and various fragments to show
development of this character-type, whose fullest expression is,

perhaps, in Aïrolo of <u>Mangeront-ils?</u>. On Hugo's colorful out-
siders, Savey-Casard states: "A travers un rêve, ils laissent
entrevoir l'âme inquiète du poète et, par delà, ses préoccupations
sociales, politiques et philosophiques." A later section deals
with Hugo's treatment of "la pénalité" in <u>Torquemada</u>.

276. Schäfer, Rotraut. "V. Hugo." In his <u>Das Eindringen schlichter</u>
<u>Sprache in das französische Alexandriner-drama</u>: 1740-1840, pp. 182-94.
Göppingen: A. Kümmerle, 1969.

Solid examination of Hugo's important rôle in introducing simple,
everyday language into French Alexandrine drama. Hugo desires, as
part of his theoretical program of <u>le grotesque</u>, to show that the
Alexandrine can accommodate all manner of language. Schäfer agrees
that Hugo reaches this goal in his plays: "Und was keinem anderem
Dramatiker vor ihm gelang, erreicht Hugo: Die Alltagssprache
verdrängt die 'langue noble' vollständig von der Bühne, sie bleibt
fürderhin die offezielle Theatersprache."

277. Schulkind, Eugene. "Hugo." In <u>French Literature and Its Back-</u>
<u>ground</u>. Edited by John Cruickshank. 5 vols. Vol. 4: 37-54. London:
Oxford University Press, 1969.

In this good overall re-evaluation of Hugo, Schulkind underlines
value of his little-known but perhaps (in Schulkind's opinion) best
poetry, like <u>Océan</u> and <u>Chansons des rues et des bois</u>. Hugo's
theatre, however, remains an inferior part of his work: "For
Hugo's theatre to have remained largely in the mould of <u>Hernani</u> was
disastrous, for this meant that it never broke free of the 1830
taste for melodrama, declamation, and ardent emotional display.
<u>Ruy Blas</u> (1838), perhaps the most effectively constructed of his
plays, could be considered as one of the most typical examples of
French Romantic drama--and the most typically Hugolian; . . . and
the present-day theatre-goer, seeking psychological subtlety or
profundity, will generally be irritated and disappointed."

278. Sée, Edmond. "Le Théâtre romantique." <u>La Revue de France</u>, 15
mars 1930. (Also in his <u>Le Mouvement dramatique</u>. <u>1929-1930</u>, I, 203-17.
Paris: Editions de France, 1930.)

Begins with origin and definition of the term "romantisme,"
continues with development and characteristics of the <u>drame</u>
<u>romantique</u>. Identifies Musset as best playwright of epoch. Of
Hugo he concludes: "Les drames en vers (<u>Ruy Blas</u>, <u>Hernani</u>)
s'imposent encore aujourd'hui à notre émerveillement, à notre
admiration, à cause du génie poétique et en dépit de la puérilité,
de l'arbitraire des intrigues (mais les drames en prose, <u>Marie</u>
<u>Tudor</u>, <u>Angelo</u>, etc., sont à proprement parler 'inécoutables'. . . ."

279. Segond-Weber, Madame. "Le Théâtre de Victor Hugo. Les Heroïnes
romantiques--les sorcières." <u>Conferencia</u> 14 (1<sup>er</sup> sept. 1920): 241-56.

This well-known sociétaire of the Comédie-Française reminisces about
her rôles in Hugo's plays from her début as doña Sol through her
parts as the witches Zineb of <u>Mangeront-ils?</u> and Guanhumara of <u>Les</u>
<u>Burgraves</u>. She tells how she prepared for rôles and employs

extensive quotations, which she acted out for the audience of this lecture. More entertainment than literary or critical information.

280. Simon, Gustave. "Sarah Bernhardt: Notes et souvenirs; lettres inédites." La Revue de Paris, année 30 (15 août, 1$^{er}$ sept. 1923): 848-72; 132-67.

Two-part article on great actress's rôles in Hugo's dramas and her ideas and opinions of them. She acted in all plays written from Marion de Lorme through Ruy Blas. Especially about her productions of Hugo's plays in her own theatre and playing lead for first time in her 1911 reprise of Lucrèce Borgia.

281. _____. "Victor Hugo et ses interprètes. Documents inédits." La Revue Hebdomadaire, année 31, t. 5 (mai 1922): 154-66, 315-29, 436-51; t. 6 (juin 1922): 39-53, 191-93.

Through "notes, lettres et documents inédits, souvenirs personnels, conversations de Victor Hugo, récits de coulisses et impressions de répétitions," Simon illuminates Hugo's warm relationships with his actors--Joanny, even the once recalcitrant Mlle Mars, Mme. Dorval, Frédérick Lemaître, Mlle George, Rachel, Marie Laurent, Mme. Favart. According to Simon, "Victor Hugo est assurément l'auteur qui a eu les plus glorieux interprètes."

282. Skwarczyńska, S. "Wiktor Hugo jako teoretyk dramatu." Pamietnik Teatralny (Warsaw) 4 (1952).

283. Sleumer, Albert. Die Dramen Victor Hugos. Eine Litterar-historischkritische Untersuchung. Litterarhistorische Forschungen, no. 16. Berlin: E. Felber, 1901. Pp. xxvi+368.

Massive collection of critical opinions of others. Helpful bibliography. Chapters on each of the ten major plays, Cromwell through Torquemada; Hugo's siècle; plays' influence; female figures; German studies; French studies; and various editions. Sleumer often stresses moral worth in evaluating the plays. Concludes: "Es lässt sich nicht in Abrede stellen, dass von den vereinigten Werken des grossen Dichters die dramatische Partie die schwächste ist; dass es--wenigstens vorläufig--diejenige ist, welche am unvermeidlichsten der Vergessenheit anheimfällt, beziehungsweise schon anheimgefallen ist."

284. _____. "Inwieweit lassen sich die Dramen Victor Hugos als Schullektüre verwenden?" Zeitschrift für französischen und englischen Unterricht, 7, 6 (1908).

285. Smet, Robert de. Le Théâtre romantique: Victor Hugo, Alexandre Dumas, Alfred de Vigny, Alfred de Musset. Avec un florilège de ces auteurs. Paris: Les Oeuvres Représentatives, 1929. (Hugo, pp. 187-206 and passim.)

Excerpts included from Hernani, Marie Tudor, Angelo, Ruy Blas and Les Burgraves. In introductory essay on the Romantic theatre, Smet declares: "Ce qui a le plus vieilli dans le théâtre de Victor Hugo et ce qu'aujourd'hui l'on pardonne le moins à son auteur, ce sont

ces appels effrontés aux bravos du parterre, ces fins de scène ou
d'acte qui accrochent l'ovation comme la note suraiguë et trillée
de la prima-donna."

286.  Smith, Horatio E.  Masters of French Literature.  New York:  C.
Scribner's Sons, 1937.  (Hugo's theatre, pp. 218-46.)

First Smith sketches trends of English and French criticism on
Hugo's plays, then chooses as Hugo's "most enduring romantic
dramas" Hernani and Ruy Blas.  Amid great poetry and lurid mélodrame, "Hugo is still, within limits, faithful to the classical
tradition of playwriting; he is even near-Aristotelian."

287.  Smith, Hugh A.  "Hugo and the Romantic Drama."  In his Main
Currents of Modern French Drama, pp. 15-35.  New York:  H. Holt & Co.,
n.d. [1925].

Standard approach of literary history.  Identifies Hernani and Ruy
Blas as Hugo's best plays, though it is for their lyricism and not
their dramatic qualities.  Complains that Hugo "lacked the specific
ability of the dramatist, without which one may, it is true, write
good literature cast in a dramatic mold, but can hardly write a
good play. . . . By temperament, then Hugo is a writer of melodrama."  Evaluates Hugo's contribution as largely negative:  "The
Romantic theatre, then, as exemplified by Hugo, is important
chiefly for its destructive work."

288.  Solente, Suzanne.  "Les Manuscrits de Victor Hugo conservés à la
Bibliothèque Nationale."  In Victor Hugo, pp. 14-116.  Paris:
Bibliothèque Nationale, 1952.

Information on all Hugo manuscripts at the Bibliothèque Nationale.
Several plays are represented by more than one manuscript (four for
Cromwell), and a few plays have with them also contracts, corres-
pondence, autographs, costume sketches, parodies, and anecdotes.

289.  Sorel, Albert-Emile.  "Parodies du théâtre de Victor Hugo."
Le Gaulois, 29 mai 1927.

290.  Souchon, Paul.  Victor Hugo, l'homme et l'oeuvre.  Paris:
Tallandier, 1949.  (Hugo's theatre, pp. 62-68, 313-20, 343-50.)

In this biography with fictionalized scenes, illustrative anecdotes
and quotations from poetry, Souchon devotes chapters to Marion de
Lorme and Hernani, Le Théâtre en liberté, and Amy Robsart and Les
Jumeaux.  Of Hugo and his Théâtre en liberté, Souchon asserts:  "Il
y a là d'innombrables témoignages de son esprit et de sa belle
humeur et il n'eût tenu qu'à lui de devenir également un grand
auteur comique."

291.  Souriau, Etienne.  Les Deux Cent Mille Situations dramatiques.
Paris:  E. Flammarion, 1950.  (Hugo's theatre, pp. 52-53, 82, 109-11,
150-51, 188-92, 240.)

Hugo's plays selected as illustrations provide mainly negative
examples.  Section on parody contains parodies of Hernani to show

Hugo's weakness in too much reliance on "un accessoire matériel," like the cor in Hernani, to move action along. Finds fault also with Hugo's use of a "coup de théâtre en renversement violent et un peu puérile (comme souvent dans le théâtre de Hugo) dans Mangeront-ils?."

292. Souriau, Maurice. Histoire du romantisme en France. 2 vols. in 3. Paris: "Editions Spes," 1927. (Hugo's theatre, I, 217-23, 250-74; II, 46-57, 204-19.)

Still perhaps the best comprehensive study of the French Romantic period. Excellent scholarship and critical finesse abound in chapters on Cromwell, Amy Robsart and Pierre Corneille; Hernani; Marion Delorme; Ruy Blas; and Les Burgraves. Souriau seeks sources, succinctly recounts history of performances and press reception, and objectively evaluates plays' worth. Balanced presentation of Hugo's many weaknesses and strengths as dramatist: "Immense comme poète lyrique, oui, mais comme poète dramatique il faut avoir le courage de dire qu'il est ordinaire. Le lyrisme de ses vers fait illusion sur la valeur scénique de ses pièces." What will remain of Hugo's theatre? Because of its transformation of theatrical language, Hernani. "C'est son oeuvre la plus vraie, la plus humaine, et par conséquent la plus scénique. Le temps lui a donné toute sa valeur, absolue et comparative."

293. Steiner, George. The Death of Tragedy. New York: A. Knopf, 1963. (Hugo's theatre, pp. 151-65, 311.)

In this well argued case that tragedy, as known in occidental literature from the Greeks through Shakespeare and Racine, is no longer possible, Hugo's role is that of helping to transform tragedy and lead it to its demise: "The plays of Victor Hugo, Vigny, and the lesser romantics are not only hopelessly dated; . . . the theatre triumphs so relentlessly over the drama. . . . Our entire interest is solicited by the manner of contrivance, not by any intrinsic meaning. . . . The limiting conditions are not those of moral insight or intelligence, but clocks nearing midnight, bolted doors, messengers racing toward scaffolds. Even the verbal form is theatrical rather than dramatic. . . . Having repudiated classical notions of the evil in man, Victor Hugo and his contemporaries replaced the tragic by the contingent."

294. Stevenson, Roger Verlin. "The Thematic Structures of Victor Hugo's Theatre." Ph.D. dissertation, University of Washington, 1978. DAI 39 (Nov.-Dec. 1978): 3622A-23A.

295. Strachey, G. Lytton. Landmarks in French Literature. London: Williams and Norgate, 1912. (Hugo's theatre, pp. 213-14.)

Very negative view of Hugo's dramas: "On the whole, the dramatic achievement of the Romantic School was the least valuable part of their work. Hernani, the first performance of which marked the turning-point of the movement, is a piece of bombastic melodrama, full of the stagiest clap-trap and the most turgid declamation. Victor Hugo imagined when he wrote it that he was inspired by Shakespeare; if he was inspired by anyone, it was by Voltaire. . . .

Of true character and passion it has no trace. The action, the
incidents, the persons--all alike are dominated by considerations
of rhetoric, and of rhetoric alone. . . . All the worst tendencies
of the Romantic Movement may be seen completely displayed in the
dramas of Victor Hugo."

296. Strowski, Fortunat. "Le Mouvement poétique en France dans la
première moitié du XIXe siècle:  le théâtre de Victor Hugo." La Revue
des Cours et Conférences, sér. 2, année 20 (28 mars 1912):  97-105.

Proposes to examine what is Romantic in Hugo's theatre, why his
plays are not, "à proprement parler, du théâtre," and why they
failed.  Claims theories and prefaces describe realistic theatre
to come, not drame romantique as Hugo achieved it.  Hugo's choice
of extraordinary subjects and characters structures his plays into
a series of lyrical odes, according to Strowski.  Thus, poetry
furnishes the Romantic content, brings about Hugo's true revolution
in style, and takes his plays out of the realm of "proper theatre."
Hugo's échec comes from his plays' lack of psychology and overabundance of antithesis.  Only "chefs-d'oeuvre" of drama he
produced are Marion de Lorme and Les Burgraves:  "Entre ces deux
pièces s'écoule toute la vie de Hugo comme homme de théâtre; . . .
tous les autres [drames] sont manqués."

297. Suarès, André. "Notes sur Victor Hugo." La Revue d'Art
Dramatique, année 17 (3-15 mars 1902):  96-108.

Suarès admires Hugo as a man but not as a poet and least of all as
a dramatist:  "Le théâtre de Victor Hugo est le scandale de la
vérité et de la nature:  il est contre toute connaissance de l'homme
et même contre toute raison. . . . Mais le génie de l'éloquence a
fait de ce néant un néant étincelant et splendide. . . . C'est le
faux Shakespeare. Et cela aussi sent l'Espagne."

298. Svevaeus, Gösta. "Uttrycksmedlens dialog:  Tecknaren Victor
Hugo--mälaren August Strindberg." Studiekamraten 49 (1967):  51-54.

299. Tephany, Jacques. "Hugo et le théâtre. L'âme publique."
Marginales, année 25 (déc. 1970):  25-30.

Examines Hugo's dramatic theory, especially in William Shakespeare,
to show his central belief that "le théâtre, plus que l'épopee ou
le roman, a pour fonction de métamorphoser la foule en public. . . ."
Divides Hugo's plays into two categories of attempts to realize
goal:  the "grands drames historiques," like Ruy Blas and Torquemada,
and the "théâtre plus confidentiel." Says Hugo eventually realized
he was far from really communicating with "le peuple" in either set
of plays, and he carried this personal obsession into Les
Misérables. Closes:  "Il demeure qu'à l'âme du peuple, Hugo a
tendu le miroir de son âme personnelle, pour qu'elle devienne l'âme
publique. Le théâtre était une tribune où cette volonté pouvait
prendre corps, avec la complicité des enfants que nous sommes."

300. "Le Théâtre de Victor Hugo, source d'enthousiasme de la jeunesse
française." Les Lettres Françaises, 10-17 avril (1952?).

Comments by M. Rostand, E. Sée, R. Kemp, R. Fauchois, Mary Marquet, J. Yonnel.

301. "Un Théâtre pour le peuple." T.E.P. Actualité, no. 67 (1970).

302. Thibaudet, Albert. Histoire de la littérature francaise de 1789 à nos jours. Paris: Stock, 1936. (Hugo's theatre, pp. 191-96.)

Expresses some interesting views on various Hugo plays. Of Cromwell he says: "Ce drame de tois mille vers, qui ne peut se jouer, est curieux, amusant, bien écrit, tient encore à la lecture-- à cause de son sujet. . . ." Antony, he argues, marks real lasting victory of Rmantic theatre, not dead Hernani. Sums up: "Ruy Blas, . . . qui fut et qui est encore le principal succès dramatique de Victor Hugo, et les Burgraves (1843) en restent deux morceaux considérables et les plus éclatants. Les invraisemblances de Ruy Blas ne l'empêchent pas d'être plein de mouvement et d'idées dramatiques, et son quatrième acte a créé pour un demi-siècle tout un style de la comédie en vers."

303. _____. "Situation de Victor Hugo." La Revue de Paris, année 42 (15 mai 1935): 258-84.

Solid personal summing up of value of Hugo and his works rather than an état présent of scholarship. In naming Hugo "le plus grand phénomène de notre littérature," Thibaudet finds his work as a whole has retained its high place in critical opinion. But Hugo is "une victime du théâtre," having entered that domain "moins pour donner des rôles que pour y jouer un rôle: le rôle d'un conquérant, quand le romantisme avait le théâtre à conquérir." Hugo's "théâtromanie" did not stop at the échec of Les Burgraves, and his problem remained the fact that he is a man of monologue rather than dialogue.

304. Thiébaut, Marcel. "Victor Hugo 1954." La Revue de Paris 61 (juin 1954): 140-56.

Personal view of Hugo's worth: "Pour le théâtre, les tentatives de résurrection théâtrale qui ont récemment appuyé ce mouvement n'ont pas été heureuses. Hernani semble décidément injouable, Ruy Blas broché de vers splendides est bien décevant, hors la partie comique qui 'tient' (comme oncle à héritage de Rostand, Hugo reste imbattable)." Also holds novels, even poetry, in rather low esteem.

305. Thomas, John H. L'Angleterre dans l'oeuvre de Victor Hugo. Bibliothèque de la Fondation Victor Hugo, vol. 1. Paris: A. Pedone, 1934. (Hugo's theatre, pp. 10-91.)

Good chapters on English sources of Cromwell, Amy Robsart and Marie Tudor. Sees influence of Ann Radcliffe's gothic novels in Hugo's early dramatic works, like Irtamène, Athélie and Inez de Castro. Scott's great importance stressed as well as Hugo's "conception superficielle de la vérité historique."

306. Tiersot, Julien. "Victor Hugo et la musique. Les Drames." Le Temps, 23 févr. 1930, p. 3. (Also in his "Victor Hugo musicien." La Revue Musicale 16 [sept.-oct. 1935]: 167-96.)

Although primarily a "visuel," Hugo was not against music as some critics claim. Convincing presentation of Hugo's deliberate use of music in Lucrèce, Les Burgraves, Hernani and Ruy Blas for atmosphere and as part of the dénouement.

307. Tomescu, Despina. "Veridicitatea in dramaturgia romantica franceza." Revista de Istorie si Theorie Literara 22 (1973): 413-25.

308. Touchard, Pierre-Aimé. "Le Dramatique." In Victor Hugo, pp. 75-93. Edité par Jacques de Lacretelle et al. Collection "Génies et réalités," no. 30. Paris: Hachette, 1967.

Rather condescending article evaluating Hugo as poor dramatic author: "Nous avons césse de croire à la sincérité du poète dramatique. . . . Il n'est même pas certain que la virtuosité verbale qui a si longtemps rassuré les admirateurs de Hugo, suffise encore à désarmer les critiques." Reviews in chronological order all Hugo's plays. Judges Cromwell superior to its reputation; Marion de Lorme only a beautiful duo d'amour; Hernani no longer believable; Marie Tudor perhaps able to survive on its historical framework as a "mélodrame honnête"; Ruy Blas Hugo's best play and "le plus classique . . . plus brillant que profond, limpide et inconsistant"; Les Burgraves bad; Torquemada "un grand drame." Finishes by suggesting that perhaps another time, needful of love and liberty as literary themes, will ressuscitate Hugo's theatre.

309. _____. "Le Drame romantique et la Comédie-Française." L'Illustre Théâtre 4 (janv. 1957): 38-41.

310. Travers, Seymour. Catalogue of Nineteenth Century French Theatrical Parodies. A compilation of the parodies between 1789 and 1914 of which any record was found. New York: King's Crown Press, 1941. (Hugo, pp. 55-60.)

Interesting listing of parodies, play by play. Marie Tudor and Ruy Blas are targets for nine each, Le Roi s'amuse and Torquemada one apiece. See also Bersaucourt (89) and Blanchard (92).

311. Treskunov, Mikhail Solomonovich. Victor Hugo: A Study of His Works. Moscow: Gos. izdvokhudozh. lit-ry, 1954. Pp. 421.

312. Triaire, Marie-Hélène. "Les Mises-en-scène des pièces de Hugo à leur création." Thèse de Doctorat d'université, Université de Paris, 1968.

313. Ubersfeld-Maille, Annie. "Les Conditions d'un refus idéologique: Hugo devant la presse de 1831 à 1840." In Hommage à Georges Fourrier, pp. 359-79. Annales littéraires de l'Université de Besançon, no. 142. Paris: Les Belles Lettres, 1973.

Reviews consistently negative press reception, 1829-1843, of Hugo's plays and suggests it was because Hugo "transgresses" bourgeois

code on four points: "l'invraisemblable," "le grotesque," "le
goût matérialiste du spectacle," "tout ce qui, dans les structures
dramatiques de l'oeuvre hugolienne, met en péril la métaphysique
et la morale bourgeoises."

314. Ubersfeld-Maille, Annie. "Une Dramaturgie de l'objet: le théâtre
de Victor Hugo." In Le Réel et le texte, pp. 229-41. Colloque du
centre de recherches dixneuvièmistes de l'Université de Lille, no. 3.
Paris: A. Colin, 1974.

Intriguing investigation of Hugo's use of objects in his dramaturgy.
Enumerates three basic functions of object: functional or utili-
tarian, picturesque, symbolic. Hugo stresses last function more
than do Dumas and Vigny, author claims, and he organizes his objects
into "un système de signes clairs et cohérents" to assure "l'unité
entre l'aspect individuel et l'aspect historico-social de l'oeuvre."

315. _____. "Hugo et le théâtre." In Manuel d'histoire littéraire
de la France, T. 4: 1789-1848, deuxième partie, pp. 286-315. Sous la
direction de Pierre Abraham et Roland Desné. Paris: Editions sociales,
n.d. [1973].

Fine presentation of literary history surrounding Hugo's theatre
and analysis of each play, using techniques of the New Criticism.
As in her other writings, author prefers ideological interpretation
of Hugo's plays and their failure: "Ainsi se fait et se défait un
théâtre du paradoxe: paradoxe d'un théâtre historique qui met en
péril le discourse de l'histoire, d'un drame du héros romantique
qui détruit le moi de l'individualisme bourgeois et le réduit à
l'épaisseur d'un masque; d'un théâtre du discours qui est théâtre
de la parole vaine et de l'objet symbolique, d'un théâtre de
l'idéologie libérale qui se retourne contre elle dans sa pratique;
d'un théâtre célèbre et ignoré, joué et refusé."

316. _____. "Job et son dernier combat." In Victor-Marie Hugo,
Oeuvres complètes, vol. 16, première partie, pp. 193-200. Editées par
Jean Massin. Paris: Club français du livre, 1970.

Introduction to the "portefeuille dramatique, 1870-1885." Unity of
theme and characters throughout stressed: "Retrouvailles qui
dessinent dans sa vie et dans son oeuvre éternellement les mêmes
figures. Le retour éternel d'un présent figé dans la malédiction
du passé se matérialise dans son oeuvre dramatique par la permanence
des mêmes thèmes et si l'on peut dire des mêmes canevas--mais aussi
par l'impossibilité de les achever."

317. _____. Le Roi et le bouffon. Etude sur le théâtre de Hugo
de 1830 à 1839. Paris: J. Corti, 1974. Pp. 686. (Précis by author
in L'Information Littéraire 26 [sept.-oct. 1974]: 155-56.)

Exhaustive, definitive work on plays of this period through Les
Jumeaux. First part offers solid, detailed background information
on epoch, theatres, plays' performances, critical receptions.
Especially good on "plans et projets," censorship, sources, genesis,
manuscript variants. Second part, less satisfying, is analysis of
structures of drames incorporating findings from her previous

scholarship and applying critical techniques of the New Criticism.
Stresses ambiguity of Hugo's theatre and his desire "non de satis-
faire un public qui serait 'un' et 'populaire,' public dont il
sait trop bien qu'il n'existe pas, mais de le constituer."
Concludes that Hugo's rupture with traditional theatre of his time,
his "libération," goes in two directions at once, "vers l'onirique"
and "vers le didactique." Suggests that Hugo's theatre leads
directly to Artaud, Brecht and Beckett. A few errors in bibliography.
a) Cellier. Revue d'Histoire Littéraire de la France 75 (1975):
   855-58.
b) Franceschetti. Studi Francesi 19 (1975): 507-11.
c) Kirton. French Studies 32 (1978): 471-72.
d) Milner. L'Information Littéraire 28 (1976): 31.
e) Nicolas. La Revue des Sciences Humaines, n.s. 156 (oct.-dec.
   1974), pp. 691-92.

318. Van Eerde, John. "Death in Hugo's Theatre." CLA Journal 10
(March 1967): 189-95.

With examples from Irtamène through Les Burgraves, shows that "in
Hugo death is above all separation from the beloved who survives."
Examines Hugo's use of ghosts and various views in plays of heaven,
hell, afterlife: "Hugo would seem to want to impress the spectator
or reader rather than his characters with the firghtfulness of
death. . . . What is more frightening than death itself in this
theatre is the callous attitude of men toward it." Finds the manner
of death, especially for men of rank, more important than death
itself: "Hugo counts on the spectator being sufficiently concerned
to allow the author to use death as a major dramatic device."

319. Van Tieghem, Paul. L'Ere romantique: le romantisme dans la
littérature européenne. Paris: A. Michel, 1948. (Hugo's theatre,
pp. 464-73.)

Faults Hugo with lack of technical expertise in dramatic construction and of "l'intuition psychologique." Only Hugo's two "pièces
espagnoles, Hernani et Ruy Blas," have remained playable. Moreover,
"Seuls, ses drames en vers, Marion Delorme, Hernani, Le Roi s'amuse,
Ruy Blas et la 'trilogie' des Burgraves, réalisaient partiellement
le programme ambitieux de la Préface de Cromwell. . . ."

320. Van Tieghem, Philippe. Dictionnaire de Victor Hugo. Paris:
Larousse, 1970. Pp. 255.

Vast amount of information handily assembled into detailed
chronology, family tree, Parisian dwellings, principal trips, and
alphabetical listing of people, works, characters, etc., all amply
defined. For plays, entries give dates of composition and performance, interesting details of history, plot, actors in rôles,
reprises of note, publication information, variants if of interest,
themes, sources, television and cinema adaptations. Various
photos, drawings, caricatures throughout accompany text. Very
helpful despite some errors of detail and omissions.
a) Bulletin critique du livre français 25 (1970): 813.
b) Bellour. Magazine Littéraire 46 (nov. 1970): 63.

c) Cabinis. Humanités Modernes 13 (juin 1970): 12.
d) Jadot. Etudes Classiques 42 (1974): 108-09.
e) Seebacher. La Revue d'Histoire Littéraire de la France 71
(1971): 311-12.

321. Van Tieghem, Philippe. Le Romantisme français. Paris: Presses
universitaires de France, 1944. (Hugo's theatre, pp. 61-70.)

Considers Musset the greatest Romantic dramatist. On Hugo's
dramatic production, summarizes: "Considéré avec le recul du temps,
et lu question du style mise à part, le drame de Hugo paraît
infiniment plus proche de la tragédie classique que ne s'en doutaient
les contemporains et l'auteur lui-même." Yet finds the Théâtre en
liberté "une réussite certaine: l'idéologie, le lyrisme, l'épique,
les acrobaties même de la versification et ce côté de grosse
bouffonerie que Hugo a si rarement exprimé, s'unissent ici avec un
naturel infiniment plus satisfaisant que le guindé sonore et
solonnel des drames."

322. Viatte, Auguste. "Nouvelles Perspectives sur Victor Hugo." La
Revue de l'Université Laval 6 (mai 1952): 710-14.

Very brief article about renaissance of études hugoliennes.
Praises poet and novelist: "Ce que nous disons du poète, nous le
dirons aussi, non sans doute de l'auteur dramatique, mais du
romancier."

323. Vigo-Fazio, Lorenzo. I Drammi maggiori di Victor Hugo: Cromwell,
Marion Delorme, Ernani, Il Re si diverte, Ruy-Blas, I Burgravi.
Catania: Edizioni Arione, 1951. Pp. 375.

Highly personal appreciation of Hugo's major plays from man with
theatrical experience himself. Literary history presented, followed
by excerpts translated into Italian for each play. Fairly competent
anthology, although hardly a detailed, scholarly approach. Signals
Ruy Blas as Hugo's masterpiece and "il gioiello del teatro romantico
francese": "Indubbiamente è in questo dramma che il genio teatrale
di Hugo ha attinto la sua totale rivelzaione; sia per l'ordito
della finzione, concepita nel teatro e per il teatro; sia per lo
scintillio delle immagini e la leggiadria del verso." No bibliography or index. See also his separate work on the Théâtre en
liberté (786).

324. Ware, Ralph H. American Adaptations of French Plays on the New
York and Philadelphia Stages from 1834 to the Civil War. Philadelphia:
University of Pennsylvania, 1930. (Hugo, pp. 9, 18-21.)

Originally a doctoral dissertation. Shows that Hugo had few
versions of his plays adapted to the American stage. First was
Richard Penn Smith's popular version of Angelo, called The Actress
of Padua and staged in Philadelphia in 1836. Discusses other
adaptations of Angelo and those of Marie Tudor, Le Roi s'amuse and
Lucrèce Borgia during period indicated.

325.  Waterhouse, Francis A.  "Victor Hugo's Operas."  Sewanee Review
29 (April 1921):  198-210.

After summarizing overwhelmingly negative critical opinion of
Hugo's plays, Waterhouse claims that Hugo's gifts are not so much
in a mélange des genres as in a mélange des arts, "at the border-
land between two arts, tragedy and opera." Therefore, Hugo's
blemishes, such as antithesis and lack of psychology, become
virtues.  Finds clearest instances of this talent, of which Hugo
was unaware, in Hernani, Le Roi s'amuse and Lucrèce Borgia, where
dénouement is accomplished through music.  There follows a comparison of Hugo's dramatic works with libretti of operas drawn from
them.  Concludes that the typical Frenchman, "the least musical"
and most appreciative of "genres tranchés," cannot love Hugo's
dramatic "operas."

326.  Weil, Félix.  Victor Hugo et Richard Wagner.  Leurs conceptions
dramatiques.  Zofingue:  Ringer, 1926.  Pp. 136.

Doctoral thesis at Berne.  Le Breton's (211) suggestion that
Hernani and Les Burgraves influenced Wagner's Lohengrin led to
this exhaustive comparison.  Weil's conclusion is negative:  "Les
rapports que nous avons pu trouver, restent superficiels en regard
des divergences considérables que présentent l'oeuvre et la pensée
des deux auteurs."  Appendix contains Wagner's comments on Hugo,
his satiric play in which Hugo is a central figure, comparative
analyses of their works and a "tableau synoptique des rapports
entre Richard Wagner et Victor Hugo."

327.  Wicks, Charles Beaumont.  The Parisian Stage.  Alphabetical Indexes
of Plays and Authors.  4 vols.  University of Alabama Studies, nos. 6,
8, 14, 17.  University, Ala.:  University of Alabama Press, 1950-1967.

List of plays includes title, subtitle, type of play, number of
acts, prose or verse, real names of authors, theatre of Paris
première, date of Paris première.  Alphabetical list of authors
serves as index.  Hugo not in vol. 1 (1800-1815); 2 plays in vol. 2
(1816-1830); 8 new entries in vol. 3 (1831-1850); 4 entries in
vol. 4 (1851-1875), one of which, #21699, attributes the play Stello
to Hugo.

328.  Wood, Kathryn L.  Criticism of French Romantic Literature in the
Gazette de France, 1830-1848.  Philadelphia:  n.p. 1934.  (Hugo's
theatre, pp. ix, 15-57, 124ff.)

1934 Ph.D. dissertation at Bryn Mawr College.  Articles in the
Gazette during the period indicated reveal disappointment in Hugo's
renunciation of royalist and Catholic cause to become chief of the
new school.  Very hostile criticism of his plays from Hernani
through Les Burgraves carries both political and literary overtones.
In particular, A. Nettement objects to "the immorality of the content
and the barbarity of the style."  Index of articles 1830-1848
included in Appendix III.

329.  Zaborov, P. R.  "Les Problèmes historiques et sociaux dans les premières oeuvres dramatiques de Hugo."  In Annuaire d'études françaises 1958, pp. 335–51.  Moscow:  Institut d'histoire de l'Académie des sciences de l'U.R.S.S., 1959.

     In Russian with summary in French.

330.  Ziegler, Henri de.  "En relisant Hugo:  la 'bonne Allemagne.'" Le Journal de Genève, 7–8 janv. 1967, p. 11.

     Brief article indicating Hugo's fascination with and admiration for Germany.  According to Ziegler, when Hugo has Queen Marie-Anne de Neuborg say in 1838 Ruy Blas, "Ah! que ne suis-je encore . . ./ Dans ma bonne Allemagne avec mes bons parents," it is Hugo Lorrain, speaking.

# Individual Plays

## Juvenilia

331. Benoît-Lévy, Edmond. La Jeunesse de Victor Hugo. Paris: A. Michel, n.d. [c 1928]. (Hugo's theatre, pp. 176-85.)

> Summary but interesting discussion of Irtamène, Athélie and Inez de Castro. Indicates their significance: "On verra les essais d'un débutant qui, malgré son âge, a beaucoup lu déjà et qui considère Racine et Voltaire comme 'les demi-dieux du Théâtre-Français.' Classique d'éducation, il laisse percevoir déjà une tendance vers la liberté, qui ne fera que s'accentuer avec les années." Book important also as that employed by J.-P. Weber in his search for overwhelming childhood experience contributing to Hugo's thème obsédant as described in La Genèse de l'oeuvre poétique.

332. Billy, André. "Sur un inédit de Victor Hugo." Le Figaro, 11 mars 1939, p. 6.

> On recently published text (see Montargis below) of Le Château du diable from fonds Juliette Drouet, who copied the manuscript. Says "la pieuse Juliette" retouched the text, correcting grammar and spelling errors.

333. Fargher, R. "Victor Hugo's First Melodrama." In Balzac and the Nineteenth Century, pp. 297-310. Studies in French Literature presented to Herbert J. Hunt by pupils, colleagues and friends. Edited by D. G. Charlton, J. Gaudon and A. R. Pugh. Leicester: Leicester University Press, 1972.

> Compares Hugo's youthful 3-act mélodrame, Le Château du diable, with 1792 play of same name by Loaisel de Tréogate. States that Hugo "saw or read Tréogate's play and remembered it with remarkable accuracy, or else . . . he wrote his version of it with Tréogate's text, or a summary of it, beside him."

334. Flottes, Pierre. L'Eveil de Victor Hugo, 1802-1822. Paris: Gallimard, n.d. [1957]. (Hugo's theatre, pp. 160-75.)

Juvenilia examined to show links with later works. Rather superficial treatment of Inez de Castro and A.Q.C.H.E.B. Better on Irtamène, seen as apology for legitimacy on throne, and Athélie, ou les Scandinaves, stressed as fore-runner of Hernani.

335. Koch, Herbert. "Fragmente zweier unbekannter Jugenddramen von Victor Hugo." Forschungen und Fortschritte 33 (Okt. 1959): 307-11.

First publication of two short 1812 plays, L'Enfer sur terre and Le Château du diable. Brief presentation of genesis and history of youthful texts and minimum of literary analysis. States: "Die Fragmente sind zu kurz, sie lassen ein abschliessendes Urteil über die dichterischen Fähigkeiten ihres zehnjährigen Verfassers kaum zu. Man darf aber wohl ohne Ubertreibung sagen, dass sie bereits den künftigen Dramatiker ahnen lassen."

336. Montargis, Jean. "La Première et la dernière oeuvre dramatique de Victor Hugo." La Nouvelle Revue Française 52 (1er mars 1939): 456-77.

First publication of Le Château du diable, a play that Hugo wrote at the age of ten in 1812. Montargis, grandson of Hugo's executor Paul Meurice, prints from the copy that Juliette Drouet made of the play, since the original manuscript is missing. (See Billy above.) Author points out possible influence of Pixerécourt's Les Ruines de Babylone and finds "la somptuosité opulente de la langue et la truculence des images" indicative of Hugo's later dramatic style. On why "la dernière oeuvre dramatique" was never published, see Gaudon (749).

337. Nozick, Martin. "The Inez de Castro Theme in European Literature." Comparative Literature 3 (Fall 1951): 330-41.

In very comprehensive article, one paragraph devoted to Hugo's youthful effort. Nozick sees influence of Houdart de la Motte's 1823 Inès de Castro in Hugo's play, which also serves as "an apprenticeship for Hernani": "The profusion of disguises, purple patches, extraneous characters, secondary plots, and lugubrious settings of this childish endeavor point to the vivid, extravagant imagination of the later genius."

338. Simon, Gustave. L'Enfance de Victor Hugo. Avec une analyse complète et des fragments d'Irtamène et de ses premières poésies inédites. Paris: Hachette, 1904. (Hugo's theatre, pp. 111-27, 140-60.)

Notable as first publication of Hugo's juvenilia, including Irtamène (1816). Simon offers fairly good analyses of it and Athélie, ou les Scandinaves (1817), A.G.C.H.E.B. (1817) and Inez de Castro (1819-20). It is interesting to see Hugo's early preoccupation with drama and his developing techniques. Irtamène is almost a pastiche of Racine's manner; Hugo began as classic, Simon indicates.

339. Simon, Gustave. "Pierre Corneille, projet de drame et scènes inédites par Victor Hugo (1825)." La Revue de Paris 6 (15 déc. 1909): 669-97.

In 1825 young Hugo identified himself strongly with the ill-treated author of Le Cid, and this shared indignation inspired him to attempt a great verse drama on Corneille. Simon publishes here for first time full scenario and the four scenes completed plus variants and notes. There is no suggestion as to why the play was not finished. Hugo's dramatic techniques and preoccupations are clarly visible here. Hugo did not abandon the epoch, as it reappears in Marion de Lorme, especially in details of the first two acts. In Act IV even verses from the original Pierre Corneille are found in toto.

340. _____. "Victor Hugo, auteur dramatique à quatorze ans." La Revue d'Histoire Littéraire de la France 11 (janv.-mars 1904): 22-41.

Reworking of material in L'Enfance (338). Does not think much of Inez de Castro--"C'est un mélodrame assez maladoit d'ailleurs et assez naïf"---despite its being accepted for performance at Panorama-Dramatique before being banned by the censor. Underscores importance of Irtamène for Hugo: "Irtamène déterminait sa vocation. . . ."

## *Amy Robsart*

341. Allais, Gustave. "Le Théâtre de Victor Hugo: Amy Robsart." La Revue des Cours et Conférences, 11$^1$ (1902): 65-71, 460-66; 11$^2$ (1903): 166-74, 464-72, 643-50, 836-48. (Also published as Les Débuts dramatiques de Victor Hugo, Amy Robsart [1822-28]. Paris: Société française d'imprimerie et de librairie, 1903. Pp. 61.)

From a series of lectures. Amy Robsart treated thoroughly as to genesis, Soumet's collaboration, Foucher's collaboration, 1828 performance and failure, character of Leicester and previous criticism. Special attention paid to interesting problem of authenticity of 1822 and 1828 versions published by Paul Meurice. Careful textual comparison leads Allais to conclude that 1828 play is more the work of Foucher than of Hugo. 1903 book contains all articles previously published plus an appendix comparing historical Amy and Leicester with play's characters and compiling all evidence then available against Hugo's authorship of play. Conjecture remained until missing 1828 manuscript was discovered and published in 1928 and Hugo alone proved author. See Curzon below.

342. Ascoli, Georges. "L'Amy Robsart de Victor Hugo." La Revue des Cours et Conférences, sér. 2, année 32 (30 mai, 30 juin 1931): 289-99, 501-16.

Definitive study on the play synthesizing work done by Glachant frères (163), Allais (341), Curzon (343). Good section on why the play failed in 1828. On Hugo's experimentation: "L'essentiel pour Hugo était de voir comment le public accepterait le mélange du

tragique et du bouffon, les audacieuses familiarités accolées aux
scènes grandioses ou terribles."

343.  Curzon, Henri de.  "Amy Robsart de Victor Hugo.  Le manuscrit pour
la représentation (1828)."  La Revue d'Histoire Littéraire de la France
35 (oct.-déc. 1928):  495-527.  (Also as "En marge des manuscrits de la
Censure théâtrale.  Le premier texte retrouvé d'Amy Robsart de Victor
Hugo."  La Nouvelle Revue, t. 108 [15 aout 1930]:  289-304; t. 109
[1er sept., 15 sept. 1930]:  49-57, 139-49.)

Curzon clears up problem of authorship of Amy Robsart by finally
locating original manuscript of 1828 performance "dans le fonds de
la Censure théâtrale, comme il y devait être, mais aux Archives
Nationales."  Handwriting conclusively proves Hugo to be author.
Comparisons made with 1822 version and with Soumet's Emilia on
same subject.  See Allais above.

344.  Faguet, Emile.  "Victor Hugo:  Amy Robsart et Les Jumeaux."  In
his Propos de théâtre, sér. 4, pp. 1-15.  Paris:  Société française
d'imprimerie et de librairie, 1907.

In this witty causerie, Faguet insists that, though the two plays
are not great, they are still worth publishing because they are by
Hugo.  Of Amy Robsart he states:  "Ce petit mélodrame n'est pas si
mauvais que cela."  However, he indicates that young Hugo was wrong
not to emphasize the tragic situation by playing up Amy's character.
Hugo's concentration, instead, upon objects produces "pur guignol"
at the end.  Considers unfinished Les Jumeaux interesting to whoever
wants to study Hugo's process of composition because in it he
"commençait par écrire et finissait par composer" without any
outline.  It is a strange method because Hugo's plays are well
organized when complete:  "On sait que les drames de Victor Hugo
sont invraisemblables et ont quelques autres défauts considérables;
mais qu'ils sont bien composés, et d'une netteté de dessin très
appréciable."

345.  Pavie, André.  "Le Premier drame romantique, Amy Robsart.  Lettres
inédites."  La Revue Hebdomadaire, année 12, t. 4 (14 mars 1903):
160-69.  (Also in his Médaillons romantiques, pp. 91-108.  Paris:
Emile-Paul, 1909.)

The grandson of Victor Pavie, friend and comrade in arms of Victor
Hugo during the romantic period, tries to throw light on the
puzzling question of authorship of Amy Robsart by publishing letters
to V. Pavie from Paul Foucher, in which the latter claims full
credit for the play.  On this basis, A. Pavie wrongly eliminates
Hugo as author.  See Allais and Curzon above.

346.  Séché, Léon.  "Les Grandes Journées romantiques au théâtre:
D'Amy Robsart à Hernani.  Documents inédits."  La Revue de Paris, année
19, t. 3 (1er mai 1912):  339-80.

Some overlapping of material presented in his previous book (365).
Part on Amy Robsart largely chronicling of collaboration with
Alxeandre Soumet and of première's fiasco under Foucher's name.
Séché blames Hugo for hiding behind his young brother-in-law,

despite Hugo's article in press claiming responsibility for play.
Concentrates next on problems surrounding Hernani. Interesting
letters from Nodier to Hugo offering constructive criticism. Pre-
performance articles in press excerpted to show how public's
curiosity was piqued. Lettres inédites about ticket distribution,
success of play, parodies. Exciting atmosphere of period evoked,
with much attention to minor details.

## Cromwell

347. Baldensperger, Fernand. "Les Années 1827-1828 en France et au
dehors. XIII: Conclusion: Cromwell et sa préface." La Revue des
Cours et Conférences, sér. 2, année 30 (30 Juin 1929): 528-42.

Sees this period and especially Cromwell and its preface as turning
point in liberation of art forever in France. Points out various
sources for play and problems encountered in trying to perform it.
Baldensperger finds in it a moderation and "toute la souplesse
nécessaire" for it to provide a new language and form for French
drama.

348. Beck, Theodore. "Alessandro Manzoni versus Girolamo Gratiani."
Kentucky Foreign Language Quarterly 11 (1964): 187-91.

Suggests possible influence of Girolamo Gratiani's 1671 preface and
play, Il Cromuele, on Manzoni and on Hugo's preface and play of
same name. See also Xavier de Courville below.

349. Benot, Yves. "Cromwell chez les rois." Les Lettres Françaises,
28 juin-4 juill. 1956, p. 8.

Written on eve of première of adaptation of Cromwell in the Cour
carrée of the Louvre. Benot quotes director Alain Trutal:
"'Cromwell m'a intéressé moins par la qualité littéraire que pour
sa valeur de pièce de cape et d'épée, une sorte de Dumas brillant
et avant la lettre.'"

350. Castellan, P. "Quelques Sources du Cromwell de Victor Hugo."
La Revue Bourguignonne, 18, 3-4 (1908).

351. Courville, Xavier de. "La Première Préface de Cromwell." La
Revue (des Deux Mondes) 15 (1er août 1956): 523-27.

Cites Graziani's Cromuele as first manifesto of new dramatic
esthetic and attempt to carry it out in a play. Says Hugo probably
did not know the Italian play. See also Beck above.

352. Dedessuslamare, M. Cromwell. Rouen: Imprimerie Gy-Laîné, 1928.
Pp. 25.

Rather disjointed essay on sources with emphasis on dominant
influence of Napoleon in Play. Sees the play as "une comédie où la
tragédie s'introduit à contre-temps," and where it is the serious
which is disconcerting. Implies superiority of Cromwell over other

Hugo plays in certain respects: "Victor Hugo composera des drames plus serrés, plus pathétiques; il n'encadrera plus un portrait historique dans un tableau d'histoire; jamais il ne saura mieux projeter sur le passé la lumière du présent." For fuller discussion see Descotes below.

353. Descotes, Maurice. L'Obsession de Napoléon dans le Cromwell de Victor Hugo. Paris: Lettres modernes, 1967. Pp. 56.

The years 1826-1827, Descotes claimes, were important for the evolution of Hugo's political ideas; and the best expression of Hugo's obsession with Napoleon is Cromwell: "Ainsi . . . le drame de Hugo apparaît-il tout plein du souvenir de Napoléon, de ceux qui le combatirent comme de ceux qui le servirent. Deux situations historiques bien précises se dessinent en filigrane sous cette intrigue qui se déroule à Londres en 1657: celle des conspirations tramées contre le Consul . . . et celle du couronnement."
a) Barbéris. Revue d'Histoire Littéraire de la France 70 (1970): 517-18.
b) Franceschetti. Studi Francesi 13 (1969): 374.
c) Bulletin critique du livre français 22 (1967): 950.

354. Des Essarts, Emmanuel. "Cromwell." Le Journal des Débats, 13 mai 1904.

355. Duchet, Claude. "Victor Hugo et l'âge d'homme (Cromwell et sa Préface)." In Victor-Marie Hugo, Oeuvres completes, III, 5-38. Edited by Jean Massin. Paris: Club français du livre, 1967.)

Fine introduction to Cromwell, which Duchet links with Torquemada on theme of "le crime au bénéfice de la vertu." Covers state of the theatre in 1827, the work's genesis, Hugo's grotesque, faults of the play, its strengths: "Ajoutons que la jeunesse, l'humour, la verve, la provocation en font une liberté qu'il se donne . . . pour briser l'étreinte d'un public trop restreint et les servitudes d'une réputation trop conformiste."

356. Fecarotta, Fabiola. L'Elemento storico del Cromwell di Victor Hugo. Palermo: Andò, 1939. Pp. 274.

Thorough presentation of background information on the play precedes examination of historical sources and the problem of accuracy in each part of the play. Shows that sources Hugo used most were not numerous. States: "In una parola il Cromwell di Victor Hugo non è per noi autenticamente storico in tutti i suoi tratti." Faults Hugo for using too many characteristic anecdotes and particular facts, which render the play confused and obscure. Results are aesthetically poor: "In questo dramma storico dunque, che però ha qualche bella scena e qualche personnagio ben rappresentato, Victor Hugo non è grande poeta, non rispetta veramente, o non intende la storia e non possiede ancora neanche la technica del drammaturgo."

357. Grillet, Claudius. "Le Pittoresque biblique dans Cromwell." In his La Bible dans Victor Hugo, pp. 67-84. Lyons: E. Vitte, 1910.

Erudite treatment of Puritans' biblical allusions in play, biblical
names used, and biblical formulas in protagonist Carr's lyricism
and oratory. Grillet sees in Carr "le personnage le plus biblique!
Il absorbe en lui la triple gloire du visionnaire, du psalmiste et
du prophète. . . . De toutes les oeuvres qui ont précédé l'exil,
il n'en est point à laquelle la Bible ait collaboré plus étroitement
qu'au drame de Cromwell."

358. Marsan, Eugène. "En relisant Cromwell." La Revue Critique des
Idées et des Livres (9 août 1927). (Also in his Pour les centenaires
du romantisme, pp. 3-10. Paris: Editions Prométhée, 1930.)

Informal essay on Cromwell, which Marsan finds too verbose and
abusive of monologues and asides. Accuses Hugo of ignoring and
deforming the natural unity of the historical moment of the play's
subject. Furthermore, the dialogue "tire d'habitude sa substance
d'un enchevêtrement d'idées fausses et de passions forcées." No
wonder, Marsan concludes, that "Cromwell nous assomme."

359. Marsan, Jules. "Cromwell et sa préface." In his Autour du
romantisme, pp. 69-85. Toulouse: Editions de l'Archer, 1937.

Good presentation of circumstances surrounding the play and of its
faults and strong points. Suggests that Lord Rochester's quatrain
is a parody of the famous sonnet scene in Le Misanthrope. Berates
Hugo's démesure and his focussing upon domestic issues and finds
Cromwell's renunciation lacking in motivation. Yet concludes:
"Cromwell n'en garde pas moins toute son importance. Il est un
acheminement de la chronique du type stendhalien au mélodrame lyrique
que l'on verra se réaliser avec Hernani. Il marque une transition
nécessaire."

360. Qualia, Charles B. "French Dramatic Sources of Bulwer-Lytton's
Richelieu." PMLA 42 (1927): 177-84.

Points out convincing resemblances between Hugo's Cromwell and
Bulwer-Lytton's play. Delavigne's Louis XI also discussed as
source. Close similarities of plot, characters, dramatic incidents,
scenes and thought lead Qualia to affirm: "In all probability
thoughts or figures of speech [in Richelieu] were often suggested
by an identical dramatic situation in Cromwell."

361. Roth, Georges. "Une Adaptation anglaise de Cromwell en 1859."
French Quarterly 9 (June 1927): 147-49.

Claims first adaptation for stage of Hugo's unwieldly Cromwell
done in 1859 by F. Phillips and put on in London at Surrey Theatre.
Unfortunately, no copy of it is to be found, but Roth quotes in toto
review article from the Times of 17 Feb. 1859. Major changes in
English version are exclusion of Milton and the four fous and
dropping of entire fifth act. Anonymous critic asserts that "an
effective melodrama is the result." Hugo seems not to have known
about this truncated translation, and Roth remarks that he probably
would not have approved of it.

362. Rozelaar, Louis A. "Le Mémorial de Sainte-Hélène et Victor Hugo en 1827; après 1827." French Quarterly 9 (mars 1927):  53-68; 10 (sept. 1928):  130-55.

In the first article, Rozelaar's goal is to "rechercher l'influence du Mémorial sur le drame de Cromwell et sa Préface au seul point de vue littéraire." Amply demonstrates through textual comparisons that Cromwell's character bears traces of former emperor and that even "le style vigoureux et figuré de Napoléon" shows up in the play.  In second article, Hernani's Charlemagne and don Carlos and Les Burgraves' Barberousse reveal marked influence of Napoleon, according to Rozelaar, and in his own mind Hugo himself becomes Napoleon--"le grand exilé."

363. Rudwin, Maximilien J. Satan et le satanisme dans l'oeuvre de Victor Hugo. Paris:  Société "Les Belles Lettres," n.d. [1926]. (Hugo's theatre, pp. 35-36, 127-33.)

In chapter 8 of first part, "Le diabolique et le grotesque: Cromwell," Rudwin argues:  "Après avoir donné les préceptes du grotesque dans la préface, Victor Hugo en fournit le modèle dans Cromwell. . . . Les personnages ont le diable incessamment sur les lèvres.  On rencontre ici aussi des chansons diaboliques avec lesquelles les bouffons du Protecteur nous entretiennent." Then in the appendix Rudwin lists diabolical characters and witches.  He furnishes a whole roster of nécromants, imagined demons and real devils.  There is at least one in each play.

364. Ruinat, Joseph.  "Victor Hugo et Talma.  Pourquoi Cromwell n'a pas été représenté." Le Correspondant 255 (25 mai 1914):  790-96.

Rejects story in Victor Hugo raconté that Talma wanted to play title role in Hugo's Cromwell and that his death before play's completion led Hugo to make drama deliberately unplayable.  Calls play "l'essai manqué d'un réformateur emporté" and thinks real reason it was not performed was that actors at the Comédie-Française rejected it.

365. Séché, Léon.  Le Cénacle de Joseph Delorme (1827-1830):  Victor Hugo et les poètes, de Cromwell à Hernani.  Documents inédits.  2 vols. Paris:  Mercure de France, 1911-1912.

Lettres inédites in Vol. 1 trace Hugo-Sainte-Beuve friendship until beginning of rupture.  Advice the critic offers the theoretician, poet and dramatist on plays from Cromwell through Hernani very astute.  Chapters 2 (Cromwell), 5 (préfaces), 7 (la bataille d'Hernani) and 9 (Sainte-Beuve au National) especially interesting. Vol. 2 contains a few lettres inédites to Hugo in praise of Hernani. Séché illustrates well importance of cénacle to Hugo's dramatic career during this crucial period.

366. _____.  "Victor Hugo et Sainte-Beuve:  De Cromwell à Joseph Delorme." Le Correspondant, année 80, t. 247 (10 avril 1912):  61-81.

Previously unpublished letter from Sainte-Beuve to Hugo after the critic has heard the first four acts of Cromwell. Sainte-Beuve encourages Hugo's general outline but in carefully chosen language criticizes "l'excès, l'abus de la force" in Acts III and IV. Wisely counsels moderation and control.

367. Sée, Henri. "Le Cromwell de Victor Hugo et le Cromwell de l'histoire." Le Mercure de France 200 (15 nov. 1927): 5-17.

Three-part article for play's centenary. After discussion of Hugo's claimed sources and his supposed total historical authenticity, Sée compares Hugo's character with real, historical man. One great difference seen is that the actual Cromwell never regretted executions, especially that of King Charles; yet Hugo portrays him as haunted by the deed. Hugo also exaggerates contrasts and "le grotesque" in personalities of both Cromwell and the Puritans: "En un mot, on a bien l'impression que le Cromwell de Victor Hugo ne ressemble que de très loin au Cromwell de l'histoire."

368. Seebacher, Jacques. "Comment peut-on être Milton?" In Le Paradis perdu, 1667-1967, pp. 241-50. Edition par Jacques Blondel. Paris: Lettres Modernes, 1967.

Treats key rôle of Milton in Hugo's inspiration. Cromwell, through character Milton, foreshadows myths, ideas to come: "Le drame de Cromwell est, en 1827 le signe avant-courreur et même prophétique du démocratisme hugolien. Milton y est campé, face au Protecteur en passe de devenir roi, d'une manière toute privilégiée. . . . Le mythe de la Fin de Satan est en germe dans le grand discours de l'acte central. . . . Si donc on accepte de voir en Cromwell, à cause du personnage de Milton, le chèque que Hugo tire sur tout son avenir et toute son idéologie, pour le laisser longtemps sans provision, . . . il faudra encore se demander quelle prédisposition morale, quelle psychologie du destin rendent possible la cristallisation du mythe de Milton chez Victor Hugo."

369. Simon, Gustave. "Va-t-on jouer Cromwell au Théâtre-Français?" Annales Politiques et Littéraires 85 (avril 1925): 353.

370. Tournier, Gilberte. "Les Points de départ du Cromwell de Victor Hugo." La Revue de Littérature Comparée 7 (janv.-mars 1927): 87-110.

Thorough examination of sources and genesis of play. In letter to Vigny on Cinq-Mars, Hugo credits passage in novel describing Richelieu with giving him first idea for Cromwell. Tournier rejects most of Hugo's stated 12-15 volumes read for documentation. Signals play's errors and local color "très plaquée, très artificielle." Declares: "Cromwell est la charge, la parodie du XVIIe siècle anglais et non sa représentation." However, Shakespearian influences, she maintains, are beneficial in play's "liberté scénique, sa fantaisie vagabonde et son louable essai de pénétration du coeur humain."

371. Triolet, Elsa. "Cromwell aux quatre vents." Les Lettres Françaises, 5-11 juill. 1956, p. 6.

Complains about cold, damp Cour carrée of the Louvre, where
production was held. Would have preferred to see the play in a
regular theatre with better accoustics. Likes the final monologue.
Little said about the play itself.

372. Ubersfeld-Maille, Annie. "Le Carnaval de Cromwell." Romantisme,
nos. 1-2 (1971), pp. 80-93.

Analyzes le grotesque in Cromwell by formulating connection between
Hugo's theory of le grotesque and notion of carnaval as conceived
by Mikhail Bakhtine. Same elements reappear in Hugo's later plays:
"Après 1839, le théâtre de Hugo se disperse dans cette poussière
de fragments qui dessine autour de Maglia-Ménippe une immense
satire ménipée, un immense carnaval; dans cette ronde infernale, le
diable et Dieu, la mort et la vie mènent le dialogue infini où
s'inscrit l'avenir encore ouvert de la société humaine."

373. Vigo-Fazio, Lorenzo. "Il Cromwell ovvero il dramma di un dramma."
Scena illustrata, anno 74 (giugno 1959): 16.

374. Wren, K. P. "Historical Sources and Literary Influence in the
Cromwell of Hugo." Thèse, University of London, Bedford College,
1974-75.

## Marion de Lorme

375. Aegerter, Emmanuel. "La Première de Marion Delorme." Le Figaro,
27 juill. 1929, p. 6.

Centenary of composition of Marion Delorme celebrated in this
informative article on events leading up to ban on the play. Implies
it was perhaps a good thing in forcing Hugo to write the more
revolutionary and lyrically beautiful Hernani. With it Hugo becomes
a real defender of freedom of art.

376. Alméras, Henri d'. "Victor Hugo et le centenaire de Marion de
Lorme." Le Journal des Débats, 28 août 1931, p. 347.

377. Arène, Emmanuel. "Marion Delorme." Le Figaro, 23 avril 1907,
pp. 5-6.

Review of 1907 reprise at Comédie-Française. Arène pleased with
everything about this production, including the play itself. After
giving a history of its genesis, original ban, première in 1831 and
critical reception, he concludes: "Elle est, d'un bout à l'autre,
intéressante: il y passe un souffle de grâce, de fraîcheur,
d'amour, d'émotion qui emplit ces cinq actes si pittoresques et si
variés d'une atmosphère chevaleresque et galante."

378. Batiffol, Louis. "Marion de Lorme de Victor Hugo et l'histoire."
Le Censeur 2 (6 avril 1907): 417-23.

Reprise gave Batiffol the idea for this investigation. Points out
errors Hugo makes in personalities of Marion and Laffemas and in

atmosphere and details of historical period. However, most serious distortion, according to Batiffol, is in Hugo's portrayal of Louis XIII and Richelieu. Batiffol defends both, quoting from historical documents as proof. Ends by claiming Louis XIII responsible for all the period's bloody executions, so that Hugo should have had him, not Richelieu, pass by Marion at the play's end.

379. Bordeaux, Henry. "Marion Delorme." La Revue Hebdomadaire (8 mars 1908). (Also in his La Vie au théâtre, sér. 1, pp. 133-38. Paris: Librairie Plon, 1910.)

On 1907 reprise of Marion Delorme, which this drama critic calls "un éclatant succès." Yet finds this persistent popularity of "le mal romantique" disturbing.

380. Braun, Sidney D. The 'Courtisane' in the French Theatre from Hugo to Becque (1831-1885). Johns Hopkins Studies in Romance Literatures and Languages, extra vol. 22. Baltimore, Md.: Johns Hopkins Press, 1947. (Hugo, pp. 17-30.)

Large portion of first chapter on "historical courtesan" devoted to Hugo's plays, especially Marion Delorme, "the first historical play of importance in which the courtesan is the central figure." Its origin seen in Manon Lescaut, but Braun finds Hugo "revolutionary" in proposing in the play "that the courtesan can be rehabilitated through pure love." Claims Hugo as the "main exponent of the Romantic expression of this time on the French stage," but says Hugo ultimately fails in "the rôle of a teacher" from plays' lack of "any convincing arguments in the garment of abstractions."

381. Brincourt, André. "Marion Delorme de Victor Hugo." Le Figaro, 4 déc. 1967, p. 19.

Television production of Hugo's play by Jean Kerchbron draws negative reaction from this critic: "Voilà beaucoup d'efforts et beaucoup d'argent pour un effet bien mince." Finds Romanticism deadly on "le petit écran."

382. Brisson, Adolphe. "Marion Delorme." Le Temps, 29 avril 1907, p. 1.

Brisson finds the reprise "fort brillante." Enjoys especially the music of Hugo's verse, yet deplores the childish elements of plot and character motivation: "[le] dernier acte . . . est le seul endroit du drame qui soit humain et propre à toucher nos coeurs."

383. Cabanis, José. "Une Lettre de Baudelaire à Hugo." La Quinzaine Littéraire, 15 juin 1967, pp. 14-15.

Lettre inédite of 25 février 1840 from ambitious young Baudelaire to established man-of-letters Hugo on recent production of Marion de Lorme. Baudelaire writes that the play "m'a tellement enchanté et m'a rendu si heureux." Admirer tells Hugo he loves him as a man for "réhabilitations" in works like Marion de Lorme. Cabanis notes that the same poet bitterly attacks Hugo in his Salons of 1845 and 1846, railing against the same play as "littérature qui consiste à prêcher

les vertus des assassins et des filles publiques." Still later
Baudelaire comes full cycle, appreciatively calling Hugo in a Figaro
article of 1858 one of the "maîtres de sa jeunesse." See also
Cellier below.

384.  Cellier, Léon.  "Baudelaire et Marion de Lorme." In his Baudelaire
et Hugo, pp. 13–44.  Paris:  J. Corti, 1970.  (Also slightly modified in
Balzac and the Nineteenth Century, pp. 311–20.  Edited by D. G. Charlton,
J. Gaudon, and Anthony Pugh.  Leicester:  Leicester University Press,
1972.)

> Traces Baudelaire's ambivalent feelings for Hugo in concentrating
> upon Marion de Lorme.  Quotes letter, previously published by Cabanis
> above, in which Baudelaire praises play to its author.  Then shows
> hate expressed in Salon de 1843 and finally indicates that the
> mature Baudelaire "retrouvera l'enthousiasm de jadis." Locates many
> references to or echoes from Marion de Lorme in later Baudelaire
> writings--"Les yeux des pauvres," letter to Marie Daubrun, "Le
> Chant d'automne," "Brumes et pluies," "Je suis comme le roi d'un
> pays pluvieux." Baudelaire obviously haunted by the play, and
> Cellier states:  "Le drame romantique nous mène droit au coeur du
> spleen baudelairien."

385.  Charles, Paul.  "Charles Nodier et Victor Hugo." La Revue
d'Histoire Littéraire de la France 39 (1932):  568–86.

> Publishes full text of two articles by Nodier on Marion de Lorme
> from Le Temps of 1831 and traces relationship of the two authors to
> that time.  Nodier praises Hugo for introducing crowd scenes "à la
> Shakespeare" and for romantic versification.  On Hugo's talent as a
> dramatic author, however, both articles express mainly negative
> thoughts "cachées par Nodier sous un verbiage d'éruduit et de bon
> homme."

386.  Citoleux, Marc.  "Afred de Vigny, Victor Hugo et Marion de Lorme."
La Revue d'Histoire Littéraire de la France 35 (juill.-sept. 1928):
439–40.

> Striking similarities between Vigny's Cinq-Mars and Hugo's Marion de
> Lorme noted:  "Il y a là bien des coïncidences pour qu'il n'y ait
> pas eu, de la part de Victor Hugo, souvenir ou réminiscence."
> Vigny, already irritated in 1829 by possible detraction of Marion
> from his "gloire dramatique" as translator of Othello, vents his
> spleen in his Journal by calling Hugo's play "un excellent ouvrage
> de style. . . . Personne n'a jamais eu autant de forme et moins de
> fond. . . ."

387.  Doumic, René.  "Marion Delorme de Hugo." La Revue des Deux
Mondes, sér. 5, 39 (15 mai 1907):  438–45.

> Doumic, generally very critical of Hugo's plays, finds Marion
> Delorme one of Hugo's most interesting dramas, containing germ for
> all his later plays.  Doumic shows Hugo's debt to Vigny for play's
> idea, which he drew from Cinq-Mars, and to Dumas, père, for technique
> of adapting novel to stage, which he learned from Henri III et sa
> cour.  Admires comic rôle of Saverny, but finds Hugo's historical

tamperings shocking. Play hasn't been performed in twenty years, and Doumic says only way to play it today (1907) is to cut out the impossible rôle of Didier.

388. Faguet, Emile. "Victor Hugo: Marion de Lorme." Le Journal des Débats, 22 avril 1907.

On 1907 reprise.

389. Flat, Paul. "Marion Delorme." La Revue Bleue 79 (27 avril 1907): 573-75.

Reprises of plays like Marion Delorme very good, Flat asserts, in showing by comparison the absence of style in popular contemporary plays. Accuses history of having given short shrift to Marion Delorme. Says that "le lyrisme, . . . la puissance et la beauté du verbe" transfigure the play and make the audience forget weaknesses of psychology. Admires especially the last scene. Finds production entirely worthy of the play.

390. Hérold, A. Ferdinand. "Marion de Lorme." Le Mercure de France 67 (15 mai 1907): 339-40.

Brief review article. Welcomes reprise: "On entend toujours avec joie les drames de Victor Hugo: ils sont pleins de fougue, de tendresse et de majesté. . . ." Appreciates also Hugo's "beaux vers" and the performance's "acteurs impeccables." Would like to see Hugo's Mangeront-ils?, "ce chef-d'oeuvre," mounted on stage.

391. Mendès, Catulle. "Marion de Lorme." Le Journal, 22 avril 1907, p. 3.

Review of reprise.

392. Nauta, G. A. "Marion Delorme: Le Chariot d'enfant." Neophilologus 20 (1935): 261-63.

Shows similarities between Hugo's play and Sanskrit play, Le Chariot d'enfant (c. 400 A.D.), attributed to King Sudraka. Concludes: "Il n'est pas douteux selon moi que Victor Hugo ait connu ce drame (traduit) car on trouve des réminiscences et des situations analogues, pareilles même, dans Marion Delorme."

393. Pommier, Jean. "Balzac et Musset; Balzac et Hugo; Balzac et . . . lui-même." La Revue d'Histoire Littéraire de la France 56 (oct.-déc. 1956): 548-61.

Among other influences on Balzac's fragment La Torpille from La Femme supérieure, Pommier identifies Marion de Lorme, especially for the idea of virginity recovered through true love.

394. Saurel, Renée. "Marion Delorme." Les Lettres Françaises 6-12 déc. 1967, p. 16.

Review of Kerchbron's television version. Says: "Grand 'western' de l'injustice et de l'amour, Marion Delorme n'est certes pas la meilleure pièce de Hugo. . . . Ici, comme ailleurs, Hugo a tant de santé et il met tant de vigueur à dénoncer l'injustice et la torture que les scories sont emportées par le torrent. Le vrai sujet de Marion Delorme est la satire de la royauté. . . . [C'est] un mélange de sublime et de grotesque, de mélodrame et de parodie de Shakespeare."

395. Séché, Alfonse et Jules Bertaut. "Les Grandes Premières romantiques: Marion Delorme." Le Correspondant, n.s. 190 (25 févr. 1907): 774-801. (Also in their La Passion romantique: Antony, Marion Delorme, Chatterton, pp. 89-158. Paris: E. Fasquelle, 1927.)

Authors attempt to give "la note pittoresque et exacte" to upcoming reprise by narrating whole story of Hugo's arranging performance of Marion de Lorme. Article explains change of title, why play was banned, why it was put on at Porte-St.-Martin, how the fifth act was changed at the request of Marie Dorval, the cold reception at its première. Good re-creation of circumstances surrounding first performance.

396. Shtein, A. "Marion de Lorme." Literaturnoye Obozreniye (Moscow) 23 (1940): 44-47.

397. Simon, Gustave. "A propos de Marion Delorme." La Revue de Paris 2 (15 mars 1907): 420-48.

Documents inédits. Publishes complimentary letter from Alexandre Soumet to Hugo after 1829 reading. Also text of what Hugo cut out of Act IV to try to get play by censors. Next letter from royal authorities indicating pension raise to placate Hugo. Then letter from Sainte-Beuve on Didier's too stolid attitude at play's original end. Author examines play's success at première and in later reprises, singling out great 1873 revival with Mounet-Sully as Didier. Closes with Mme. Favart's memories concerning her rôles in Hernani and Marion de Lorme.

## *Hernani*

398. Achard, Marcel. "Hernani." Conferencia 54 (15 déc. 1949): 499-516. (Also published as "La Bataille d'Hernani" in Historia 21 [févr. 1957]: 129-39.)

Urbane, enthusiastic recalling of "aventure" of the bataille d'Hernani through both well known and obscure anecdotes and quotations from the témoins, author of Victor Hugo raconté, Gautier and Dumas. Closes with sad affirmation: "Il faut l'admettre: Hernani prête à rire. Et les parodistes sont souvent bien près de l'original. Malgré cela, le dernier article de Théophile Gautier . . . était consacré à Hernani. La dernière ligne qu'il écrivit . . . était celle-ci: 'Hugo a des traits de génie révoltants.'"

399. Alguazils, Les. "Le Centenaire d'Hernani." Le Figaro, 1$^{er}$ mars, 1930, p. 7.

Brief review of criticism on Hernani from Auguste Trognon and Gustave Planche through Robert Kemp.

400. Allan, Blaise. "Récririez-vous Hernani?" Bravo, 21 févr. 1930, p. 14.

In special issue of Bravo celebrating centenary of Hernani. Allan asks dramatists of that day if they would rewrite Hernani. Marcel Achard, Marcel Pagnol, and Armand Salacrou answer negatively. André-Paul Antoine would make Hugo's play into a silent film, and Maurice Rostand would rewrite it for the Grand Guignol. While Bernard Zimmer would adapt it as "vaudeville," Steve Passeur finds the play's subject impossible for 1930. Fernand Crommelynck would try to illuminate the play's characters "par l'intérieur" in his version.

401. Alméras, Henri d'. "Le Centenaire d'Hernani. Cabales et parodies." Le Journal des Débats, 23 févr. 1930.

Short article on the bataille d'Hernani and parodies of the play. Today, of all that fatras there remain only "un chef-d'oeuvre, Hernani, et une parodie très amusante, presque un chef-d'oeuvre aussi, mais pas du même genre, Harnali ou la Contrainte par cor."

402. Ambra, Lucio d'. "Celebrazioni romantiche: il centenario dell' Hernani." Nuova Anthologia, vol. 270, ser. 7, raccolta 348 (1 marzo 1930): 65-77.

Re-creation of the bataille and première, résumé of principles in preface, and importance of Hernani and romantic triumph suggested: "25 febbraio 1830: la data più illustre del Romanticismo francese, il punctum saliens del centenario che quest'anno celebrano, dovunque, quanti di noi nel mondo non si vantano ancora antiromantici."

403. Avrett, Robert. "Ochoa's Translation of Hugo's Hernani: A Study in Racial Psychologies." Modern Language Journal 38 (Nov. 1954): 362-65.

Comparison of French and Spanish texts shows that "Ochoa seems to have thought it advisable, if not essential, to alter the original French in order to bring it more into conformity with Spanish nationalistic spirit, as well as decorum." For example, Ochoa's changed references to the Pope omit blasphemy and reduce irony; don Carlos, a popular monarch among the Spanish, becomes "a strong man in the grip of a strong passion, rather than . . . the lecherous and thorough-going scoundrel represented in Hugo's lines." Other changes made "to protect the Spanish sense of propriety" or, as Ochoa says in a footnote, "porque somos tan morales!"

404. Baguley, David. "Drama and Myth in Hugo's Hernani." Modern Languages 52 (March 1971): 16-22.

In elegant prose author points out coherence of play as "reiteration of the familiar romantic myth of redemption through the suffering of unadulterated passion" in lineage of Tristan and Yseut legend. Because the play centers upon spiritual regeneration in "fallen world," Hugo minimizes its historical significance.

405. Banachévitch, N. "A propos d'un vers des Contemplations sur un vers d'Hernani." La Revue de Littérature Comparée 28 (avril-juin 1954): 206-11.

"Réponse à un acte d'accusation" in Les Contemplations defends, among other things, don Carlos's famous line in Hernani, "Quelle heure est-il?" Banachévitch tries to show it an echo of Hamlet's Act IV question "What hour now?" Other similarities between the two plays suggested.

406. Bastia, Jean. "Hernani, les petits chevaux, le dancing et la trompette du funiculaire." Comoedia, 21 mars 1927.

Amusing parody of Hernani.

407. Bauër, Gérard. "Le Centenaire de Hernani à la Comédie Française." Les Annales, no. 2354 (15 mars 1930), p. 268.

Review of this successful event. Praises actors and costumes but dislikes décor: "Le théâtre de Victor Hugo est fait de conventions qu'on a déjà de la peine à supporter, par ces temps d'ironie, mais il ne faut pas encore y ajouter par les détails qui défient toute vraisemblance." Says Act V least worthy of drama, yet throughout play there are still lots of beautiful verses.

408. _____. "La Critique d'Hernani." Bravo, 21 févr. 1930, pp. 7-10.

Summarizes both negative and positive criticism of Hernani. Says that both enthusiastic admirers of play, such as Gautier, and more critical reviewers, such as Planche, were right in their judgments. Bauër admits that he does not like the play, but sees some merit in it: "La chance d'Hernani (et l'adresse de Victor Hugo), c'est que ce drame a toujours résumé une passion lorsqu'on l'a joué ou repris."

409. _____. "Une Interprétation d'Hernani." L'Opinion 14 (8 déc. 1922): 1219-26.

On a reprise. Audience conquered by "l'entraînement supérieur du lyrisme" of the play and by the great talent of Mme. Piérat as doña Sol. Calls performance "un miracle qu'on doit aux interprètes, et peut-être aussi, n'est-il pas vrai? à ce 'stupide' Victor Hugo."

410. Bernard, Jean-Jacques. "La Nouvelle Bataille d'Hernani." Adam International Review, 19, 229-30 (1952): 6-7.

On 1952 reprise (to celebrate 150th year since Hugo's birth), which begins new critical and political battle over the play. Concludes: "Il y a du ridicule, oui, dans Hernani, et les contemporains ne se sont pas fait faute de le souligner. Mais ils se sont battus aussi

pour la grandeur qu'il y avait dans cet ouvrage . . . qui, avec
toutes ses faiblesses, demeure pourtant un des moments pathétiques
de la scène française."

411. Bertaut, Jules. "La 'Batille d'Hernani.' Du côté des perruques."
Le Temps, 2 mars 1930, p. 3. (Also as "Les Perruques à la bataille
d'Hernani." In his Visages romantiques, pp. 177-86. Paris: J.
Ferenczi, n.d. [1947].)

Amusing vignettes of such "perruques" present at première of
Hernani, as Brifaut, Lemercier, Baour-Lormian, Ancelot and others,
"aussi incapables les uns que les autres de comprendre une pièce
romantique. . . . Tous ne moururent pas, mais tous furent frappés
ce soir-là."

412. Berton, Claude. "Hugo le père." Les Nouvelles Littéraires,
3 sept. 1927, p. 6.

Apology for Hernani occasioned by reprise at Théâtre-Français:
"Hernani, le drame le plus jeune, le plus chargé de passion qu'ait
écrit Victor Hugo . . . un chef-d'oeuvre de poésie."

413. Bertrand, J. J. A. "Charles-Quint et Victor Hugo." In
Gesammelte Aufsätze zur Kulturgeschichte Spaniens, pp. 203-09.
Spanische Forschungen der Görregesellschaft, vol. 14. Münster:
Aschendorffsche, 1959.

Finds Hugo's portrait of Charles V and of Spain's political situation in Hernani "d'une rare justesse." That Hugo first meant to
focus on the young emperor is revealed in the play's original title,
"La Jeunesse de Charles-Quint." Summary of composition, bataille,
plot, fantasies and minor historical errors. Hugo presents fairly,
Bertrand feels, Charles V's good side: "Grace à Victor Hugo,
Charles-Quint a régné un temps, longtemps après sa mort, et règne
encore aujourd'hui dans le ciel de la poésie."

414. Bertrand de Muñoz, Maryse. "Hernani et le théâtre romantique
espagnol." Mosaic 10, i (1976): 91-102.

Comparative study of Hernani, La Conjuración de Venecia of Martínez
de la Rosa and El Trovador of García Gutiérrez. Traces influence
of Hernani on the Spanish plays.

415. Bidou, Henry. "Hernani." Le Journal des Débats, 30 sept. 1912.

416. _____. "Hernani." Le Journal des Débats, 27 févr. 1930.

Review of centenary production at Comédie-Française.

417. Borgerhoff, Joseph, ed. Nineteenth Century French Plays. New
York and London: The Century Co., n.d. [c 1931] (Hugo, pp. 179-241.)

Text of Hernani presented in this anthology as most representative
of Hugo. Standard biographical and historical introduction. Hugo
lacks "le sens du théâtre, but Hernani and Ruy Blas still hold their
place on the stage on account of the splendor of their style."

418. Borgerhoff, Joseph, ed. Le Théâtre anglais à Paris sous la restoration. Paris: Hachette & Cie, n.d. [1913]. (Hugo's theatre, pp. 209-212.)

In last chapter on effect of the English troupe's Paris performances in 1827-28, Borgerhoff quotes contemporary critics of Hernani who refer to Shakespeare's influence in the play--then offers own views: "Ce n'est pas le drame shakespearien malgré quelques dépendances de détail et malgré le culte que Victor Hugo prétend vouer au barde de l'Avon. Ce qu'il y a de shakespearien dans Hernani (comme d'ailleurs dans ses drames subséquents) . . . c'est l'antithèse qui est pour Hugo la grande marque distinctive du dramaturge anglais. . . . Chez Hugo . . . elle est amenée violemment, pour elle-même et d'une manière qui sent trop le parti pris. . . . Avec moins d'étalage et peut-être moins de moyens, Shakespeare a plus d'éloquence. . . ."

419. Brétaras, Claude. "Victor Hugo. La volonté d'enseigner et la volonté de plaire." Cahiers du Théâtre, no. 6-271 (1973?).

420. Brisson, Adolphe. "Les Deux Batailles d'Hernani." Le Journal de l'Université des Annales, année 5, t. 1 (15 déc. 1910): 17-38.

Lecture. First part deals with modifications made by Hugo in Hernani before and after première on advice from friends. Lettre inédite from Emile Deschamps included as illustration. Second part shows drama's triumph at 1867 reprise, despite expected second "bataille" with Emperor. Described through quotations from Mme. Hugo's letters to her husband.

421. Brisson, Pierre. "Le Centenaire d'Hernani." Le Temps, 3 mars 1930, pp. 2-3. (Also in his Au hasard des soirées, pp. 65-71. Paris: Gallimard, n.d. [1935].)

Centenary performance leads Brisson to evaluate Hugo's place in French dramatic history: "L'oeuvre dramatique d'Hugo . . . est soutenue par la gloire du poète, par l'éclat des mots, par un retentissement historique dont il est peu d'exemples dans les lettres. Une pièce comme Ruy Blas, plus cohérente dans l'artifice et plus complète que les autres, maintiendra son prestige. . . . L'influence d'Hugo sur la destinée du théâtre est à peu près nulle. . . . Le poète dramatique du XIXe siècle, . . . c'est Musset. . . ."

422. Bruner, James D. "The Characters in Victor Hugo's Hernani." Sewanee Review 13 (April, Oct. 1905): 209-15, 444-53. (Also in his Studies in Victor Hugo's Dramatic Characters, pp. 3-31. Boston: Ginn & Co., 1908.)

Sympathetic discussion of Hernani, don Ruy Gomez, don Carlos and doña Sol. Blames uncomprehending critics for missing Hernani's "poetical temperament." Explains Hernani's behavior thus: "Out of this fatalism grows his morbid melancholy, which leads to doubt, distrust, irresolution, weakness." Doña Sol, "an almost perfect woman . . . dies, a martyr to love." Somewhat simplistic and partial study. (See 98.)

423. Bruner, James D. "Parallel Situations in Hernani and Filippo." MLN 20 (Nov. 1905): 209-10.

"The 'I guilty, she pure' situation in Victor Hugo's Hernani, Act III, sc. 5, was probably borrowed from a similar situation in Alfieri's Filippo, Act V, sc. 3," according to Bruner. Yet he makes no attempt to ascertain if Hugo saw or read Alfieri's play.

424. _____. "The Probable Source of a Couplet in Hernani." MLN 19 (Jan. 1904): 32.

Shakespeare's Henry IV, Act III, scene ii, 11, 97-98, where Lady Jane Gray says to King Edward II: "I know I am too mean to be your queen,/ And yet too good to be your concubine," supposedly furnished Hugo with doña Sol's line to don Carlos as he tries to kidnap her: ". . . fille noble, et de ce sang jalouse,/ Trop pour la concubine, et trop peu pour l'épouse." (Hernani, II, ii, 501-02.)

425. Cabanis, André. "Actualité théâtrale. Hernani de Victor Hugo, mise en scène de Robert Hossein, à la Comédie Française." L'Ecole des Lettres, 23 nov. 1974, pp. 45-46.

426. Carlson, Marvin. "Hernani's Revolt from the Tradition of French Stage Composition." Theatre Survey 13 (May 1972): 1-27.

Important article detailing Hugo's innovations in staging, scenery, costumes and interpretation in Hernani. Oddly, critics accepted these changes more readily than "iconoclasm" of the plays' language, style. Prompt-book of the play illustrates that "the blocking patterns throughout show how much more Hugo utilized the entire stage space than any director earlier in the century." Concludes: "Thus the boulevard tradition and the immediate inspiration of the contemporary English theatre were both used by Hugo in 1830 to develop a new approach to the drama at the Comédie, the stronghold of conservatism."

427. Carr, Philip. "Hernani Has a Birthday." New York Times, 23 March 1930, IX, p. 2.

Review of centenary performance at Comédie Française. Presents literary and stage history of Hernani; criticizes characters, plot. Concludes: "And yet the play itself has an unquestionable life. It has fire and a splendid enthusiasm."

428. Charlier, Gustave. "Hernani et Le Figaro." Le Mercure de France 305 (1er mars 1949): 459-65. (Also in his De Montaigne à Verlaine, pp. 117-26. Brussels: La Renaissance du livre, 1957.)

Examines anonymous article in Le Figaro of 27 février 1830, hailing Hugo as one more good dramatic poet, but failing to recognize Hernani as the long-awaited new dramatic form. Charlier describes the article as "un petit chef-d'oeuvre de démolition perfide et de savant abattage" and suggests the author was perhaps Hugo's rival dramatist Latouche, who hoped to create a new genre with his own Reine d'Espagne. See also (429).

429. Charlier, Gustave. "Hernani jugé par Le Figaro." La Revue
d'Histoire du Théâtre, 2, 4 (1950): 473-78.

Refers to his previous article (428) on authorship of anonymous
negative review of Hernani in Le Figaro of 27 février 1830. Cites
article of proposed author Latouche in Le Mercure du Dix-neuvième
Siècle on Hugo's Cromwell to show style and manner the same,
especially "cette alternance, en douche écossaise, de blâme et
d'éloge." Complete text of anonymous review follows.

430. Chassé, Charles. "Victor Hugo, Dumas père et le tombeau de
Charlemagne à Aix-la-Chapelle." La Revue des Sciences Humaines, no. 95
(juill.-sept. 1956), pp. 331-34.

Wonders what Hugo's side is in debate over Charlemagne's burial
position. At time of Hernani, Hugo, unaware of legend that the
emperor was buried seated, has him lying down. After 1842 trip to
Aix-la-Chapelle, however, Hugo adopts in Le Rhin the legend of the
seated position.

431. Clark, R. J. B. "Hernani Reconsidered or Don Carlos Vindicatus."
Modern Languages 53 (Dec. 1972): 168-74.

Agrees generally with Baguley's 1971 article (404), but says author
minimizes historical dimension too much. Focuses attention upon
don Carlos, especially upon his moral choice in Act IV, which Clark
sees as tending toward le sublime: "The character is distinguished
psychologically from all the others in that he alone is the agent
of his own destiny rather than the victim of some uncontrollable
fatality. . . ."

432. Claudel, Paul. "Le Cor d'Hernani." Le Figaro Littéraire, 18 oct.
1952. (Also in his Oeuvres en prose, pp. 479-80. Paris: Bibliothèque
de la Pléiade, 1965.)

Opening sentence sets tone of article: "Pourquoi les deux émotions
théâtrales les plus fortes de ma vie sont-elles dûes à des poètes
pour qui mon admiration n'a cessé de décroître, Victor Hugo et
Richard Wagner?" Recounts then his memories of having seen, at
age 10, the "reprise désastreuse" of Hernani at the World's Fair in
1878 with Mounet-Sully and Sarah Bernhardt. The horn that night
moved him greatly although in retrospect he feels it represented a
very bad technique: "Les tristes obligations d'une dramaturgie
maladroite ont ramené sur terre l'ange rauque et lui ont substitué
le souffle, hélas! d'un machiniste indubitable!" Claudel sees 1952
reprise and writes sadly about the "représentation d'Hernani qui a
marqué les funerailles définitives du théâtre de Hugo." It is of
interest to delve into views on Hugo of this dramatist with whom Hugo
is often compared and who is said to have been perhaps subconsciously
influenced by Hugo.

433. Cluzel, Etienne. "Les Démêlés de Hugo avec Mlle Mars lors de la
première d'Hernani." Bulletin de la Librairie Ancienne et Moderne,
année 48 (nov. 1968): 169-73.

Investigation of the anecdote concerning "Vous êtes mon lion superbe et généreux," rendered famous in Dumas' Mémoires. Compares it with version in Victor Hugo raconté and 1830 printed editions of the play. Concludes that Mlle Mars, not Hugo, won the battle and that "monseigneur vaillant" replaced "lion superbe" until the 1836 edition and the 1838 performance with Marie Dorval.

434. Comfort, William. French Romantic Plays. New York: C. Scribner, n.d. [c 1933]. (Hugo, pp. xxix, 109-436.)

French text of Hernani and Ruy Blas included in this anthology. Fairly good introduction offers these observations on Hugo: "His plays are conceived rather as a succession of impressive and moving tableaux, dealing with extraordinary and violent events, but set forth in poetry of matchless beauty and exhibiting an imagination which knew no bounds. Hernani and Ruy Blas especially may be studied as a series of effective tableaux."

435. Couët, Jules. "Les Etapes d'un chef-d'oeuvre." Le Journal des Débats, 19 juill. 1926.

On production of Hernani.

436. Dedessuslamare, M. Hernani. Rouen: Albert Laîné, 1932. Pp. 12.

Treats sources of the play and provides some interesting speculation on this subject, such as possible influence of Les Plaideurs in Act III.

437. Delorme, Hugues. "A propos de Hernani." Le Figaro, 1er mars 1930, p. 5.

Delorme obtains first edition of the play and notes that acts are printed without the titles that appear in later editions. Also indicates changes demanded by censor.

438. Derème, Tristan. "Hernani et son H." In his Le poisson rouge, pp. 217-19. Paris: Bernard Grasset, 1934.

Amusing essay showing that even in the play itself Hugo sometimes makes "H" of Hernani non-aspirated, sometimes aspirated.

439. Deschamps, Gaston. "Avant la bataille d'Hernani." Le Figaro, 20 févr. 1930, p. 5.

Succinct summary of events leading up to the bataille and the contested première. Hugo's amazing, unbroken chain of successes before Hernani were bound to cause resentment. Deschamps admires Hugo's admirable behavior toward detractors. Evokes spirit of event: "Les passions échauffées autour de ce drame ont atteint, dans la société parisienne, un rare degré d'effervescence."

440. Dubech, Lucien. "Cent Ans après." L'Action Française, 28 févr. 1930.

441. Dubech, Lucien. "Hernani." Candide, 20, 27 févr. 1930.

442. _____. "Le Theatre: D'Hernani à M. Baty." La Revue Universelle 40 (15 mars 1930): 762-64.

On centenary performance, which Dubech describes as "une cérémonie officielle, sans chaleur, sans couleur et sans joie. . . . Il n'est pas plus possible de contester le génie lyrique et poétique d'Hugo qu'il n'est permis de nier ses faiblesses d'auteur dramatique. . . . Cette machine montée avec peine grince et tourne mal et sent l'effort; les personnages, les situations et les sentiments ne s'engrènent jamais avec justesse parce qu'ils sont eux-mêmes toujours faux."

443. Dussane, Madame. "Le Centenaire d'Hernani." La Revue Hebdomadaire, année 39, 2 (15 févr. 1930): 259-80. (Also in shortened form as "les Interprètes d'Hernani." Franche-Comté et Monts Jura, année 17 [mai 1939]: 83-85.)

Lecture given before la Société des Conférences on 31 January 1930. Reads many passages from Hernani and concentrates on actors who have played famous roles. Sarah Bernhardt's voice enchanted audiences and Mounet-Sully "savait bien qu'il ne fallait demander à Hernani que la joie un peu sensuelle d'un débauché de lyrisme et de couleur." At end Mme. Dussane affirms: "Hernani vit toujours."

444. Duval, Jacques. "Un Cinna romantique: Hernani." La Revue Latine 3 (25 juill. 1904): 425-31.

In 1830 journalists merely suggested a similarity between the two plays, and only now does a critic indicate the extensive parallels: "Faites passer l'amour d'Emilie et de Cinna au premier plan, la clémence d'Auguste au second, vous trouvez Hernani. . . . Lisez les quatre premiers actes d'Hernani, lisez ensuite Cinna; vous aurez lu la même pièce en deux langages différents. Lisez enfin le cinquième acte d'Hernani, et vous verrez, à côté des similitudes, les dissemblances de deux génies qui, à deux cents ans de distance, se sont exercé sur une même matière."

445. Engel, Claire-Elaine. "Une Traduction anglaise de Hernani." La Revue de Littérature Comparée 14 (juill.-sept. 1934): 542-49.

On James Kenney's version of Hernani, The Pledge or Castilian Honour. Suggests that changes made by Kenney to please English taste eliminate "le romantisme exalté" of the original: "Il a fait disparaître tout le lyrisme de Hugo, toute la passion qui anime son drame, bien plus, tous ses mots à effets."

446. Esquerra, Ramón. "Sur les origines d'Hernani." Annales de la Faculté des Lettres de l'Université de Bordeaux et des Universités du Midi, Bulletin Hispanique 40 (juill.-sept. 1938): 313-14.

Author finds, in Pompeu Gener's Amigos y maestros (1897), an anecdote supposedly told by Hugo. According to the story, Hugo's 1811 entrance into Hernani was preceded by hold-up, in which "un joven, alto y buen mozo, que aunque envuelto en una manta tenía todo el

aspecto de un perfecto caballero," gallantly lets women and children
pass unharmed.  Of course, this character supposedly inspired the
hero of Hernani; but there is no other known support for the story.

447.  Etiemble.  "Balzac critique."  Les Temps Modernes 6 (nov. 1950):
926-37.

Finds Balzac quite a judicious critic in admiring La Chartreuse de
Parme and condemning Hernani before these views became fashionable.
Examines Balzac's two articles in La Revue Parisienne on Hernani--
those of 24 mars and 7 avril 1830--and claims each time that Balzac
"voit juste; . . . il va droit à l'essentiel. . . . Vers 1830, tous
les gens à la page admirent Hernani.  Balzac écrit:  ça ne vaut
rien."

448.  Evans, David O.  "The Hegelian Idea in Hernani."  MLN 63 (March
1948):  171-73.

Locates in Hernani evidence of Hugo's having read Victor Cousin's
Cours de philosophie:  "Hugo's symbolic drama anticipates the
Hegelian definition of art as 'a spiritual idea represented in
sensuous form'. . . . The esthetic principle  in Hugo is total.
Hernani is a "Gesamtkunstwerk' breathing the whole spirit of the
Romantic Age."

449.  _____.  "Hernani, IV, 2."  MLN 47 (Jan. 1932):  21-24.

Tries to show genesis of verses 1524-39.  Traces image of powerful
masses as a wave breaking from "Ce qu'on entend sur la montagne"
and especially "A la Colonne" through manuscript to final form in
published edition.  Evans remarks:  "Hernani is a dynamic version of
this image, a transposition from the auditive to the visual sphere."
Prefers manuscript to final printed form, however.

450.  _____.  "A Source of Hernani:  Le Paria by Casimir Delavigne."
MLN 47 (Dec. 1932):  514-19.

According to Evans, Delavigne's play contributed to Hernani the
outline of two lyrical scenes (I,2 and II,4), the motif of renunica-
tion, and certain features of the hero's Byronic character.  In
addition, Evans claims, "Le Paria is instructive because it shows
the tendency which the tragedy was following before the advent of
Hernani."

451.  Faguet, Emile.  "Victor Hugo:  Hernani."  Le Journal des Débats,
10 déc. 1900.

452.  Falk, Eugene.  "The Formative Effects of Romantic Commitments."
Symposium 23 (Fall-Winter 1969):  225-34.

Intriguing investigation of influence of both Descartes's notion of
the formative effect of love and the "concept of its unconscious and
involuntary aspects" on Romantic drama.  Both strains found in Hugo:
"In terms of these distinctions in perspective Hugo's Hernani
reveals an emphatically Cornelian orientation. . . . In another of
Hugo's plays, Ruy Blas actually recognizes the involuntary and

unconscious origin of his love as an inscrutable, bewildering, and overpowering force, an irresistible destiny."

453. Frick, Reinhold. Hernani als litterarischer Typus. Plieningen: Druck von F. Find, 1903. Pp. 80.

Originally an inaugural dissertation. Sees Hernani as the last of a long line of rogue-heroes, including Robin Hood, Roque Guinart, le Chevalier des Grieux, Byron, Ivanhoe, and especially Karl Moor.

454. _____. "Hernanis Stammbaum." Zeitschrift für Vergleichende Literaturgeschichte n.s. 17 (1909): 239-61, 385-413.

Article based on his longer work above on Hernani's literary and real-life ancestors. This description ties together Hernani's basic characteristics, drawn from many disparate sources: "Hernani als Typus ist der edle, vornehm denkende Held, der durch die Macht der Verhaltnisse--sei es die Niedertracht der Menschen oder die Leidenschaft seines Charakter, seien es Gesetz seines Landes und seiner Zeit oder Ziele, die er auf anderem Weg nicht zu erreichen glaubt--dem Banditenleben in die Arme getreiben wird."

455. Galdemar, Ange. "Hernani in der spanischen Stadt Hernani." Comoedia, 26 févr. 1927.

456. Galey, Matthieu. "Ahurissement mais irrésistible." Les Nouvelles littéraires, 21 oct. 1974, p. 15.

Favorable review with some reservations of Robert Hossein's reprise of Hernani with actors of the Comédie-Française at the Théâtre Marigny. Agrees with "les réactionnaires" that "Hernani est un monument d'enflure et de ridicule grandiloquent." Yet feels: "Il y a dans cet ouragan de mots quelque chose d'irrésistible. . . . [Hossein] va dans les sens des défauts, et c'est une façon de mettre en valeur ce monument délirant. . . . Avec Hugo, on rejoint le burlesque surréaliste, on bascule dans la démesure d'un mauvais goût . . . proche de génie."

457. Gandon, Yves. "L'Opinion d'Yves Gandon sur la reprise d'Hernani." France-Illustration, no. 334 (8 mars 1952), p. 235.

Henri Rollan's 1952 attempt to rival 1830 première of Hernani viewed as failure by this critic: "Ce drame romantique à tous crins porte plus de rides que le Cid du vieux Corneille." Jean Yonnel the only good actor. Critic admits that don Carlos's monologue in Act IV is stirring and that the duo d'amour in Act V contains "quelques-uns des plus beaux vers d'amour qui aient été écrits." Includes photos from the reprise.

458. Gandrey-Rety, Jean. "Reprise d'Hernani à la Comédie-Française." Les Lettres Françaises, 28 févr. 1952, p. 7.

Affectionate view of play. Finds doña Sol "le type complet et parfaitement réussi de l'amoureuse brave," like Chimène and Racinian heroines. Forgives bizarre "invraisemblances" because "la vérité

interne des personnages" touches his heart, and torrents of words
define their characters and lend them credence and life.

459. Gara, Eugenio. "Donne belle e stravaganti nella storia dell'
Ernani." Il Nuovo Corriere della Sera, 25 febbr. 1959, p. 3.

Recounts rôles of three leading ladies involved in productions of
Hernani and of Ernani: Adèle Hugo, Mlle Mars and Soffia Loeme,
Verdi's prima donna.

460. Genov, Geno. "Xarakteri i obstojatelstva v romantičeskite drami
na Viktor Jugo: Ernani, Kraljat se zabavljava, Rjui Blas." Trudove na
Velikotărnovskija universitet 'Kril i Metodij' 13, i (1977-78): 239-86.

461. Giraudoux, Jean. "De siècle à siècle." In his Littérature, pp.
201-28. Paris: B. Grasset, 1941.

Lecture given for centenary of Hernani, in which Giraudoux tries to
show apparent similarities of the epochs represented by 1830 and
1930. States that Hernani brought about no real revolution:
"Hernani faisait rentrer notre littérature, échapée du cercle royal,
dans le cercle bourgeois. . . . Libre au vocabulaire de 1830 d'être
excessif et vide." Calls for artists of 1930 to forge a new
language so the theatre can extend its realm to all people.

462. Glaesener, Henri. "A propos d'un centenaire romantique: Hernani
et ses sources." Le Mercure de France 218 (15 févr. 1930): 511-34.

Recounts the bataille and the première. Identifies sources of the
play in events of Hugo's youth and works of Alarcón, Calderón and
Schiller. Importance of Hernani is establishment of "le drame-type
du romantisme."

463. Grant, Elliott M. "'Car le géant est pris.' Hernani, 1911."
MLN 44 (nov. 1929): 458.

Detects origin of "bold metaphor" of article's title in Hugo's poem
"Lui."

464. _____, ed. Chief French Plays of the Nineteenth
Century. New York: Harper, n.d. [1934]. (Hugo, pp. 71-318.)

Anthology contains French texts of Hernani and Ruy Blas. In
perfunctory introduction, Grant offers: "Hernani is beyond doubt
the most famous Romantic play. . . . [It is] typical of many aspects
of Hugo's genius."

465. _____. "Victor Hugo, Vesuvius and Etna." In Vincent
Guilloton, Autour de la Relation du voyage de Samuel Sorbière en
Angleterre, pp. 31-61. Smith College Studies in Modern Languages,
vol. 11, no. 4. Northampton, Mass.: Dept. of Modern Langs. of Smith
College, 1930.

Extension of previous note (463) on volcano image in Hernani.
Examines Hugo's life-long devotion to volcanoes. Triboulet described
as one in last act of Le Roi s'amuse, but verse 1911 of Hernani is

still "the most extraordinary instance of the metaphor." Grant
finds its origin in geological, archeological, artistic and literary
events of the early nineteenth century.

466. Gregh, Fernand. "Le Centenaire d'Hernani." Les Nouvelles
Littéraires, 1er mars 1930, pp. 1-2. (Also as "Allocution prononcée
à la cérémonie du centenaire d'Hernani à la Comédie-Française." Effort
Clartéiste, année 7 [mai 1935]: 2-7. Also as "La Bataille d'Hernani."
Franche-Comté et Monts Jura, année 17 [mai 1935]: 81-83.)

Affectionate, laudatory official acclaim of Hernani for centenary
at the Comédie-Française. Personal recollections mixed with literary
history. Hugo a great poet, and "le style de la pièce n'a pas une
ride."

467. Guillemin, Henri. "Une lettre inédite de Victor Hugo à la veille
d'Hernani." Points et Contrepoints, n.s. no. 18 (Oct. 1952), pp. 1-2.

Letter dated 9 févr. 1830 to Alexandre Soumet reprinted here.
Short, witty, it congratulates Soumet and Belmontet on their
successful play at the Odéon. Hugo writes that they are "au port,
quand peut-être je touche au naufrage."

468. Guillot de Saix, Léon. "Le Manuscrit de Hernani. 19 août-24 sept.
1829." In L'Ami du lettré, pp. 41-51. Paris: Editions de France,
1929.

On manuscript found in archives of Comédie-Française. Many changes
for première and even afterwards. Concludes: "L'étude de ce
manuscrit nous montre mieux encore combien en dépit des apparences,
le style de Victor Hugo était proche encore du style de la tragédie
de son époque, et l'influence de Walter Scott ajoute à l'ensemble
cette nuance 'troubadour' propagée alors par la lithographie en
couleurs."

469. Guilloton, Vincent. "Hernani ou l'honneur castillan." In Essays
in Honor of W. A. Neilson, pp. 103-09. Smith College Studies in Modern
Languages, no. 21. Northampton, Mass.: Dept. of Modern Langs. of
Smith College, 1940.

Claims that Hugo's pundonor is just another term for his own
romantic concept of honor as a youth. Furthermore, Guilloton
agrees with Souriau (292) that Hugo's real source for play,
especially for the last act, is himself from other, earlier works,
particularly Bug Jargal, perfected this time into "une scène
vraiment tragique" at Hernani's close.

470. Halbwachs, Pierre. "A propos de la 'Bataille d'Hernani.'" In
Romantisme et politique, 1815-1851, pp. 99-109. Colloque de l'Ecole
Normale Supérieure de Saint-Cloud (1966). Paris: Colin, 1969.

Reinterpretation of meaning of the bataille d'Hernani. Identifies
in the play's detractors a sort of literary and political coalition
against Hugo's "libéralisme": "Hernani est suspect au gouvernement
parce que pour la deuxième fois la personne d'un roi y est ravallée,
et peut-être surtout parce qu'est mise en cause la sacro-sainte

hiérarchie sociale, en ébranlant le respect dû à la classe encore dirigeante, la noblesse." Yet finds Hernani championing outdated theatre style even in 1830: "Contrairement aux apparances, . . . il faut appeler la victoire d'Hernani le triomphe d'une esthétique déjà dépassée dans d'autres domaines littéraires, son apothéose mais son couchant. . . ."

471. "Hernani." Paris-Match, 2 nov. 1974, p. 133.

Describes Hossein's production as "très cinématographique." Approves music, acting, scenery: "Tout cela sert la pièce avec un maximum d'efficacité. C'est beau, c'est grave, c'est noble. C'est Hugo."

472. Hess, John A. "Goethe's Egmont as a Possible Source of Hugo's Hernani." Modern Philology 27 (Nov. 1929): 193-99.

Parallels between two plays brought out, especially endings: "The significant thing . . . [is] the fact that [the couple's] union in death overwhelms the rejected suitor in each case and makes his lot intolerable."

473. Houghton, Norris, ed. The Laurel Masterpieces of Continental Drama. Vol. 2: The Romantic Influence. New York: n.p., n.d. [Dell Publishing Co., 1963]. (Hugo, pp. 281-379.)

Introduction gives basic facts on European Romantic drama and Hugo's part in its development: "The regrettable thing is that . . . he was unable to lead the romanticists very far foreward--even though he lived to be eighty-three." English version of Hernani by Linda Asher follows. Other plays in volume are Faust, Part I, Schiller's Mary Stuart and Rostand's Cyrano de Bergerac. For general reader.

474. Houville, Mme. Gérard d'. "Toujours Hernani." Le Figaro, 3 mars 1930, p. 5.

Tribute to the play occasioned by centenary.

475. Jaloux, Edmond. "La Bataille d'Hernani." Le Temps, 21 févr. 1930, p. 3.

Regrets that we no longer have batailles, like that of Hernani, because we accept everything in all domains of art. Fond recounting of the première.

476. Jasinski, René. "La Bataille d'Hernani." La Nouvelle Revue des Jeunes, année 2 (10 mai 1930): 635-43.

Excellent article. By examining press of times, Jasinski re-evaluates meaning of the bataille d'Hernani and concludes that it was only the opening campaign of a continuing war between classical defenders and new idealists who saw themselves fighting for political freedom as well as freedom from authority in literary matters. Investigates ambiguities and contradictions in ideals of the group's leaders.

477.  Jeuland-Meynaud, Maryse.  "De l'Hernani de Hugo à l'Ernani·de Giuseppe Verdi."  Cahiers d'Etudes Romanes 3 (1977):  117-51.

478.  Kemp, Robert.  "La Bataille d'Hernani."  France-Illustration, no. 334 (8 mars 1952), pp. 236-37.

Says perhaps it because hernanistes were young and healthy and we moderns are old and sick that we can no longer appreciate Hernani: "Certes, oui! le Cid, l'aîné de près de deux cents ans, est plus beau, plus vrai, plus jeune qu'Hernani.  Mais la 'querelle' du Cid, qui dura longtemps, est moins superbe que la 'bataille' d'Hernani gagnée un soir, le 25 février 1830."  Furnishes details of composition, bataille, play's 1867 success.  Good illustrations of première and photos of reprise.

479.  _____.  "Le 'Lion' est-il toujours superbe et généreux?" Bravo, 21 févr. 1930, p. 12.

Calls Hernani both absurd and sublime.  The play's characters are "des fous," yet the beautiful music in Hernani compensates for the lack of psychological truth.  The play represents an entire era: "Le romantisme n'est pas mort.  Et, de tout le théâtre romantique, il ne subsiste guère qu'Hernani. . . . Hernani résume et cristallise tout un siècle."

480.  Kociecka, M.  "Hernani w Polsce."  Ruch Literacki (Cracow), 1, 4 (1963):  36-39.

481.  Lancaster, Henry C.  "A Note on Hernani, IV, 1."  MLN 43 (Nov. 1928):  467.  (Also in Festschrift presented to him, Adventures of a Literary Historian, p. 353.  Baltimore, Md.:  Johns Hopkins Press, 1942.)

Brief note on origin of thirteen stars as indication that don Carlos is to be elected emperor, echoing Genesis, XXXVII, 9, in which "the thirteen heavenly bodies . . . did obeissance to Joseph . . . and thus predicted his elevation to power in Egypt."

482.  Larroumet, Gustave.  "Hernani."  Le Temps, 10 déc. 1900, p. 1.

Review of reprise celebrating the rentrée of Mme. Weber, outstanding sociétaire de la Comédie-Française.  Larroumet praises the production's sets and costumes as well as Hugo's play:  "Le drame de Victor Hugo, a soulevé un long enthousiasme.  On se serait cru, à certains moments, en présence d'une oeuvre tout récente. . . ."

483.  Le Breton, André.  "Les Trois Batailles de 1830.  I.  La Batille d'Hernani."  Lectures pour Tous, janv. 1930, pp. 68-71.

Provides details of events leading up to première and lively evocation of the famous night.

484.  Levaillant, Maurice.  "Le Premiere Bulletin d'Hernani."  Le Figaro, 22 févr. 1930, p. 5.

Exact figures of box office receipts for première and following
night given to show play a moderate financial success.

485. Levaillant, Maurice. "La Première Edition d'Hernani. Documents
inédits." Le Figaro, 22 févr. 1930, p. 5.

An altered text of Hernani. Original manuscript reveals "divers
inédits et des variantes admirables. . . . Victor Hugo, cependant,
dans l'édition originale, avait adouci un grand nombre de ses vers;
il attendit quelques années--jusqu'en 1836--avant d'oser publier son
drame tel qu'il l'avait écrit. . . ."

486. Lièvre, Pierre. "Hernani." Le Mercure de France 255 (1er oct.
1934): 136-40.

On reprise at the Comédie-Française. Declares play's characteristics can be seen as faults or merits depending on viewer's mood.
Blames lack of psychological complexity on Hugo's optimistic belief
in never-ending moral and technological progress. Calls for
"simplicité grandiose" and "fantaisie" in performing Hugo's plays.

487. Losfeld, Georges. "Ponctuation d'Hernani." In his Le Cahier
d'Alceste, pp. 232-34. Essais et critiques, no. 14. Paris: Didier,
1974. Pp. 324.

Upon consulting six different editions of the play, author finds
six different versions of punctuation for verses 975-76. Goes to
the manuscript and establishes correct seventh version. Calls for
more care in publishing texts.

488. Lote, Georges. En préface à Hernani--cent ans après. Paris:
Gamber, 1930. Pp. 200.

This study is stronger on literary history and Hugo's theories than
on sources, criticism and bibliography. Lote tries to prove that
Hernani is basically only a mélodrame with two dénouements. Its
only saving grace, he adds, is its lyric poetry. Disappointing
underestimation of play's style and general significance.

489. McLean, Malcolm D. "The Historical Accuracy of Hugo's Hernani."
South Central Bulletin 22 (Winter 1962): 26-30.

Catalogue of Hugo's errors in characters, numbers, dates, scenes,
titles, behavior of Carlos V. McLean asks rhetorically: "Did
Hugo respect the facts of history in writing his plays? The answer
is . . .: He most certainly did not." See also Pietri (260) and
Martinenche (495).

490. Maillet, Henri. "Structure d'un drame romantique: Hernani."
L'Information Littéraire 23 (mai-juin 1971): 139-49.

Indicates basic "moule classique" of Hugo's plays, then shows
special technique of composition Hugo uses. With Hugo the word
comes first, and characters and action follow from what author wants
said: "La genèse même du personnage est de l'ordre de la poésie et
de la rhétorique, . . . et l'action quant à elle, s'accommode des

exigences du verbe, avec, il faut le reconnaître, toute la souplesse
que peut lui conférer une intelligence remarquable des possibilités
du théâtre et de la scène."

491. Maillard, Lucien. "On répète Hernani à Marigny." Comédie-
Française 31 (sept. 1974): 8-11.

492. Mambrino, Jean. "Hernani de Hugo au Théâtre Marigny, par la
Comédie-Française." Etudes 341 (déc. 1974): 729-30.

Very favorable review of Hossein's production: "On sent bien tout
ce que cette oeuvre avait de subversif à l'origine, d'une incroyable
audace, et qui nous parle encore, en notre époque de partisans et
de guérillas, dont l'amour ne connaît pas de frontières! . . .
Enfin, c'est la jeunesse du théâtre, le col ouvert, cheveux au vent.
Insouciante et grave. Elle ne changera jamais."

493. Marsan, Jules. "1830." L'Archer (juin 1930). (Also in his
Autour du romantisme, pp. 87-103. Toulouse: Editions de l'Archer,
1937.)

Passes over the bataille and the première of Hernani to focus on
"le somptueux éclat de son lyrisme" as a major contribution of
romanticism, still the great literary fact of the last century:
"enthousiasme légitime certes, si l'on considère non pas la valeur
théâtrale ou la valeur humaine du drame, mais ce déploiement de
poésie, cette ardeur frémissante, cette jeunesse."

494. Martin du Gard, Maurice. "Le Centenaire d'Hernani." Les Nouvelles
Littéraires, 1er mars 1930, p. 12. (Also in his Carte rouge, pp. 262-
70. Paris: Flammarion, n.d. [1930].)

Tone of amused tolerance in this review of a centenary performance.
Points out weaknesses of this mélo and suggests: "Si Hernani
peut passer pour un chef-d'oeuvre, c'est à la lecture, et pris par
petites doses."

495. Martinenche, Ernest. Histoire de l'influence espagnole sur la
littérature française. L'Espagne et le romantisme français. Paris:
Hachette, 1922. (Hugo's theatre, pp. 115-53.)

Thorough treatment of Spanish influence in Hernani, Ruy Blas.
Sees no direct work of which Hernani is an imitation, but cites
many Spanish works Hugo must have known for both plays. Finds
exaggeration and errors of geography, history, spelling, customs.
Ends on positive note: "Victor Hugo n'a pas eu, en tout cas, à se
repentir d'avoir cédé à l'élan naturel de son imagaination et aux
sympathies réfléchies qui le poussaient vers l'Espagne. Il n'est
guère dans son théâtre que deux drames qui vivent vraiment d'une
vie ardente et toujours jeune. Et sur l'un comme sur l'autre flotte
le panache espagnol." More reliable treatment than that of Huszár
(190).

496. Morand, Hubert. "La Bataille d'Hernani et Le Journal des Débats."
Le Journal des Débats, 25 févr. 1930.

497.  Morel, Louis.  "Sur un passage de Hernani, Acte III, scène iv."
La Revue d'Histoire Littéraire de la France 27 (1920):  579-80.

Morel points out possible influence of Balzac's youthful novel,
Argow le Pirate (1824) on Hernani.  Intriguing similarities between
novel's chapter 13 and play's Act III, scene 4.

498.  Nozière, Pierre.  "Hernani."  L'Avenir, 9 sept. 1912.

On reprise.

499.  _____.  "Hernani."  L'Avenir, 3 mars 1930.

500.  Oudon, Noël.  A la manière d'Hernani.  Parodie en 2 actes, en vers.
Senlis:  Oudon, 1931.  Pp. 32.

In prologue Oudon asserts that today Hernani seems "un peu démodé,
trop haut en couleur, trop déclamatoire, trop romantique, enfin."
Offers this play as up-dated version.  It is funny, light nonsense
with a "happy ending."  Englishmen--Sherlock Holmès, Bob and Jim--
amusing stereotypes.

501.  Paire, André.  "La Bataille d'Hernani."  L'Echo de Paris, 25 févr.
1930.

502.  Palache, John G.  "A Rose-coloured Waistcoat."  In his Gautier
and the Romantics, pp. 15-19.  London:  J. Cape, n.d. [1927].

Pleasant, undetailed account of Hernani's famous première and of
Hugo's relationship with Gautier.  On Hernani:  "As Brandes has
pointed out, Hugo closely resembles Corneille as a rhetorician. . . .
There is much of the college undergraduate in Romanticism in its
most self-assertive moments."  On Gautier's première attire:  "The
whole point of his gaudy costume was that it should be moyenâgeux.
All Hugo's friends insisted on the Middle Ages as the keynote to
Romanticism."

503.  Pannetier, Odette.  "Que pensez-vous d'Hernani?"  Bravo, 21 févr.
1930, p. 18.

Author asks ten people randomly selected their opinions of Hernani.
Most do not even remember play.

504.  Passillé, Guy de.  "Le Centenaire d'Hernani.  Au camp des
Perruques."  Le Figaro, 23 févr. 1930, p. 5.

Amusing one-line description of each of the "perruques" opposing
Hernani.  Underscores fact that they were not true "classiques" but
hack writers whose poetry was "purement descriptive et didactique,"
men for whom "[la] tragédie . . . n'était plus qu'un métier."  See
also Bertaut (411).

505.  Pavie, André.  Médaillons romantiques.  Paris:  Emile-Paul, 1909.
(Hugo's theatre, pp. 91-108, 109-23, 127-31.)

First section on Amy Robsart published previously (345). Second illustrates tumultuous period of the "bataille d'Hernani" by quoting lettres inédites from Paul Foucher to Victor Pavie and from V. Pavie to his father in which they describe conditions before, during and after première. Third, through more lettres inédites, depicts competition between Vigny's Chatterton and Hugo's Angelo in 1835. Angelo triumphs at the time because it was understood by everyone.

506. Plinval, Georges de. "Hernani que nous avons connu." Les Ecrits de Paris, no. 90 (avril 1952), pp. 81-87.

Appreciative review of the reprise. Voices strange link between Hugo and existentialist hero: "Hernani, dans sa sinistre beauté de légende, c'est le portrait de l'aventurier moderne, l'épopee du maquis. . . . Nous avons eu Sartre et Malraux. Ce sont eux qui nous ont aidé à mieux comprendre et qui nous ont fait reconnaître en Hernani, brute lucide, le nouveau 'héros' des temps modernes."

507. Pollin, Burton R. "Victor Hugo and Poe." La Revue de Littérature Comparée 42 (oct.-déc. 1968): 494-519.

Cites Hernani as source for "The Masque of the Red Death." Claims Poe saw Zanthe, Barrymore's pilfered version of Kenney's translation of Hernani, in January of 1842. It is that production, rather than the written text, he asserts, that carries over into the tale: "The chief point is that the essential source lies in the presentation of the contrast between the bal masqué and the spectral figure of Don Ruy, who brings death." Indicates that Poe acquired considerable respect for Hugo's works.

508. Portal, Georges. "Chronique dramatique: Sur Hernani à la Comédie-Française." Ecrits de Paris, no. 343 (janv. 1975): 123-28.

Review of Hossein's production. Praises director's talents, but concludes that "Hernani n'est qu'une pantalonade héroïque. . . . La seule qualité indéniable de l'ouvrage c'est le mouvement," on which Hossein capitalizes.

509. Praviel, Armand. "L'Année romantique: 1830." Le Correspondant, année 102, 321 (25 nov. 1930): 580-96.

Insists that 1830 is a truly important date in literary history for production of many plays embodying Zeitgeist, but not for masterpieces. On Hugo: "Hernani n'a rien de shakespearien; c'est un mélodrame, écrit en vers souvent hâtifs et qui ne reste au repertoire que comme une pièce de musée. . . . Plus son oeuvre dramatique se développera, plus il rencherira sur les hardiesses d'Hernani."

510. "Une Première d'Hernani en province (à Lons-le-Saunier, 1834)." L'Information, 22 août 1927.

511. Régnier, Henri de. "Hernani." Le Journal des Débats, 7 mars 1910.

Sees première of Hernani as having created a new dramatic genre
destined to resist time and political persecution.

512. Ridge, George Ross. The Hero in French Romantic Literature.
Athens: University of Georgia Press, n.d. [c 1959]. (Hugo's theatre,
pp. 8-9, 98-99, 114-15, 126-28.)

Hernani seen as exception to general Romantic type of social rebel
because he is unaware of the reason for his rebellion. Yet he does
share some typical characteristics: "Hypersensibility is also
interwoven with fatality in Hugo's Hernani. His rôle as a man of
fate springs from his hypersensibility as expressed in the social
context." Ruy Blas is a Romantic hero, "yet at times he displays
the most lamentable weakness. . . . As a fusion of the hero and
anti-hero Ruy Blas is admittedly more the former than the latter."

513. Roger, Noëlle. "A Genève. Le Centenaire d'Hernani." Le Figaro,
11 mars 1930, p. 5.

La Société d'étudiants reënacted the bataille and the première of
Hernani to the last detail "et jamais peut-etre, à Genève, Hernani
ne remporta plus éclatant succès." See below.

514. "Le Romantisme chez les Genèvois. Hernani à Genève en 1830."
Le Figaro, 19 févr. 1930, p. 5.

In marked contrast to the success of the 1930 performance of Hernani
(see above), in 1830 "le bourgeois de Genève est resté hostile au
romantisme." Two articles quoted from Le Journal de Genève reflect
this cold reception: "C'est le style, dit-on, qui fait vivre les
ouvrages; dans ce cas, Hernani serait menacé d'une fin prochaine."

515. Rousseaux, André. "Victor Hugo Européen." La Revue Universelle
40 (15 mars 1930): 693-710.

Examines various works for Hugo's pan-european thought: "Hugo se
laissait éblouir avec délices par tout ce qu'il y a de majestueux
et de surhumain dans cet aspect du passé de l'Europe. . . . C'est
notamment l'idée maîtresse des Burgraves et, pour une part,
d'Hernani. . . . L'esprit [de Hugo] y a perdu, dans la vision de
tout un passé, l'intelligence nationale." See also Schinz below.

516. Rouveyre, André. "Le Centenaire d'Hernani à la Comédie-Française."
Le Mercure de France, sér. moderne, t. 219 (1er avril 1930): 162-64.

Lukewarm praise for Hugo's play: "A certains points de vue, elle
est ridiculement surannée. A d'autres, elle est restée chaude et
généreuse." Complains also that actors lack fire needed to perform
play adequately.

517. Rudler, Gustave. "La Source de la scène des portraits dans
Hernani." Modern Language Review 13 (July 1918): 329-32.

Rudler closely examines statue scene in Shiel's Eviradné as possible
source for portrait scene in Hernani. He agrees with anonymous
author of 1830 Le National article that Hugo took his scene from

Shiel's play but indicates it not "mot pour mot" as charged:   "il
a pris, de la scène anglaise, l'idée, le mouvement général,
l'insistance de don Ruy Gomez sur son père, l'exaltation de'honneur
et de gloire. . . ." Hugo, however, adapted the idea of feminine
honor and chevalric devotion in the English original to the concept
of warrior grandeur and gentleman's honor appropriate to Hernani's
setting and characters.

518.   Salomon, Michel. "A la veille d'Hernani. Vers inédits de Victor
Hugo à Charles Nodier." Le Journal des Débats, 22 févr. 1902.

519.   Salvan, Jacques L. Le Romantisme français et l'Angleterre
victorienne. Paris: H. Champion, 1949. (Hugo's theatre, p. 66.)

Very brief mention of Hugo's influence on the young Swinburne, who
tried to equal "l'éclat oratoire" of Ruy Blas and Hernani in his
early plays, The Queen Mother and Rosamond.

520.   Saragea Guberman, Solange. "Analyse des vers 1461-1480 d'Hernani
(Acte IV, scène ii)." Culture Française (Bari) 24 (1977):  251-53.

521.   Schaffer, Aaron. "A Letter of Auguste Vacquerie Concerning a
Performance of Hernani." MLN 66 (March 1951):  182-83.

Comparison of this undated lettre inédite, signed only A. V., with
letters written by Madame Hugo during days just preceding and
following the famous reprise of Hernani in 1867 "makes the deter-
mination of its authorship and date a relatively simple matter."
Date in question is Monday, 10 June 1867.

522.   Schinz, Albert. "L'Unité dans la carrière politique de Victor
Hugo." La Revue d'Histoire Littéraire de la France 39 (1932):  15-44.

Finds in Hernani "la première expression claire et consciente de
l'idée . . . de Victor Hugo en politique: il faut un homme d'élite,
et non un assemblage anonyme et incohérent de cerveaux moyens.  En
outre, nous avons en germe deux autres idées . . .: que Napoléon
avait été l'homme taillé pour cette tâche de reconstruction de
l'Europe après le cyclone de la Révolution; cette idée qu'un jour
il formulera par ces mots aujourd'hui dans toutes les bouches:  les
Etats-Unis d'Europe."

523.   Schneider, Erwin. "Victor Hugos Hernani in der Kritik eines
Jahrhunderts (1830-1930)." Romanische Forschungen 47 (1933):  1-146.

Examination of critical opinion on Hernani in France, Spain, Italy,
Germany and England through the centenary. Bibliography and critical
summaries quite helpful. In Schlusswort, Schneider resumes trends:
"Hernani ist in der Kritik eines Jahrhunderts als ein hohes
poetisches Stilkunstwerk anerkannt worder. . . . Sein positiv zu
wertender Gehalt liegt in seinem Charakter als Jugendwerk eines
grossen lyrischen Dichters begründet. . . . Hernani kann auf die
Dauer nur in Frankreich und ausserhalb Frankreichs nur in
französischer Sprache erfolgreich sein."

524. Schneider, Louis. "La Première d'Hernani." Le Temps, 26 févr. 1930, pp. 4-5.

Standard literary criticism and colorful anecdotes. Quotes some of lines most sifflés at première.

525. Séché, Léon. "La Reprise d'Hernani en 1867." La Grande Revue, année 16, t. 74 (1912): 296-310.

Through Mme. Hugo's letters to exiled husband and contemporary reviews, Séché reconstructs triumphant reprise. Empress Eugénie behind project of mounting play for Exposition Universelle. Most interesting quotations come from Francisque Sarcey's review. He admires "les beaux vers et la langue lyrique, mais était-ce bien du théâtre?" he wonders.

526. Sénart, Philippe. "Hernani (Comédie-Française)." La Nouvelle Revue des Deux Mondes, déc. 1974, pp. 691-93.

Voices opinion that Hernani won no real victory: "Hugo n'est arrivé que pour occuper le terrain et consolider des positions déjà conquises. Il a passé la revue, après la victoire des autres." Accuses Hossein of being too restrained and calculating in his production: "Malheureusement, ainsi assagi, ainsi régularisé, Hernani paraît un peu figé." Yet there is still a saving grace in play: "Il reste pourtant dans ce spectacle le merveilleux air de poésie du cinquième acte."

527. Shipley, Joseph T. Guide to Great Plays. Washington: Public Affairs Press, n.d. [1956]. (Hugo, pp. 322-25.)

Includes only Hernani and Ruy Blas. Offers snappy résumé of plot, bataille, press reaction and revivals. Evaluation emphasizes plays' poetic value: "Dynamic in mouvement, superb in the vivid rhetoric of its verse, Hernani opened the French theatre to the romantic drama; it remains an outstanding example of the type. . . . [Ruy Blas], though summary in its psychological development, is stark and strong in its emotional appeal, and one of the most striking of romantic melodramas in the amplitude and verve of its lyric outpouring, the power and beauty of its poetic form."

528. Souriau, Maurice. "La Bataille d'Hernani." La Vie Intellectuelle, année 3, t. 6 (janv. 1930): 210-22.

Best article, with that of Jasinski (476), of this centenary year on Hernani. After brief discussion of "la légende" of the bataille and première, Souriau recounts "la manoeuvre d'Hernani," stressing important rôle of politics in the play's campaign. Emphasizes also "classique" journalist Armand Carrel's influence on Hugo. Indicates that victory was not really won by Hugo until the 1867 reprise. Offers own view of the play's lasting value: "Le drame sifflé en 1830, démoli par Carrel, applaudi en 1867 contre l'Empire, maintenant s'impose aux critiques les plus sourcilleux et enflamme toujours le coeur des jeunes, des poètes."

529. Spinelli, Louis. "La Bataille à Marseille." Le Soleil (Marseille), 25 févr. 1930.

530. Stock, P.-V. "Des Contrats entre auteurs et éditeurs." Le Mercure de France 233 (1er févr. 1932): 622-30.

Details of Hugo's contract for Hernani indicate that Hugo had good business sense. Stock says Hugo's most famous and widely circulated works in his lifetime never made much money for the publishers.

531. Stocker, Leonard. "Hugo's Hernani and Verdi's Ernani." Southern Quarterly 8 (July 1970): 357-81.

Solid comparison of the two lyrical masterpieces. Says Verdi "probably attracted to Hernani by its strong characters and its powerful dramatic situations." Piave changed the play in his libretto to adapt it to dominant musical pattern: "Piave retained Hugo's three themes but changed many details of plot. . . . In adapting the play, Piave lost most of Hugo's literary values through translation, condensation, and ineptitude." Hugo so displeased with the opera as "crude treatment" of his tragedy that he insisted title and character names be changed (to Il Proscritto) for 1846 Paris performance. Stockard finds both authors "share a common gift for lyrical expression," though they employ different media. See also Stringham (533).

532. Stremoukhoff, D. "Témoignages russes sur Victor Hugo." L'Information Littéraire, no. 3 (mai-juin 1952), pp. 95-101.

General article showing Hugo as "un des écrivains préférés de la Russie." However, Turgenev, living in Paris during height of romantic theatre, did not think much of Hugo as a dramatist in Hernani: "Alexandre Tourguénev, lui aussi, semble s'intéresser bien plus aux parodies qu'à la pièce elle-même, tout en admettant plus tard que le talent de Mlle Mars cache les défauts d'Angélo."

533. Stringham, Scott. "Giuseppe Verdi and Victor Hugo: Some Notes on the Transformation of Hernani into Ernani." West Virginia University, Philological Papers 18 (Sept. 1971): 42-50.

Shows changes Verdi made in creating this most effective opera. Extremely compressed action makes libretto incomprehensible without pre-reading, Stringham notes: "The irrational behavior and reactions of characters in Hugo's play become positively lunatic in the opera." Verdi eliminates humor from play and has only Hernani die at end, which author thinks "an improvement on Hugo's original." Concludes: "Verdi transformed a great play into a great opera." See also Stocker (531).

534. Tanquerey, F. J. "Pousset de Montauban et Victor Hugo." La Revue d'Histoire Littéraire de la France 43 (avril-juin 1936): 289-90.

In Act III, scene 4 of "une comédie assez médiocre de Pousset de Montauban: Les Aventures et le Mariage de Panurge," Tanquerey discovers "certaines énumérations pseudo-héroïques de Victor Hugo, spécialement la scène des portraits d'Hernani." Says it is

definitely only coincidence and not influence, since Aventures was
in manuscript form only at the time of Hernani's composition.

535. Thomas, Louis-Jacques. La Bataille d'Hernani à Montpellier
(avril-mai 1830). Montpellier: Causse, Graille et Castelnau, 1930.
Pp. 60.

Through contemporary documents Thomas traces the bataille d'Hernani
in Montpellier. It was largely "de plume" without much "éclat,"
and the event caused few ripples: "C'est que ce pays n'est pas de
tempérament romantique. . . . A Montpellier, cette bataille mit aux
prises . . . le public lui-même, de simples bourgeois curieux de
bonnes lettres, qui avaient bien d'autres soucis, et plus sérieux,
que la rivalité de deux écoles littéraires." See also Fourcassié
(143).

536. Thompson, Howard. "Stage: Hernani Thrills at Open Eye." New
York Times, 2 Aug. 1974, p. 14.

Favorable review of revival of Hernani, first performance of it in
New York for 103 years, by the Gamma troupe, directed by Albert
Takazauckas. Finds the Off Off Broadway production "a small miracle
of crisply vivid, compelling theater, when every word counts."
Characterizes play as "a courtly melodrama of love, lust, intrigue
and fatal, ironclad honor, marked by tightly stitched construction
and vibrant, poetical language. Portions sound almost
Shakespearean. . . ."

537. Touchard, Pierre-Aimé, ed. Le Drame romantique. Choix établi
avec une préface et des notices. 3 vols. [Evreux]: Cercle du
bibliophile, n.d. [1969]. (Hugo, II, 9-158, 293-450.)

Includes complete text of Hernani and Ruy Blas. Introductory essay
to each play contains literary history and editor's personal views.
Underscores puerility of Hernani and seems to think it incapable of
being mounted on modern stage, yet praises play's beauty in reading:
"J'ai été une fois de plus entraîné, charmé, vaincu par ce
ruissellement d'images, cette splendeur du vers, ce mouvement de
jeunesse irrésistible." In Ruy Blas, Touchard criticizes especially
the poor characterization of its "personnages de mélodrame" and
Hugo's summary tableau of decadent Spanish monarchy. Finds that
"le véritable intérêt de la pièce est pour nous dans ce qu'elle a
d'involontairement classique, c'est-à-dire de rigoureux dans san
construction." Says the 1960 Rouleau reprise at the Comédie-
Française just shows how much the play "parut avoir vieilli."

538. Treille, Marguerite. Le Conflit dramatique en France de 1823 à
1830, d'après les journaux et les revues du temps. Paris: Picart,
1929. Pp. 180.

1929 Ph.D. dissertation at University of Wisconsin. Through articles
of such critics as Charles Magnin, Pierre Dubois, Philarète Chasles
and Duvicquet, Treille recaptures varying opinions current during
this important period. First chapter on theatrical censorship quite
informative about Hugo's struggles with it. Last chapter good on

press reception of Hernani and meaning of play's acceptance: "Après Hernani le drame est définitivement reconnu comme oeuvre littéraire. . . ."

539. Tronquart, G. "Le Vers 1028 d'Hernani." L'Ecole Vosgienne, année 22, no. 1 (1953-1954): 19-20.

Marshals strong argument to show that doña Sol's famous "Vous êtes mon lion superbe et généreux" is not "un péché de jeunesse" but rather a line which "s'accorde bel et bien avec la vision cosmique que le poète se faisait de son héros."

540. Truffier, Jules. "Le Théâtre romantique." Conferencia 22 (20 janv., 5 mars, 5 mai 1920): 161-71, 330-42, 520-34.

Three of ten lectures with illustrative scènes commentées on beauties and flaws of Romantic theatre. Above articles talk about Hernani, Lucrèce Borgia and Ruy Blas, respectively. In presentation of last play, Truffier stresses musicality of Hugo's language and verses and his brilliant comic gift as seen in Act IV: "C'est un comique tout particulier qui résulte tout entier de la sonorité de l'alexandrin et du contraste de cette sonorité avec l'idée exprimée par les vers ou les mots employés par lui."

541. Ubersfeld-Maille, Annie. "La Jeunesse d'Hernani." Comédie-Française 31 (sept. 1974): 11-12.

542. Van Tieghem, Philippe. "Avant et après Hernani." Les Nouvelles Littéraires, 12 avril 1930, p. 8.

Point of departure is Lote's book (488). Recreates ambiance of the première, then reviews Hugo's evolution as dramatist from "classique à la Boileau" to revolutionary in Hernani. Attention to press reaction and parodies. Van Tieghem poses modern judgement of the play as correct: "Mais nous sommes infiniment plus sensibles qu'eux à la poésie, qui sauve le drame à nos yeux. . . . Enfin Hugo nous revèle, outre sa sensibilité propre, ses ambitions personnelles; . . . il voulait être par la plume ce que Napoléon fut par l'épee."

543. Villeroy, Auguste. "Hernani ou le prestige de la poésie." La Revue française (16 oct. 1927).

544. Warren, F.-M. "Some Notes on Hernani." MLN 42 (Dec. 1927): 523-25.

Warren contends: "There is little in Hernani that may be traced to earlier plays." Then lists many "echoes" from such disparate sources as Andromaque, Polyeucte, Les Natchez, Voltaire's Adelaïde du Guesclin, Brutus and Nanine, Bossuet's sermon Sur les devoirs des rois, and Vigny's Le Cor.

545. Wedkiewicz, Stanislaw. "Victor Hugo et la Pologne. Contributions nouvelles." Académie polonaise des sciences et des lettres. Centre polonais de recherches scientifiques de Paris. Bulletin, no. 11 (mai 1953), pp. 76-83.

First two parts of article deal with Hernani's première "jugée par un témoin polonais" and with first Polish translation of Hernani. The Polish témoin writes that Hernani is "un monstre" in "mauvais goût et style atroce," yet his attendance at second performance allows him to see more beauty in the play. The 1830 Polish translation is in prose and better than mediocre, according to author. Best of the four translations of the play, however, were done by Joseph Conrad's father in 1862.

546. Williams, M. A. "A Precursor of Hernani." French Studies 13 (Jan. 1959): 18-25.

Locates in Anthony and Leopold's 1826 mélodrame, Le Corregidor, ou les contrebandiers, many resemblances with elements in Hernani. Since there is no proof that Hugo read or saw the play, author would explain similarities by "an almost unavoidable conformity to certain current trends dominating the literary world in that period, and especially by the conception of Spain common in France."

547. Worms, G. "Le Dernier Acte d'Hernani à la représentation d'adieu de Mme Baretta-Worms. Une lettre de M. Worms." Le Gaulois du dimanche, 25-26 janv. 1902, p. 7.

Mme. Baretta-Worms chose the famous acte d'adieux from Hernani as her last vehicle at the Comédie-Française. In this open letter, M. Worms remembers his role as don Carlos in the reprise of 1879. Accompanying illustrations good: Hugo's drawing of don Ruy's castle, sketches of Sarah Bernhardt and Mounet-Sully in the second and fifth acts.

548. Wright, C. H. Conrad. History of French Literature. London: Oxford University Press, 1912. (Hugo's theatre, pp. 682-707.)

Highly personal, often judicious criticism. Asserts mélodrame most successful contribution of nineteenth century to dramatic literature and Romantic drama only "an outgrowth or a passing phase" of it. Hugo's dramas deserve study today for their lyricism and their historical importance. Claims: "Hernani is an excellent example of Hugo's virtues and vices. It is a beautiful poem and a grotesque picture." Presents an amazing list of "echoes" he finds in Hernani, ranging from Dryden's Palomon to Hamlet. Hugo's plays offer "an ensemble of gorgeous pictures, of magnificent scenery and costumes, a swinging and sonorous verse, a series of startling episodes." However, to Hugo Wright still prefers Vigny for intellectual content, Musset for Shakespearean fantasy and Dumas for dramatic technique.

549. Yarrow, P. J. "Three Plays of 1829 or Doubts about 1830." Symposium 23 (Fall-Winter 1969): 373-83.

Revisionist criticism calling Hernani's traditional importance "exaggerated." Examines the three "victories" won by Romanticism in 1829 with Dumas' Henri III et sa cour, Casimir Delavigne's Marino Faliero and Vigny's More de Venise and suggests that "the significance of Hernani is a matter of personalities, not of principles, of form, not of substance."

## Le Roi s'amuse

550. Abram, Paul. "De Triboulet à Rigoletto: les incarnations d'un bouffon royal." Les Annales-Conférencia 75 (janv. 1968): 21-34.

Le Roi s'amuse continues to live only through Verdi's superior creation, Rigoletto, based on Hugo's drame. Complete story of play and opera given here; comparison of Piave's libretto shows it quite close to original. Hugo at first opposed to opera's performance in France, then liked it when finally persuaded to see it.

551. Alméras, Charles. "Deux Procès littéraires sous la monarchie de juillet--Le Roi s'amuse et La Revue des Deux Mondes. 1832-1833." La Croix, 4-5 févr. 1951, p. 4.

Really about the lawyer Odilon Barrot, who pleaded both cases. Hugo's suit to have ban on play lifted argued grandiloquently 19 déc. 1832 in courtroom packed as though for a première at the Théâtre Français. Quotations from the Gazette des Tribunaux making fun of lawsuit show that "au début, le romantisme était raillé par des partis de gauche." Hugo loses suit but remains grateful to Barrot. See also Cadroy below.

552. Austruy, Henri. "Le Roi s'amuse." La Nouvelle Revue, sér. 3, t. 21 (1er juin 1911): 425-27.

Author has overwhelming praise for reprise of play at Comédie-Française: "nos maîtres d'aujourd'hui ne peuvent qu'applaudir à ces pages éloquentes et fougueuses où les excès du pouvoir absolu semblent être le thème de la pièce." Says Hugo did not mean play to be satiric but rather "humaine." In evaluating cast, Austruy approves Mounet-Sully's François I and suggests that, although too athletic in build, M. Silvain reveals well Triboulet's soul.

553. Bertaut, Jules. "La Première de Le Roi s'amuse." La Revue des Deux Mondes, sér. 8, t. 12 (15 nov. 1932): 431-43.

Discusses in detail colorful, "political" première of this play to celebrate its centenary. Play generally recognized as inferior and disapproved: "L'interdiction de la pièce, provoquée par le gouverne-ment, devint même la défaite honorable, souhaitée en secret par l'auteur et ses partisans, qui tira tout le monde d'embarras. . . . Une sorte de désapprobation générale saluait, pour la première fois, l'ouvrage d'un écrivain qui avait déjà été violemment attaqué."

554. Bidou, Henry. "Le Roi s'amuse." Le Journal des Débats, 24 juin 1911. (Also in his L'Année dramatique, 1911-1912, pp. 64-69. Paris: Hachette, 1912.)

Begins with quotation from Francisque Sarcey's completely negative review of 1882 reprise, indicating disappointment at eagerly-awaited second performance of play. Bidou reluctantly agrees with Sarcey's evaluation: "Ce texte spendide, que rien ne peut rayer ni changer, se trouve être précisément le plus prodigieux assemblage d'invraisemblances. Il résiste aux acteurs, et ne se plie pas à la vie. . . . Le rôle de Triboulet ne peut être joué."

555. Bordeaux, Henry. "Le Roi s'amuse." La Revue Hebdomadaire (24 juin 1911). (Also in his La Vie au théâtre, sér. 2, pp. 437-42. Paris: Librairie Plon, 1911.)

Cites essential fault in play as lack of psychology with no compensating factors such as Hernani's "fougue de jeunesse" or Les Burgraves' "magnifique poésie légendaire." Wonders why, then, performances are so well received by public this time. Offers as possible explanation that play is being presented as opera. Dislikes combined themes of democratic hatred of royalty and paternal love because Triboulet, he feels, is not "un personnage pathétique." Yet in character of François I, Bordeaux perceives "le premier chapitre des Châtiments."

556. Cadroy, Michel. "Une Plaidoirie de Victor Hugo." Actes de l'Académie Nationale des Sciences, Belles-lettres et Arts de Bordeaux, sér. 4, t. 15 (1955-1957): 101-08.

On Hugo's attempt to have ban on Le Roi s'amuse lifted legally. Event re-created through trial's inédits. See also Alméras above.

557. Daudet, Léon. "Reprise du Roi s'amuse." In his Fantômes et vivants. Souvenirs des milieux littéraires, politiques--de 1880 à 1905, pp. 121-27. Paris: Nouvelle Librairie Nationale, 1914.

Remembrance of the unsuccessful reprise of 1882 leads Daudet to evaluate Hugo's theatre as a whole: "La vérité est que son théâtre est la partie la plus caduque de l'oeuvre de Hugo. Lyrique et peu scénique, il a construit des drames grandiloquents, mais vides, avec des réminiscences de Shakespeare, sur lesquelles sont plaquées quelques effets contrastés et plats. . . . La vie est absente de ces enluminures, ainsi que le sens légendaire, historique, psychologique et politique. Il reste, ici et là, un chant mélodieux et noble. . . ."

558. Doumic, René. "Reprise de Le Roi s'amuse de Victor Hugo." La Revue des Deux Mondes, sér. 6, t. 3 (15 juin 1911): 929-35.

Another very unfavorable review. Doumic begins: "Je pense que la Comédie-Française a repris Le Roi s'amuse pour en finir, une bonne fois, avec cette méchante pièce." Of all of Hugo's dramas, he assesses this one as "le plus mauvais, . . . le plus pénible et le plus irritant." Outside of a few great verses, the play offers nothing but rhetoric and declamation. Triboulet is "artificiel, arbitraire, incohérent,--un monstre."

559. Du Bos, Maurice. "Le Roi s'amuse et son destin." Le Figaro, 19 nov. 1932, p. 6.

Strange history of this "médiocre mélodrame" traced for the centenary. Play seen as "l'oeuvre inférieure du répertoire dramatique de Hugo. . . ." Du Bos attributes its échec to several

causes, but thinks Romanticism's honeymoon with the public was
already ending in 1832.

560. Du Bos, Maurice. "Une Source inconnue des erreurs historiques du
Roi s'amuse." Le Mercure de France 240 (15 nov. 1932): 23-42.

Discovers in a popular novel, Les Deux Fous, of Paul Lacroix (le
bibliophile Jacob) Hugo's idea for the play and some of his
historical errors, especially modification of personalities of
Saint-Vallier and his son-in-law Louis de Brézé. See also Richer
(566).

561. Ernest-Charles, J. "Une Représentation du Roi s'amuse."
L'Opinion, année 2 (11 sept. 1909): 343-45.

Review of performance at Comédie-Française organized by Gustave
Simon. Author says première a flop, 1882 second performance
"exécrable," and this recent one a "douleureux effondrement." Why?
Play too prolix, melodramatic, puerile, full of "tout l'attirail
démondé." Bemoans the fact that Hugo has dominated the French stage
for sixty years, then ironically selects Rostand as just the young
playwright to throw off the yoke of the Romantic theatre.

562. Guichard, Léon. "Autour du Roi s'amuse." Le Lingue Straniere 14
(nov.-dic. 1965): 16-25.

Offers new information on play. First part identifies as among
play's sources Mélesville et Xavier's 1831 vaudeville Le Bouffon du
prince, Paul-Louis Courrier's 1821 Simple Discourse à l'occasion
d'une souscription pour l'acquisition de Chambord, and Goethe's
Marguerite as prototype for Blanche. In second part explains
different dates given for reading to committee at the Comédie-
Française and affirms from correspondence that Hugo did carefully
supervise rehearsals. Last section invalidates story from Victor
Hugo raconté that assassination attempt on the king helped create
échec of play. Guichard seems to be unaware of Lambert's fine
study below on this play.

563. Lambert, Françoise. Le Manuscrit du Roi S'amuse. Annales Littéraires de l'Université de Besançon, vol. 63. Paris: Les Belles
Lettres, 1964. Pp. 127.

Complete listing of manuscript variants from "le texte de l'édition
Ollendorff, dite de l'Imprimerie Nationale." Preceded by brief
explanation of method and procedure and an outstanding essay on
genesis of play. Appendices contain sketches, outline and notes, a
list of play's editions and their variants, and the reliquat of
inédits with manuscript. When taken with the Imprimerie Nationale
text, this work amounts to a critical edition. Although no literary
criticism is included per se, Lambert offers valuable glimpses into
Hugo's creative process. Her investigation of changes and errors
in the manuscript reveals a great deal about Hugo's techniques and
method of composition. A comparison of play's manuscript with that
of Les Contemplations shows a "nette continuité des méthodes de Hugo
entre 1832 et 1855." Book's format somewhat awkward, however, and
critical abbreviations obfuscating.

a) Journet. Revue d'Histoire Littéraire de la France 65 (oct.-déc. 1965): 709.
b) M[ilner]. L'Information Littéraire 18 (mars-avril 1966): 7-8.
c) Onimus. Revue des Sciences Humaines, n.s. fasc. 119 (juill.-sept. 1965): 454.

564. Lanson, Gustave. "Le Roi s'amuse." La Grande Revue, année 15 (juin 1911): 638-42.

Review of reprise. Says Hugo at his worst and falsest in this "vulgaire mélodrame . . . manqué." Glad public not taken in by its "absurdités, invraisemblances et artifices grossiers." Particularly rejects characters; Blanche is "un mannequin," Triboulet false and Hugo's mouthpiece, Saltabadil incoherent. Only in a few places do beautiful verses break through to relieve the terror that comes straight out of Perrault's tales. In Lanson's opinion the role of Triboulet is so bad that no one could do it well.

565. Péladan, Joséphin. "Victor Hugo et Le Roi s'amuse." Les Annales Romantiques 9 (1912): 129-35.

1911 reprise of play provoked this author to an investigation of Hugo's historical inaccuracies. Concludes: "Que Victor Hugo ait ignoré l'importance historique de Diane [de Poitiers], cela pourrait s'attribuer à une vue superficielle de l'histoire: mais il a calomnié François I, il a faussé sa physionomie." There follows an attempt to rehabilitate Lucretia Borgia from Hugo's slanderous defamation of her character in his play about her. Péladan closes by linking the historical distortions in both plays to the same dominating idea: "Le grand poète offre au peuple, au mauvais peuple, un tableau jacobin: Le Roi s'amuse et Lucrèce Borgia appartiennent au théâtre de la Révolution prolongée."

566. Richer, Jean. "Deux Lettres de Victor Hugo à Paul Lacroix: P. Lacroix, Vigny, Hugo--une source probable du Roi s'amuse." La Revue des Sciences Humaines, n.s. nos. 98-99 (avril-sept. 1960), pp. 199-201.

In letters Hugo tells Lacroix he has read latter's Deux fous. Richer concludes: "Il suffit de lire l'ouvrage de P. Lacroix pour constater qu'il fut très probablement une source du Roi s'amuse." See also Du Bos above.

567. Roz, Firmin. "Le Roi s'amuse de Victor Hugo." La Revue Bleue 37 (20 mai 1911): 633-35.

Kind words for Hugo's theatre, as whole. In Le Roi s'amuse, however, Roz finds that "toutes ses faiblesses s'y étalent, tous ses défauts y éclatent, et l'oeuvre manquée apparaît trop souvent comme une parodie du drame romantique en général, de la manière de Hugo en particulier. . . . Et il y a au fond du drame une prétention puérile, énorme." Poetically inferior to Hernani, Ruy Blas and Marion Delorme, this play lacks even historical truth. Yet the reprise does have value as a "document."

568. Trompeo, Pietro Paolo. "I capricci del pedante--La donna è mobile." Corriere d'informazione, 8-9 agosto 1955, p. 3.

On origin of François I's song from Le Roi s'amuse: "Souvent femme varie,/ Bien fol est qui s'y fie!" Traces idea of "varium et mutabile semper femina" from Vergil's Aeneid through François I to Tasso and Hugo and on to Piave's Rigoletto.

569. Tyler, Parker. "The Education of a Prince: The Elements in Drama." Prose 6 (Spring 1973): 185-215.

Sees Hugo in Le Roi s'amuse, Shakespeare in Troilus and Cresida and Calderón in La vida es sueño as "critics of the social crystallization which gave honor as a prerogative to the ruling caste and morality as opportunism to those beneath it." Finds François I prophesying "the reverse: the increased burden of tragedy which the love-frustration of the clown was to assume in the theatre and prose fiction." Narrow reading of play.

570. Ubersfeld-Maille, Annie. "Les Drames de Hugo: Structure et idéologie dans Le Roi s'amuse et Lucrèce Borgia." In Littérature et idéologies, pp. 162-67. Colloque de Cluny, no. 2. Paris: La Nouvelle Critique, 1970.

Examines Le Roi s'amuse and Lucrèce Borgia as a simultaneous "projet idéologique" imperiled by Hugo's techniques or "structures dramatiques." Hugo attempts to introduce "le peuple" into historical tragedy via le grotesque in Le Roi s'amuse and thus to unite lower class with audience of Comédie-Française composed of aristocratic and bourgeois élite. At the same time (summer of 1832) "Hugo cherche à 'remonter' le mélodrame" with Lucrèce Borgia, to be presented at semi-popular Théâtre Porte-Saint Martin. Again Hugo's instrument is le grotesque, this time through "le bon monstre," Lucrèce. Both attempts to "faire un théâtre à la fois théâtre populaire et théâtre de l'élite" fail for same reason, according to author: "Le grotesque, direct dans Le roi s'amuse, transposé dans Lucrèce, met en péril le sujet historique. C'est l'ensemble de l'idéologie bourgeoise libérale qui bascule dans le néant." Subject interesting, but article's jargon at times obfuscates its point.

## Lucrèce Borgia

571. Augustin-Thierry, A. "Le Centenaire de Lucrèce Borgia." Le Temps, 3 févr. 1933, p. 5.

On all circumstances involving composition and production of the play. Hugo's goals in it were revenge for ban on Le Roi s'amuse and propagation of his social ideas. It was quite popular, embodying "le goût et l'esthétique du jour." By later standards, however, Augustin-Thierry notes: "Ce n'est même pas une bonne pièce tout court. L'outrance des situations, l'exagération des caractères, la truculence ampoulée des tirades, font aujourd'hui sourire."

572. L'Avant-Scène 574 (1 nov. 1975).

Issue devoted to Silvia Monfort's production at Le Nouveau Carré of Lucrèce Borgia, presented earlier at the Avignon Festival. Comments by Monfort, Fabio Pacchioni, director, and Yoshihisa Taïra, composer.

573. Bell, Gerda. "Georg Büchner's Translations of Victor Hugo's Lucrèce Borgia and Marie Tudor." Arcadia 6 (1971): 151-74. (Shorter version published as "Traduttore-traditore? Some Remarks on Georg Büchner's Victor Hugo Translations." Monatshefte 63 [Spring 1971]: 19-27.)

Examines "how far Büchner's own personality becomes visible behind these translations." Finds two kinds of errors in them: misunderstanding of French words or phrases and too literal translations. Yet finds translator "improved" on original in several places to express his own personality: "Their [originals'] rhetorical eloquence has been toned down slightly and social or religious glosses of the German rebel have been slipped in. . . ." See also Furness below.

574. Bersaucourt, Albert de. "Un Procès de Victor Hugo." In his Etudes et recherches, pp. 408-45. Paris: Mercure de France, 1913.

Interesting account of Hugo's successful suit in 1842 against Etienne Monnier for having translated Donizetti's opera based on Lucrèce Borgia and against Bernard Latte for having published the French version. Previously Hugo had stopped performances of Donizetti's work at the Théâtre Italien in Paris. Hugo also wins appeal. Details of trial and arguments given here.

575. Du Bos, Maurice. "Lucrèce Borgia (2 févr. 1833)." Le Figaro, 8 févr. 1933, p. 5.

This play, Hugo's first uncontested and greatest popular success on stage, Du Bos names "le chef-d'oeuvre du mélodrame. . . ." and he adds: "Par ses caractères bien dessinés, son dialogue vif, ses mouvements pittoresques, son impulsion fébrile, Lucrèce Borgia, en dépit des invraisemblances, reste, même à la lecture, d'un attrait singulièrement fascinateur."

576. Dumur, Guy. "Lorenzaccio le petit." Le Nouvel Observateur, n.s. no. 3 (déc. 1964), p. 33.

On Raymond Rouleau's production of Lucrèce Borgia.

577. Funck-Brentano, Frantz. "Les Crimes de Lucrèce Borgia." La Revue Bleue, année 68 (4 oct. 1930): 577-83. (Also in his book Lucrèce Borgia, pp. 9-11. Paris: Editions Nouvelle Revue Critique, 1930.)

Contrast between portrayal of Lucrezia Borgia in Hugo's play and contemporary picture of her as sweet, innocent maiden started author's project to check contemporary historical sources on her character. Rejects Hugo's version and rehabilitates Lucrezia's reputation.

578.  Furness, N. A.  "Georg Büchner's Translations of Victor Hugo."
Modern Language Review 51 (Jan. 1956):  49-54.

Examines types of changes Büchner made in translating Lucrèce Borgia
and Marie Tudor.  Finds consistent reduction of degree of dramatic
tension through omission and modification of melodramatic elements
and also faulty rendering of numerous phrases.  Büchner disliked
mélo and did translations for money only.  Furness claims that
Büchner's versions employ dramatic technique nearer to modern taste
than that in Hugo's plays.  See also Bell above.


579.  Green, Julein.  "Journal sans date."  La Revue de Paris, année
56 (juin 1949):  3-13.

Short entry in Green's diary on 1948 reprise of Lucrèce Borgia.
Play "médiocrement jouée" as if actors were ashamed of "ce texte
aujourd'hui impossible."  Yet "toutes ces réserves faites, ce
mélodrame est amusant à voir."


580.  La Force, Le Duc de.  "Lucrèce Borgia, drame en trois actes . . .
et en vers de Victor Hugo."  La Revue des Deux Mondes, sér. 8, t. 31
(1er janv. 1936):  171-79.

Points out forty-nine perfect Alexandrines in the play's prose
dialogue, which he offers as proof that Hugo "abandonnait le vers
à regret."

581.  Martin du Gard, Maurice.  "Hugo en scène."  Les Nouvelles Littéraires, 1er juin 1935, p. 8.  (Also in his Harmonies critiques, pp.
131-37.  Paris: Editions du Sagittaire, n.d. [1936].)

On reprise at the Comédie-Française of Lucrèce Borgia, some parts
of which he finds laughable.  Stresses, however, importance of
theatre in Hugo's life.  General evaluation of plays: "On ne peut
vraiment pas accepter en bloc son oeuvre dramatique, sauf peut-être
les Deux Trouvailles de Gallus, qu'on joue rarement."

582.  Miard, Louis.  "Les Premières de Lucrèce Borgia de Victor Hugo
en Espagne et au Portugal."  Interférences 4 (juill.-déc. 1973):  47-62.

583.  Ortiz, Ramiro.  "Sull'influsso della Leyenda de los siete Infantes
de Lara su Lucrèce Borgia di Victor Hugo."  In Mélanges Drouhet.
Bucharest:  J. E. Toroutiu, 1940.

584.  Parrot, Jacques.  "Malgré ses 115 ans passés, Lucrèce Borgia
n'accuse aucune ride."  Les Lettres Françaises, no. 217 (1948).

585.  Pawlowski, Gaston de.  "Lucrèce Borgia."  Le Journal, 1er mars
1918.

586.  Poirot-Delpech, B.  "Lucrèce Borgia."  Le Monde, 30 oct. 1964,
p. 18.

Likes very much production at Vieux-Colombier:  "Il reste la
savoureuse audace d'avoir arraché le drame de Hugo à sa réputation
de mélo risible. . . .  Il était juste que l'auteur de la Préface de

Cromwell participât à sa manière à la célébration de son maître Shakespeare, et qu'il y participât si brillamment."

587. Poirot-Delpech, B. "Lucrèce Borgia au Festival du Marais." Le Monde, 27 juin 1964, p. 16.

Criticizes Lucrèce for not revealing to Gennaro her true identity, yet admires production's acting, directing and splendid setting, l'Hôtel de Soubise. Considers it a success: "Le public vient en foule retrouver ce théâtre sauvé de sa naïveté par le génie de l'excès et par une réalisation somptueuse."

588. Poizat, Alfred. "A propos de la reprise de Lucrèce Borgia au Théâtre-Français." Le Correspondant, année 90, t. 271 (10 avril 1918): 104-19.

Reprise of Lucrèce Borgia, "ce genre de pièces [qui] n'est guère l'affaire de ce théâtre," leads Poizat to criticize its tone, style and historical inaccuracies. A consideration of the rest of Hugo's theatre brings forth this evaluation: "Hernani, Ruy Blas et Les Burgraves, en dépit de leurs défauts, peuvent être considérés comme les trois plus originales et plus belles tragédies que notre théâtre ait produites depuis Racine. . . ."

589. Portal, Georges. "Couleur locale." Les Ecrits de Paris 235 (mars 1965), pp. 123-28.

Calls Lucrèce Borgia production at Vieux Colombier a "dégringolade." Compares Hugo very unfavorably to Musset. No hope for Hugo's plays: "La convention sommaire, enfantine et, pour tout dire, imbécile autant que mensongère, voilà sans doute le vice irrémédiable du théâtre hugolien."

590. Roux, François de. "Lucrèce Borgia à la Comédie-Française." L'Epoque, 6 juill. 1948, p. 2.

On a reprise at the Odéon. Lucrèce Borgia is "un simple mélodrame écrit par un homme de génie." Although "le théâtre actuel qui est ultra romantique méprise le mélodrame," still Hugo's play is not boring, and is worth putting on as a negative example: "Tous les drames d'Hugo . . . sont un exemple à ne pas essayer de suivre. Ils sont le témoignage d'une époque et d'une école littéraire qui eurent leur grandeur et qui ont renouvelé la sensibilité française. . . ."

591. Sénart, Philippe. "Lucrèce Borgia au Nouveau-Carré." La Revue des Deux Mondes (janv.-mars. 1976):181-82.

592. Sion, Georges. "Madam Lucrèce Borgia." La Revue Générale Belge, no. 12 (déc. 1965), pp. 119-22.

Sees November 1965 production by Compagnie des Galeries of Lucrèce Borgia as an attempt to renew the theatre, robbed of a positive vision of man by the théâtre de l'absurde. Yet Hugo is not the answer to the problem, at least not in Lucrèce.

593. Souday, Paul [P. S.]. "Au tripot comique. Lucrèce Borgia." Le Temps, 15 avril 1918.

Above information listed in Talvart et Place, Bibliographie des auteurs modernes de langue française, Vol. 9, p. 223. However, the article does not appear in the issue of Le Temps indicated.

594. Ubersfeld-Maille, Annie. "D'un commandeur à l'autre ou la chanson de Gubetta." Littérature 9 (févr. 1973): 74-85.

Comparison of first and final versions of song in Act V of Lucrèce Borgia. Hugo was forced to change Gubetta's song, "une sorte de condensé du grotesque dans tous ses niveaux de l'écriture," to save the play from official and audience censure. Heart of the scene was lost as a result: "Mais l'insigne platitude de la chanson substituée nous permet peut-être de saisir sur le vif comment la réécriture d'une séquence pourtant limitée--la microséquence chanson--met en péril l'ensemble d'une signification idéologique qui s'inscrit à tous les niveaux du texte. La déconstruction poétique emporte avec elle l'idéologie."

595. Vandérem, Fernand. "Lucrèce Borgia." La Revue de Paris, 15 avril 1918. (Also in his Le Miroir des lettres, I, 42-47. Paris: Flammarion, n.d. [1919].)

On reprise at Comédie-Française. Points out play's defects, yet demands more than "une indulgente déférence" toward it from critics since it is more than a mere mélo. Underscores play's importance to Hugo's destiny in bringing Juliette Drouet into his life.

## Marie Tudor

596. Beigbeder, Marc. "Séduction et fraîcheur de Marie Tudor." Les Lettres Françaises, 21-28 juill. 1955, pp. 1, 7.

597. Blanchard, Marc. Marie-Tudor: Essais sur les sources de la pièce avec des notes inédites de Victor Hugo. Paris: Boivin, 1934. Pp. 396.

Reproduces Catalogue de sources for Marie Tudor that Hugo published in 1837 and finds list too comprehensive since Hugo did not use all sources claimed. Review of criticism indicates that Hugo was often accused of plagiarism in the play, but Blanchard says Hugo was not guilty. Concludes: "Ne cherchons pas l'histoire: nous sommes dans la fantaisie. . . . Pourtant, ne nions pas l'histoire: la pièce est une création de l'imagination, à base de matériaux historiques." Exhaustive treatment. Good index and bibliography.
  a) Kurz. Romanic Review 25 (April 1934): 167-69.

598. Bocchi, Lorenzo. "Al Théâtre National Populaire. Jean Vilar, anno quinto, rispolvera Victor Hugo." Il Corriere Lombardo, 21-22 dic. 1955.

599. Bracker, Milton. "French Troupe in a Stunning Performance of Marie Tudor." New York Times, 22 Oct. 1958, p. 39.

Favorable review of T.N.P. production in French at Broadway Theatre. Special praise for Maria Casares as Marie, "but the triumph was basically collective. . . . It seems not too much to say that this was one of the best performances of classic theatre seen in New York in a decade."

600. Brisson, Adolphe. "Marie Tudor." Le Temps, 4 déc. 1916, p. 4.

On reprise at Odéon. Critic favorably views acting and production but has mixed feelings about play's text: L'audition de Marie Tudor, comme celle d'Angelo, précise ce malentendu entre l'idéal romantique et l'état d'âme actuel. . . . D'abord on est amusé. . . . L'oeuvre se soutient par la fougue de l'exécution, par le tourbillon des épisodes et l'éloquence enflammé du discours."

601. Decaunes, Luc. "Marie de la nuit." T.E.P. Actualité no. 66 (1970).

602. Descotes, Maurice. "A propos de la reprise de Marie Tudor." La Revue d'Histoire du Théâtre, 8, 4 (1956): 333-36.

Favorable review of Jean Vilar's production of play at T.N.P. Suggests Vilar manages "tour de force" of presenting this play, "avec Angelo la plus extravagante et la plus plate des oeuvres dramatiques de Victor Hugo," only by cutting out and changing the text so much that even Hugo would not have recognized it: "La leçon n'est pas nouvelle: le drame romantique est l'expression de la sensibilité et surtout du style très particulier d'une époque."

603. Dringenberg, Willibert. "Das Englandbild Victor Hugos." Geist der Zeit 18 (Nov. 1940): 672-86.

Examination of Hugo's conception of England in Marie Tudor and Cromwell. First play seen as artistically poorest and least important. Second judged more an historical study of Puritan England than a viable work for the stage. Asserts that Hugo emphasizes religion based on Old Testament vindictiveness rather than New Testament love in portraying Puritans.

604. Dubech, Lucien. "Marie Tudor." Candide, 21 juill. 1938, p. 15.

On the reprise. Indicates that reader or spectator must admire Hugo's genius, yet smile at his puerile dramatic techniques.

605. Du Bos, Maurice. "Juliette Drouet comédienne: à propos du centenaire de Marie Tudor." Le Mercure de France 248 (15 nov. 1933): 26-43.

The day after the première of Marie Tudor, Sainte-Beuve writes to Victor Pavie that Juliette Drouet played Jane so badly that Hugo was forced to take the role from her. Sympathetic article on her acting career.

606. Duvignaud, Jean. "Marie Tudor, mise en scène de Jean Vilar, avec le Théâtre Populaire, au 9e Festival d'Avignon." Théâtre Populaire, no. 14 (juill.-août 1955), pp. 84-86.

   Play called "inutile" by reviewer. Says T.N.P. should produce quality plays, not those of Hugo. Play appeals to public's confused passion for detective novel, critic claims, but movies fulfill this need better than Hugo's plays.

607. Filon, Augustin. "Les Drames de Victor Hugo et l'histoire d'Angleterre." Le Journal des Débats, 26 nov. 1902.

608. _____. "Marie Tudor." Le Journal des Débats, 24 déc. 1902.

609. Fitch, Girdler. "Favras and Hugo's Marie Tudor." MLN 55 (Jan. 1940): 24-30.

   Suggests Hugo saw Favras, an 1831 play of Merville and Sauvage, and changed the ending of his Marie Tudor as a result: "Nearly all the important elements of the latter part of Marie Tudor have proto-types of some sort in Favras. It is no exaggeration to say that Dumas' Christine plus Favras will account for so much of the plot of Marie Tudor that Hugo's contribution is less one of invention than of fusion, rearrangement, transference into another setting and expression in a richer style."

610. Hensel, Georg. "Hugo sehen und Georg Büchner hören. Hugos Maria Tudor übersetzt von Büchner, im Wiener Burgtheater." Frankfurter Allgemeine Zeitung für Deutschland, 2 Febr. 1977, p. 23.

611. Hill, Louis A. The Tudors in French Drama. Johns Hopkins Studies in Romance Literatures and Languages, vol. 20. Baltimore, Md.: Johns Hopkins Press, 1932. (Hugo's theatre, pp. 72-76, 85-88.)

   Considers Marie Tudor first, then Amy Robsart. Shows the plays' flaws, especially the not very true-to-life picture of monarchs, and implies that this is one reason for the dramas' lack of success.

612. Lièvre, Pierre. "Marie Tudor." Le Mercure de France 286 (15 août 1938): 169-70.

   Review of the reprise at the Arènes de Lutèce of this "mélodrame extraordinaire." Talks largely about Juliette Drouet's brief acting career.

613. Schneider, Louis. "Le Centenaire de Marie Tudor." Le Temps, 7 nov. 1933, p. 4.

   Recounting of the première, popular acclaim and bad press. 1873 reprise not very successful. Schneider likes and quotes the Jew's song and that of Fabiani. Concludes: "En vérité, Marie Tudor n'est inférieure aux autres oeuvres que parce que c'est un drame en prose."

614. Triolet, Elsa. "Plus fort que le peuple." Les Lettres Françaises, no. 506 (1955).

## Angelo, tyran de Padoue

615. Aderer, Adolphe. "Angelo." Le Temps, 3 févr. 1905, p. 2. (Also in his Hommes et choses de théâtre, pp. 47-51. Paris: Calmann-Lévy, 1905.)

Revival of play by Sarah Bernhardt after fifty-five years of neglect. Aderer noncommittal on play's worth. Stresses excellent actresses who have played in it. Its 1835 popular, not critical, success due to acting duel between Mlle Mars (La Tisbé) and Mlle Dorval (Catarina). In 1850 Rachel's début in Romantic rôle as La Tisbé and her younger sister as Catarina well received at Théâtre-Français. Sarah Bernhardt excellent as La Tisbé. She puts back into play on-stage murder of spy Homodei that Hugo was forced to cut out for première in 1835.

616. Ambrière, Francis. "Les Cent Ans d'Angelo, tyran de Padoue." Le Mercure de France 259 (15 avril 1935): 405-11.

Article for the play's centenary. "Le pire drame de Victor Hugo" draws interest solely because of the battle between actresses Marie Dorval and Mlle Mars, who originally created rôles of Catarina and La Tisbé: "En somme, Angelo, tyran de Padoue, ne mérite plus de vivre dans la mémoire des hommes autrement que par le pittoresque de ses à-côtes." See also P.V.S. below.

617. "Angelo au théâtre." Le Gaulois du dimanche, supplément hebdomadaire littéraire et illustré, 18-19 févr. 1905, pp. 1-2.

Entirely devoted to reprise at Théâtre Sarah Bernhardt. Excellent photos of scenery, actors, Hugo. Facsimiles of pertinent letters. Quotations from Hugo, Victor Hugo raconté, Auguste Vacquerie, Théophile Gautier.

618. Borer, Alain. "Le Traître mot." Romantisme 19 (1978): 90-93.

This structural analysis of Angelo finds that "la 'puissance' de la mise en scène réside ici moins dans la représentation des personnages que dans les figures géométriques." Two patterns are identified: "Alors que la circulation 'actantielle' reproduit les schémas du théâtre classique, c'est encore dans les diagonales que ce drame infiltre des éléments romantiques et politiques, à travers le conflit hommes-femmes. . . ."

619. Brisson, Adolphe. "Angelo, tyran de Padoue." Le Temps, 9 févr. 1905, p. 1.

This well known theatrical reviewer has reserved praise for Angelo: "L'impression qu'éveille cet ouvrage chez les spectateurs d'aujourd'hui est des plus singuliers. D'abord on est amusé . . . On l'écoute avec stupéfaction, mais sans ennui. [La pièce] porte, malgré tout, la souveraine empreinte du génie."

620. Crump, Phyllis. "Victor Hugo's Italian Plays." French Quarterly 4 (juin 1922): 107-24.

Drawn from her M.A. thesis at University of London in 1919.  In first section on genesis and sources of Lucrèce Borgia and Angelo, tyran de Padoue, Crump identifies both historical and literary sources.  In second part dealing with Hugo's method of using sources, she concludes that Hugo depends little on historical fact, which furnishes only background, atmosphere, local color.  Literary predecessors, however, offer parallel for almost every important scene.  Yet, she asserts, "the lyrical qualities, . . . the symbolical representation of a noble idea and the author's wonderful 'flair' for a dramatic situation, all these and other qualities raise the Italian plays above the rank of contemporary melodrama, and at times bring them to the level of real tragedy."

621.  De Carli, Antonio.  L'Italia nell'opera di Victor Hugo.  Turin: Chiantore, 1930.  (Hugo's theatre, pp. 18-38.)

Tries to demonstrate Hugo's ignorance of Italy, her language and literature.  Insists that Hugo did not use sources he claims for Lucrèce Borgia and Angelo.  Author attempts to rehabilitate Lucrezia Borgia and repair slanderous prejudices apparent in the plays: "Nella descrizione della vita italiana, publica e privata, in quel depravato cinquecento, l'immaginazione dell 'Hugo si sbizzarrisce fino al punto da rasentare l'allucinazione. . . . Il suo lavoro è accampato in aria; gli manca un solido fondamento storico. . . ."

622.  Doumic, René.  "Angelo."  La Revue des Deux Mondes, sér. 5, 25 (15 févr. 1905):  932-33.

Excoriating review of 1905 production:  "Effort doublement malheureux d'un grand poète pour s'abaisser aux inventions des plus vulgaires dramaturges et d'un dramaturge inférieur pour se hausser aux conceptions d'un penseur."  Angelo worse than all other dramas of Hugo except, perhaps, Lucrèce Borgia and Marie Tudor.

623.  Faguet, Emile.  "Victor Hugo:  Angelo, tyran de Padoue."  Le Journal des Débats, 13 févr. 1905.  (Also in his Propos de théâtre, sér. 3, pp. 240-47.  Paris:  Société française d'imprimerie et de librairie, 1906.)

Very intelligent article.  Gives play's history and importance in Hugo's dramatic career.  Stresses his desire for popular success in Angelo, which Faguet calls "la littérature dramatique industrielle, . . . le type même, ramassé et synthétique, de tous les défauts et de tous les ridicules du romantisme populaire de l'époque. . . ."  Faguet praises Sarah Bernhardt and her "reprise assez brilliante" of unfortunate Angelo, "qui a paru presque à tout le monde prodigieusement ridicule."

624.  Hérold, A. Ferdinand.  "Angelo, tyran de Padoue."  Le Mercure de France 54 (1er mars 1905):  130-32.

Another unfavorable review of the reprise.  Even Sarah Bernhardt's great talent not enough to redeem the play.  Hérold tells circumstances of composition and original production.  In an interesting presentation of the play's sources and influence, he cites Spanish

traits in the play and two Italian operas based on it, il
Giuramento (1837) and La Gioconda (1876). Dislikes reinserted death
scene of Homodei.

625. Jullien, Jean. "Angelo au Théâtre Sarah-Bernhardt." La Revue
Universelle 5 (7 févr. 1905): 129-30.

Favorable review. Jullien defends Hugo's play in attributing its
weaknesses to "le goût de la foule" of 1835. Plot summary and
précis of preface provided. Concludes: "Le canevas sur lequel le
génie du maître broda les arabesques de ce drame fantasque montre
les ressources surprenantes de sa prodigieuse imagaination."

626. Mendès, Catulle. "Angelo, tyran de Padoue." Le Journal, 8 févr.
1905, p. 3.

High praise from one poet for another in this review: "Dans ce
pittoresque, parfois excessif et fantasque, toujours saisissant,
toujours amusant, dans ce romanesque, parfois chimérique, toujours
intéressant, émouvant, poignant drame, il y a le vrai amour, la
vraie passion, la vie, le drame, la beaute! il y a, parmi la
splendeur de la mise en scène et le charme musical des danses, le
plus grand des poètes interprété par la plus grande des
comédiennes."

627. Patin, Jacques. "Sur un exemplaire d'Angelo." Le Figaro, 21 mars
1931, pp. 5-6.

Original edition to be sold contains four manuscript letters about
the work: three either to or from Marie Dorval about a role in the
play; one from Delphine Gay, thanking Mme. Hugo for tickets and
praising the performance.

628. S., P. V. "Les Cent Ans d'Angelo, tyran de Padoue." Le Mercure
de France 260 (15 mai 1935): 216-17.

In response to Ambrière's article above asking for information on
Auguste Jouhaud, author of a parody of Angelo, tyran de Padoue.

629. Sardou, Victorien. "Le Cas Angelo: l'opinion de M. Victorien
Sardou." Le Figaro, 13 févr. 1905, p. 4.

This dramatist considers the general question of whether or not one
should change the work of a deceased author to put it on stage.
Specific case involves Homodei death scene, which Hugo cut from
Angelo's 1835 première and which Sarah Bernhardt replaced in her
version. Sardou not in favor of change: "En effet, le grand mérite
d'Angelo c'est la rapidité de l'action qui, une fois lancée, ne
s'arrête plus et rebondit, de coup de théâtre en coup de théâtre.
. . ." Reinserted death scene causes unfortunate break in pace.
Works should always be left as they are, he asserts.

630. Thouvenin, Jean. "La Reprise d'Angelo." Les Annales Politiques
et Littéraires, année 23 (12 févr. 1905): 106.

Even the great Sarah Bernhardt cannot save this "mélo à la
Pixerécourt" from seeming démodé today, according to Thouvenin.
Finds it too transparent to be chilling and calls it "un succès de
curiosité dû à l'évocation d'une époque disparue."

## La Esmeralda

631. Croze, J. L. "La Esmeralda de Victor Hugo et de Louise Bertin."
Le Temps, 7 déc. 1937.

On centenary of Hugo's opera libretto.

632. P., J. G. "A propos de La Esmeralda de Victor Hugo." Le Mercure
de France 275 (15 avril 1937):  446.

On a lettre inédite from Hugo to Paul de Saint-Victor, thanking him
for favorable comments on Notre-Dame de Paris in his article on
Lebeau's Esmeralda, an opera based on Hugo's libretto.

633. Tiersot, Julien. "La Esmeralda (Centenaire)." La Revue Musicale
17 (déc. 1936):  389-405.

Offers a complete, interesting history of the unsuccessful opera.
Analysis of Hugo's libretto, "une suite de tableaux," partially
reveals reasons for failure: "A une epoque où, dans l'opéra, l'air
était tout, il en est réduit ici à presque rien. . . . Par surcroît,
le poète avait adopté une forme de versification rare et bien digne
de lui, mais très peu favorable à la musique."

## Ruy Blas

634. Atkinson, Brooks. "Theatre:  Ruy Blas." New York Times, 14 Dec.
1957, p. 16.

Unfavorable review of performance of J. D. Cooper's adaptation,
directed by Andrew Szekely, at the Royal Playhouse: "Ruy Blas is
more interesting as a phenomenon than a play, and Hugo is more
interesting as a historical figure than a dramatist."

635. Bainville, Jacques. "Un Compte rendu de Ruy Blas." L'Action
Française, 9 nov. 1913. (Also in his Une Saison chez Thespis, pp.
88-90. Paris: Editions Prométhée, 1929.)

Reviewer has just attended performance of Ruy Blas where plot
summary in program form was handed to spectators upon arrival.
Bainville complains about this insult to his intelligence: "Ruy
Blas est quelque chose d'un peu bête. Mais tout de même! . . .
Voilà où en est le public."

636. Baldick, Robert. "Frédérick Lemaître à l'heure de Ruy Blas."
Le Figaro Littéraire, 5 nov. 1960, p. 11.

History of Hugo's play, emphasizing importance of great actor in
its creation. Lemaître had expected to play comic rôle of don César
because of character-typing from his rôle as Robert Macaire. He
was overjoyed at breadth allowed him in the new rôle; he even
helped to rewrite certain scenes in the play. Baldick attributes
play's success, as did contemporary press, to Lemaître's great
acting. Interesting focus, but unbalanced view of the play.

637. Barrère, Jean-Bertrand. "Victor Hugo, Ruy Blas, eux et nous."
In Ruy Blas, pp. 5-10. Etabli par S. Chevalley. Paris: S.I.P.E.,
1960. (Also as avant-propos to Victor-Marie Hugo, Ruy Blas, pp. 4-6.
Présenté par Francis Lafon. Paris: Didier, 1966.)

Intelligent introduction to work, giving important details of
inspiration, sources, composition and keen analysis of play's worth:
"Chaque acte donne un échantillon de son talent: le premier,
d'intrigue; le second, élégiaque; le troisième, historique et
politique; le quatrième, comique et fantasque; le cinquième, qui
les unit tous, poignant d'espoir et d'anxiété jusqu'à l'explosion
finale qu'attendrit une dernière touche d'idylle." Because Ruy
Blas is least rhetorical and most human of Hugo's dramas, Barrère
suggests it is also apparently the most successful.

638. Bart, B. F. "Ruy Blas, IV, 7." MLN 68 (Dec. 1953): 549-51.

Examines changes Hugo made even after the première in lines of
don César describing duègne: ". . . affreuse compagnonne,/ Dont
la barbe fleurit et dont le nez trognonne." Finds: "The line
became a weapon in a minor quarrel with the two grammarians and
critics, Trognon and Cuvillier-Fleury."

639. Barthes, Roland. "Ruy Blas, mise en scène Jean Vilar, avec le
Théâtre National Populaire." Le Théâtre Populaire, no. 6 (mars-avril
1954), pp. 93-95.

Scathing review of the play, which Barthes finds totally unworthy
of being staged at the T.N.P. He cannot see Ruy Blas "sans être
emporté par un sentiment irrésistible de dérision. Ce théâtre ne
supporte plus que la parodie." Says, furthermore, that the play is
dangerous in that it can lead "un public mal armé à confondre les
signes extérieurs du théâtre et le théâtre lui-même. . . ."

640. Bauër, Gérard. "Ce soir, Ruy Blas." In Ruy Blas, pp. 3-4.
Etabli par S. Chevalley. Paris: S.I.P.E., 1960.

Quotes his article (below) on 1938 reprise of Ruy Blas. Adds that
although twenty-two years have passed, neither his feelings nor
tastes have changed: he still finds the play a delight. Praises
actors and scenery of 1960 production.

641. _____. [Guermantes]. "Ruy Blas à la Comédie-Française."
Le Figaro, 23 mai 1938, p. 5.

On play's centenary reprise at the Comédie-Française. Loves Ruy
Blas even though it is accused of being dated. Admits faults and

that "le goût n'y serait plus." Praises M. Yonnel's "fougue romantique" in title role.

642. Beerbohm, Sir Max. "Ruy Blas." In his Around Theatres, II, 394-96. New York: Alfred A. Knopf, 1930.

On the London production 20 February 1904 of John Davidson's adaptation of Ruy Blas, A Queen's Romance. Finds Romantic drama "depressing" when stripped of "its proper romantic trappings." Language barrier cited: "There is no means of truly conveying into English the spirit of Ruy Blas, just as there is no possible synonym in our vocabulary for the word 'panache.'"

643. Benedetti, Mario. L'Estetica romantica nel Ruy Blas di Vittor Hugo. Perugia: Tip. Guerra, 1912. Pp. 38.

Scathing attack on Romantic aesthetic as applied to drama and best exemplified in Ruy Blas. Many pages concerned with impossible psychology of the hero. Good words only for Act IV as true to life. Benedetti attacks especially Hugo's conception of life. Only element he admires is play's democratic spirit: "Ma il fatto che questo popolarismo sia l'unico motivo riuscito, è la riprova che all'autore, nel momento di soffiare nella gran tromba tragica, è mancato il fiato: e il lirismo dei particolari non salva il tutto dalla meritata condanna." Essay with few divisions and no index. Many complaints lodged against "new" aesthetic principles resemble those of Lasserre (208).

644. Brisson, Adolphe. "Remarques sur Ruy Blas." Le Temps, 17 juin 1918, p. 3.

Reprise elicits great enthusiasm from this reviewer: "De tous les drames de Victor Hugo, celui-ci est le plus vivant, et sans doute le moins rapidement périssable. . . . L'aventure de Ruy Blas peut encore exprimer symboliquement la disproportion entre nos moyens et nos désirs, l'essor de l'homme . . . tenté par un grand dessein, . . . l'écroulement de ses illusions, sa chute et sa mort."

645. Bruner, James D. "The Characters in Victor Hugo's Ruy Blas." Sewanee Review 14 (July 1906): 306-23. (Also in his Studies in Victor Hugo's Dramatic Characters, pp. 32-94. Boston: Ginn & Co., 1908.)

Same type of character analysis as for Hernani (422). Finds Ruy Blas's behavior difficult to interpret. He, like Hernani, Bruner finds, is prey to "morbid melancholy" caused by the "fatality" of his situation. His "lyrical nature" and "religious nature" make him sympathetic to us. Bruner points out in an interesting section Hugo's use of disguises and antithesis to indicate "real character" and "assumed character." Bruner's theory of Ruy Blas's "infatuation" with don Salluste to explain the former's puzzling actions is expanded in article described below (646). See also (98).

646. _____. "The Infatuation of Ruy Blas." MLN 21 (June 1906): 162-66.

Ruy Blas does not kill don Salluste or have him arrested, because the hero is literally under the villain's spell. Bruner claims: "The central thought of this explanation is the suggestion that the will and intellect of Ruy Blas have been infatuated by the powerful personality and fascinating presence of his villainous master, Don Salluste." Theory based on Act III, scene v. Compares this process of conquest by fascination to that used by Shakespeare in King Richard III and Antony and Cleopatra. Less felicitous examples from "real life" add nothing to this unconvincing argument for hypnotism as motivation.

647. Bryuelle, Roland. "Le Théâtre de Victor Hugo: l'histoire, less caractères, et le drame dans Ruy Blas et Hernani." La Nouvelle Revue Pedagogique, année 6 (1er janv., 1er, 15 févr. 1952): 1-3 in each.

Defends Hugo's two Spanish plays in discussing prefaces, characters, form. Much attention to "sublime et grotesque," especially in Ruy Blas, "le mieux écrit et le mieux versifié" of all Hugo's plays. At end presents disjointedly version of Mithridate, "mise sous forme de drame romantique."

648. Cam, Francis. "En marge de Ruy Blas." Les Paroles Françaises, année 2 (8 août 1947): 4.

On parodies of Hugo's play. Says they are among the most pene- trating and "distrayantes" of the genre, if not wittiest. Asserts poetic value of Hugo's plays will continue to be appreciated but that other aspects are weaker: "Mais c'est surtout dans ses drames que Hugo prêta le flanc à de faciles plaisanteries par ses exagéra- tions et ses invraisemblances de toute nature."

649. Camp, André. "Ruy Blas vu par Raymond Rouleau." L'Avant-Scène, no. 232 (1er déc. 1960), p. 42.

On reprise at Comédie-Française. Finds drame "poussiéreux." Yet finds poetry still beautiful: "Or, Raymond Rouleau a su vêtir les vers de Hugo de somptueuse façon. . . . Ceci dit, Ruy Blas . . . est un fort beau spectacle."

650. Chaine, Pierre. Ruy Blas 38. Pièce en 4 actes d'après "Jean" de Bris Fekete, précédée de Ruy Blas centenaire, avant-propos fantaisiste. Paris: L'Illustration, 1938. Pp. 30. (Also in La Petite Illustration, no. 889 [24 sept. 1938].)

Avant-propos is one-act gentle parody. Ruy Blas 38 is four-act comedy put on 6 March 1938 in Paris at the Théâtre de l'humour.

651. Charensol, G. "Le Cinéma. Ruy Blas." Les Nouvelles Littéraires, 26 févr. 1948, p. 8.

Review of Cocteau's film, which he finds a totally different work from Hugo's play: "Cette tentative, pour doter le drame romantique de sentiments et d'un langage modernes . . . se solde par un échec. . . . Ruy Blas est un beau, un magnifique spectacle. On peut regretter qu'il ne soit que cela mais il est impossible de ne pas s'y plaire."

652. Chevalley, Sylvie. "Les Interprètes de Ruy Blas." In her Ruy Blas, pp. 39-45. Paris: S.I.P.E., 1960.

Reviews and judges all French actors and actresses who starred in title rôle, from Frédérick Lemaître through Sarah Bernhardt to modern actors. Discusses also lesser rôles of don Salluste and don César. States that Hugo originally wanted "deux Frédérick Lemaître" for rôles of both Ruy Blas and don César. See also Baldick above.

653. _____. "Les Parodies de Ruy Blas." In her Ruy Blas, pp. 25-28. Paris: S.I.P.E., 1960.

Considers ten parodies of Hugo's play from Maxime de Redon's 1838 Ruy-Brac to Albert Chanay's 1904 Guignol Ruy Blas. Suggests that their function was that of "bouffon du roi" and they represent "la rançon du succès." Claims Hugo was particularly susceptible to parody because of the lack of naturalness and human simplicity in his dramatic characters and the invraisemblance of his intrigue.

654. _____, ed. Ruy Blas. Monographie établie à l'occasion de la reprise du 2 novembre 1960 (809e représentation). Paris: S.I.P.E., 1960.

Mme. Chevalley, bibliothécaire-archiviste de la Comédie-Française, compiled articles in this volume to celebrate the play's 809th performance at the Comédie-Française. Monograph also includes iconography; quotations from Mme. d'Aulnoy's Mémoires de la cour d'Espagne, Victor Hugo raconté, and Zola's 1879 article in Le Voltaire on poetry of Ruy Blas; Henri de Régnier's poem "En relisant Ruy Blas"; a series of amusing anecdotes; and a list of all Hugo plays and adaptations put on at the Comédie-Française.

655. _____. "Ruy Blas à la Comédie-Française." In her Ruy Blas, pp. 29-35. Paris: S.I.P.E., 1960.

Play admitted to the répertoire 27 January 1879. In April of the same year Hugo was publicly acclaimed at "l'événement de la saison, . . . la consécration suprême d'un chef-d'oeuvre en présence de son glorieux auteur." Graph of performances from 1879 to 1960 shows that play was not performed in only five years and that a total of 808 performances had been given by 1953. List of all actors in four main rôles follows.

656. Cocteau, Jean. "Ruy Blas (dialogue pour un film)." Nef, année 4, no. 37 (déc. 1947): 26-31.

Preliminary notice and Cocteau's adaptation of two famous scenes printed here. Cocteau discusses problems of physical resemblance between Ruy Blas and don César and of diversification needed in adaptation. In actual film version, there is, perhaps, more of Cocteau than of Hugo, but there is also striking similarity in their manner of conceiving and presenting the world dramatically. Both employ in plays large doses of le grotesque and trucs like moving portraits and trap doors.

657. Cocteau, Jean. Ruy Blas (motion picture). Adapté pour l'écran par Jean Cocteau. Mis en scène par Pierre Billon. Paris: P. Merihien, [c 1948]. Pp. 129.

Changes carried out by Cocteau seem to make drame even more melodramatic. Effect is that of seeing Hugo's play through a distorting mirror. Cocteau appends at end speeches left out through his process of "simplification."

658. Colette. "Ruy Blas." Quoted in Jean Gaudon, Victor Hugo dramaturge, p. 153. Paris: L'Arche, 1955.

On the 1938 reprise. "Je ne pense pas que se puissent recruter aujourd'hui, dans aucune troupe en France, les acteurs qui joueraient romantiquement le drame romantique. Le théâtre de Victor Hugo demande à être joué tel que son auteur l'a conçu, c'est-à-dire avec grandiloquence, flamme, grands éclats, égarement, contrastes de lumières et d'ombres, expressions démesurées."

659. Crémieux, Benjamin. "Ruy Blas à la Comédie-Française." Lumière, 3 juin 1938.

660. Dauzat, Albert. "Un Espagnol contemporain de Victor Hugo fut le prototype de Ruy Blas." Les Nouvelles Littéraires, 24 juill. 1952, p. 5.

Identifies Manuel Godoy as model for Ruy Blas. Godoy's biography was well known in France even before French translation of his memoirs appeared in 1836. Dauzat does not exclude other sources, like Rousseau's Confessions and Hélène de Mecklembourg: "Le dramaturge comme le romancier prend son bien où il le trouve: dans l'histoire ou dans la vie."

661. Dubech, Lucien. "Ruy Blas." In his Le Théâtre, 1918-1923, pp. 24-29. Paris: Plon, n.d. [1925].

On a recent performance of the play, which, Dubech judges, "manque aux deux premières de toutes les lois, au bon sens et à la vérité du coeur." Yet, he continues, "on entend Ruy Blas sans élan, mais avec attention. Pour notre compte, nous avons écouté jusqu'au bout, sans ennui. Ruy Blas, le sujet est beau à souhait." Dubech agrees that Act IV is "un tiroir inutile': however, he adds that without it, "la pièce perdrait ce qu'elle a de meilleur."

662. Dumesnil, René. "L'Origine du quatrième acte de Ruy Blas." Le Figaro, supplément littéraire, 3 juin 1911, p. 3.

Dumesnil follows up on original suggestion by Charles Maurice in the Courrier des spectacles that don César's comic gestures and incidents in Act IV of Ruy Blas have their source in "une sorte de trilogie bouffonne de M. de P." Identifies the probable author as Maurice de Pompigny and presents performance dates for the three plays in question--Le Ramoneur-Prince (1784), Barogo ou la suite du Ramoneur (1785) and Le Mariage de Barogo (1785). Claims plays' direct influence on don César's entering house through chimney,

finding fine clothes and delicious meal, becoming involved in love
imbroglio, and being led off by alguazils at end.  Convincing
argument.  See Rigal below.

663.  Dumur, Guy.  "<u>Ruy Blas</u> de Victor Hugo, mise en scène de Raymond
Rouleau à la Comédie-Française."  <u>Théâtre Populaire</u>, no. 40 (4e trim.
1960), pp. 146-49.

Play's only virtue is its spontaneity, Dumur asserts, and that is
lost here in the solemnity of Rouleau's production.  Finds Hugo's
language dated except in moments of excess and describes play as
a "morne spectacle" in all scenes but those where "le burlesque"
predominates.  Says Rouleau lacked focus and could not find "un
sens" for the play.

664.  Escholier, Raymond.  "Le Mystère de <u>Ruy Blas</u>:  Pourquoi Victor
Hugo ne confia pas le rôle de la reine de <u>Ruy Blas</u> à Juliette Drouet."
<u>Les Nouvelles Littéraires</u>, 1$^{er}$ avril 1939, pp. 1-2.

Occasioned by Souchon's book (below).  Cites examples of Juliette's
poor style in letters, then discusses Adèle Hugo's letter to Joly,
director of the Théâtre de la Renaissance, asking that rôle of
queen not be given to poor actress Juliette.

665.  Escholier, Raymond.  "<u>Ruy Blas</u>, pièce à clé."  <u>Les Nouvelles
Littéraires</u>, 18 juin 1938, p. 4.

<u>Reprise</u> leads Escholier to offer his view "que <u>Ruy Blas</u> est
l'histoire romancée des amours platoniques du poète et de la
duchesse d'Orleans."  In this reconstructed version of Hugo's life
in 1838, Sainte-Beuve, Escholier believes, becomes don Salluste.
Hugo's hopes to be made the duchess's regent were dashed by the
Revolution of 1848.

666.  Florenne, Yves.  "<u>Ruy Blas</u>, la vision et le songe."  <u>Médecine de
France</u>, no. 198 (1969), pp. 43-48.  (Also in Victor-Marie Hugo, <u>Hernani</u>.
<u>Ruy Blas</u>, pp. 5-13.  Edition annotée et présentée par Yves Florenne.
Paris:  Le Livre de Poche, 1969.)

Urbane apology for Hugo as dramatist and for <u>Ruy Blas</u>, his best and
most representative play in Florenne's opinion.  Argues that Hugo's
theatre must be treated on level of vision and dream, not as part
of traditional psychological drama.  Says Hugo lacks depth and
misjudges at times proper dosages of tragic, sublime, grotesque
and comic, but manages to create some great characters; in <u>Ruy Blas</u>,
moreover, "la truculence et l'outrance comiques sont, ici, parteuses
de tragédie."  Adds:  "S'il a borné son oeuvre dramatique, c'est
parce qu'il s'est heurté à une société et qu'il n'y a jamais
rencontré son public."  Calls for rehabilitation of Hugo's theatre.

667.  Gamarra, Pierre.  "Romantique mort ou pas mort?  <u>Ruy Blas</u> de Hugo
au T.G.P. de Saint-Denis."  <u>Europe</u>, année 52 (avril-mai 1974):  254-56.

Concludes from enthusiastic reception of José Valverde's <u>reprise</u> of
<u>Ruy Blas</u> that Romanticism is not dead:  "C'est pourquoi il faut
remercier José Valverde et son équipe de nous offrir ce juste et

beau spectacle. L'alexandrin de Hugo n'a pas vieilli. . . . C'est
pourquoi José Valverde a eu raison de jouer le jeu, c'est-à-dire
de jouer Hugo d'être fidèle au drame et au romantisme de cet
important moment du théâtre français comme de la pensée (politique,
littéraire) du poète. . . ."

668. Gerling, George F. "Central City, Colorado, and Ruy Blas."
New York Times, 24 July 1938, IX, p. 2.

Review of Robert Edmond Jones's production of Hooker's adaptation,
presented in old gold camp theatre in mountains by Broadway actors.
Praises costumes and stage sets, "an ideal production for Designer
Jones." Says Hooker's version "streamlines the action" but keeps
poetry and emotions of original.

669. Hallays, André. "Ruy Blas à la Comédie-Française." Le Journal
des Débats, 23 avril 1900.

670. Henriot, Emile. "Autour de Ruy Blas." Cahiers de Radio-Paris 9
(15 oct. 1938): 1025-32.

For the centenary, Henriot recreates in detailed causerie the
atmosphere surrounding the play's première. Claims Latouche's
La Reine d'Espagne as point of departure for Hugo's immensely
superior play. Recounts Juliette Drouet's distress in having rôle
of queen taken from her. Finds Ruy Blas a masterpiece: "C'est une
merveille de théâtre, d'imbroglio dramatique, de verve lyrique, de
bouffonerie éloquente et de somptuosité verbale."

671. _____. "Le Centenaire de Ruy Blas." Annales Politiques et
Littéraires, 10 févr. 1938, pp. 125-28.

672. _____. "Ruy Blas et La Reine d'Espagne." Le Temps, 1928.
(Also in his Romanesques et romantiques, pp. 197-204. Paris: Plon,
n.d. [1930].)

Critic rereads Latouche's Reine d'Espagne and indicates that "Ruy
Blas ne doit pas grand'chose à cette pièce, qui n'a pour elle que
la priorité de fait."

673. _____. "Victor Hugo, Ruy Blas et Madame d'Aulnoy." Le Temps,
12 avril 1927, p. 3. (Also in his Esquisses et notes de lecture, pp.
176-82. Paris: Editions de la Nouvelle Revue Critique, n.d. [1928].)

Examines Hugo's unadmitted reliance upon Mme. d'Aulnoy's Mémoires
de la cour d'Espagne, from which he drew "quelques-uns des épisodes
les plus typiques de Ruy Blas, et toute cette atmosphère espagnole
qui baigne l'admirable drame." Indicates what Hugo borrowed and
how it was used. Also accuses Mme. d'Aulnoy of having plagiarized
her work from a manuscript of the memoirs of Villars, French
ambassador to Spain 1679-81.

674. Houston, John P. "Style and Genre: The Example of Hugo and
Musset." In his Demonic Imagination: Style and Theme in French
Romantic Poetry, pp. 21-43. Baton Rouge, La.: Louisiana State
University Press, 1969.

Examines Hugo's success with Ruy Blas "in introducing a noteworthy range of metaphor and imaginative diction into the drame." Focuses on new style, in which sentences brief, colloquial in syntax and vocabulary, function apart from prosodic form: "It becomes clear, I think, that Hugo had deeply modified the whole conception of French dramatic prosody by 1840." Identifies Hugo's real contribution as rejection of traditional aesthetic of the couplet, which he then carries over into his lyric poetry, "a decisive step in the breaking up of neoclassical genre theory."

675.  Jamieson, D.  "Ruy Blas, ou le degré zéro de l'homme."  In Proceedings of the Fifth Inter-University French Seminar. University of Waikato, Section de français, Hamilton, New Zealand, 1975.

676.  Kemp, Robert.  "Le Centenaire de Ruy Blas."  Le Temps, 6 juin 1938, p. 2.

Laudatory review of centenary performance: "Il faut se laisser emporter, sans réfléchir un instant, par la chevauchée des rythmes et des images; éblouir par le ruissellement des mots. . . . Cette musique n'a pas la jeunesse, les élans, la volupté de celle d'Hernani, la grandeur épique, les sublimes folies des Burgraves; son éloquence est chargée de clichés. Elle reste belle cependant. Il faudrait la chanter. Ruy Blas est un opéra."

677.  Labadie-Lagrave, G.  "Les Origines historiques des personnages de Ruy Blas."  La Revue Hebdomadaire, année 11 (3 nov. 1902): 190-202.

Cites Fernando de Valenzuela, a lackey loved by a Spanish queen and made an hidalgo, as model for Ruy Blas. Discusses Hugo's sources and defends plays' historical inaccuracies: "Toutes les critiques relevées dans Ruy Blas au point de vue de l'histoire, paraissent justifiées . . . [mais] son unique souci était de donner au spectateur une sensation générale de la décadence espagnole pendant les dernières années du règne de Charles II."

678.  La Force, Le Duc de.  "A porpos de Ruy Blas."  La Revue des Deux Mondes, sér. 8, t. 45 (15 juin 1938): 937-40.

Witty, favorable article reviewing centenary performance of Ruy Blas. La Force points out resemblances between Hugo's play and François Coppée's Severo Torelli and between Ruy Blas and Paul Meurice's Struensée (1898).

679.  Lancaster, Henry C.  "The Genesis of Ruy Blas."  Modern Philology 14 (March 1917): 641-46.  (Also in Festschrift presented to him, Adventures of a Literary Historian, pp. 354-60.  Baltimore, Md.: Johns Hopkins Press, 1942.)

Continues work already published by Rigal (702) and Lanson (680). After summary of recent scholarship, Lancaster finds in Jersey diary of Hugo's daughter Adèle supposed first scene visualized by Hugo for play--a minister at height of his powers has unknown man walk in and command him as his master. Says version is more or less supported in Victor Hugo raconté. Asserts: "It seems safe to conclude that the original idea of the play was that of a minister's fall from power under very dramatic circumstances, rather than as story of vengeance and love." See also Moore below.

680. Lanson, Gustave. "Victor Hugo et Angelica Kauffmann. Notes sur les origines de Ruy Blas." La Revue d'Histoire Littéraire de la France 22 (juill.-déc. 1915): 392-401.

Suggested by Rigal's article (702). Says Hugo did not know English; so Lanson looks for common source for both Ruy Blas and Bulwer-Lytton's Lady of Lyon. Identifies life story of artist Angelica Kauffman as shared link of inspiration. Léon de Wailly's novel on the topic, definitely read by Hugo, was published too late to be a source of Bulwer-Lytton's play. Therefore, Lanson hypothesizes, English author knew of story through other sources available at time. Ends by asserting that Lady of Lyon not necessary to explain genesis of Ruy Blas. See Showalter (708).

681. Lardner, James. "Comédie Française: Vivid Ruy Blas." Washington Post, 16 May 1979, pp. B1, B8.

Review of Ruy Blas, part of J. F. Kennedy Center, "Paris: The Romantic Epoch." Derides "shabby conventions" of play; lauds its "passages of rich dramatic verse." Details particular inconveniences for non-Francophones: "Little portable radios and earphones are provided, along with an act-by-act plot synopsis; . . . but the experience takes some getting used to, and even then gives you the feeling of looking into a museum diorama rather than being in a theater."

682. Laubreaux, Alain. "Ruy Blas à la Comédie-Française." Candide, 2 juin 1938, p. 17.

Reviews centenary performance. Recognizes weaknesses of the play but appreciates beauty of many verses.

683. Lebois, André. "Ruy Blas est-il . . . Charles Lassailly?" Revue Quo Vadis? 9 (1955): 43-50, 83-85. (Also in his Admirable XIXe siècle, pp. 35-49. Paris: Editions Denoël, n.d. [1958].)

Calls Ruy Blas "plus plausible que les autres ténébreux de Hugo" and identifies poor, young writer Charles Lassailly as character's real life prototype: "C'est un portrait fidèle, et criant, jusque dans ses inconséquences, d'un contemporain 'de taille.'"

684. Levaillant, Maurice. "La Genèse de Ruy Blas." Le Figaro, supplément littéraire, 25 nov. 1933, p. 5.

Survey for general reader of scholarship on question of sources and composition from Rigal (702), Lanson (680), Lancaster (679), Moore (694). Hugo's genius lies in combining history, life, theories of "le grotesque" and "le sublime": "C'est dans cette opération qu'allait triompher la virtuosité dramatique de Victor Hugo."

685. _____. "Le Premier Ruy Blas et les trois 'Don César.'" Le Figaro, 2 déc. 1933, p. 5. (Also in Mélanges de philologie, d'histoire et de littérature offerts à Joseph Vianey, pp. 369-78. Paris: Les Presses françaises, 1934.)

Don César-like character Maglia dated from 1833 in Hugo's inspiration, according to Levaillant. He appeared in Ruy Blas only to
provide comic relief until Hugo changed the plot and needed a double
for his hero. From manuscript variants Levaillant finds that Hugo
rejuvenated forty-year-old don César to make him sosie for Ruy Blas
on 8 July 1838 and decided at the last minute to give him his own
act. Hugo dreamed of creating comédie picaresque around César-
Maglia later on, but character's potential was not fully realized
until Rostand's Cyrano de Bergerac.

686. Lièvre, Pierre. "Ruy Blas." Le Mercure de France 285 (15 juill.
1938): 428-31.

More on Juliette Drouet than on Hugo's play. Suggests that Hugo
did not really want her to return to stage, so allowed rôle of queen
in Ruy Blas to be taken from her. See also Du Bos above.

687. Ludwig, Albert. "Victor Hugos Ruy Blas." Zeitschrift für
französischen und englischen Unterrichten 27 (1928): 338-48, 413-23.

Author states his purpose to show Ruy Blas a work unusually
characteristic of Hugo, Romanticism, and the French. First part
of informal essay examines sources, strengths and weaknesses of
the play. Second section offers Ruy Blas as fine example of
Romantic folk art and of Hugo's drama of antithesis. Interesting
comparison also with drama of German Romanticism.

688. Lyonnet, Henry. "Ruy Blas a-t-il existé?" Comoedia, 6 sept.
1927, p. 1.

Review of proposed sources for play from Mme. d'Aulnoy and
Rousseau's Confessions through Bulwer Lytton's Lady of Lyon and life
of Angelica Kauffmann. Then claims true story of Struensée, Danish
minister and former doctor of Charles VII, to be real nucleus of
Ruy Blas. Nothing new. See Rigal below.

689. Lyons, Constance L. "Tragedy and the Grotesque: Act IV of Ruy
Blas." French Review, special issue no. 4 (Spring 1972), pp. 75-84.

Act IV is not only coherently linked with the rest of the play, it
prefigures the dénouement, according to Lyons. She states: "With
its emphasis on matter, falsity, and disintegration, Act IV has thus
been the necessary key to understanding the emergence of spirit,
truth, and permance [sic] in the play's final scenes."

690. Maillet, Henri. "Explication française. L'Aveu d'amour de Ruy
Blas à Don César. Etude de structure." L'Information Littéraire 21
(mars-avril 1969): 86-92.

Traditional explication de texte. Tries to show that Hugo uses as
much "art" or "artifice," under pretext of passion, as necessary to
achieve desired effects: "Admirons plutôt l'excellence, la grande
allure, l'éclat, l'aisance, la vie, la beauté de cette rhétorique."

691. Marion, M. P. "Ruy Blas." Le Journal des Débats, 9 avril 1912.

Repeats Dumesnil's (662) observation that Act IV of Ruy Blas could have come from Maurice de Pompigny's trilogy.

692. Mas, Emile. "Le Centenaire de Ruy Blas. 1838-1938." Le Petit Bleu, 21 mai 1938.

693. Maurois, André. "Juliette Drouet et Victor Hugo. En marge de Ruy Blas." In Ruy Blas, -p. 19-21. Etabli par S. Chevalley. Paris: S.I.P.E., 1960.

Readable summary of situation described fully in Souchon's Autour de Ruy Blas (713). Explains rôle of queen in Ruy Blas originally designed for Juliette to appease her for interruption in her acting career since the débâcle of Marie Tudor. Quotes from Adèle Hugo's letter to Joly, director of the Théâtre de la Renaissance, asking that rôle be given to more talented actress than Juliette to prevent flop. Hugo pleads "cabale" and "préjugés" when the part was given to Atala Beauchêne, Frédérick Lemaître's mistress, while Juliette accepts final blow to her career calmly.

694. Moore, Olin H. "How Victor Hugo Altered the Characters of Don César and Ruy Blas." PMLA 47 (Sept. 1932): 827-33.

Comparison of two versions of Ruy Blas, one begun 5 July 1838 and other 8 July 1838, leads Moore to conclude: "The manuscript thus shows clearly that shortly before July 14, 1838, when Act I was completed, Victor Hugo was attempting to graft upon his tragedy materials drawn from Angelica Kauffman," a novel of Léon de Wailly. See also Rigal (702), Lanson (680), Lancaster (679).

695. _____. "Victor Hugo as a Humorist before 1840." PMLA 65 (March 1950): 133-53.

More humor is discovered in Hugo's plays than one would imagine. Hernani in original conception was to have been "a masterpiece of comic relief." Judges one reason for Ruy Blas's popularity to be Hugo's revived interest in the comic: "Ruy Blas represented at once the climax and virtually the conclusion of Hugo's comic relief. Even in the play itself there were already evidences of a tendency to collect amusing anecdotes purely for local color, and with no apparent thought of antithetical effect."

696. Picard, Gaston. "Emile Zola, Ruy Blas et la génération de 1869." Le Figaro, supplément littéraire, 3 oct. 1925, p. 2.

Zola detested Hugo, Picard claims, and quotes Zola's acerbic review of successful 1879 reprise of Ruy Blas. Then Picard offers Abraham Dreyfus's pastiche of the play rewritten to please Zola and his public. It is amusing to see Maria Neuborg transformed into "la femme d'un brave bourgeois, qui a la manie de passer ses journées à la chasse" and Hugo in employment offices looking for "documents humains." Part of the scene where don Salluste hires Ruy Blas is imagined in dialogue form and concerns how many bottles of wine the latter is entitled to.

697. Pichois, C. "Une Source possible d'un épisode de Ruy Blas."
L'Ecole, 15 nov. 1952.

698. Porché, François. "Le Centenaire de Ruy Blas à la Comédie-
Française." La Revue de Paris, année 45, t. 4 (15 juill. 1938):
456-60.

> First presents literary history of the play. Of the play itself,
> Porché remarks: "Je dirai qu'elle est à la fois absurde et
> magnifique, et cela à l'extrême dans les deux sens opposés. . . .
> Toutefois, dans cet étrange Ruy Blas, il y a des moments où le
> lyrisme est autre chose que le merveilleux accompagnement musical
> d'une fable insensée." Like Colette (658) and Vilar (719), Porché
> calls for "le jeu sans arrière pensée . . . une candeur absolue
> . . . la folie" in acting of this drame romantique. In this
> production only M. Yonnel attains such a goal.

699. Praviel, Armand. "Jules de Rességuier." Le Correspondant, année
86 (25 févr. 1914): 765-83.

> Prints the three variations of the king's famous letter to the
> queen in Ruy Blas that Jules de Rességuier sent to Hugo (e.g.,
> "Nous n'avons pas chassé les cerfs du duc d'York,/ Mais nous avons
> tué, chez nous, un fameux porc.") No mention of how Hugo reacted
> to them.

700. Régnier, Henri de. "En relisant Ruy Blas." La Revue des Deux
Mondes 15 (1er août 1923): 608-19. (Also in his Flamma tenax, pp.
93-116. Paris: Editions du Mercure de France, 1928.)

> Series of six poems in Hugo's manner on "moments" or "verses" of
> play. Interesting to see one poet creating as reaction to another's
> work.

701. _____. "Sur un vers de Ruy Blas." La Revue de France 3
(15 juin 1928): 596-600.

> Poem inspired by line from Act III. See other poems above.

702. Rigal, Eugène. "La Genèse d'un drame romantique: Ruy Blas."
La Revue d'Histoire Littéraire de la France 20 (oct.-déc. 1913):
753-88.

> Seminal article on sources and composition of Ruy Blas. Rigal tries
> to show logical construction of work from three principal sources--
> Bulwer-Lytton's Lady of Lyon, Gaillardet's Struensée ou le Médecin
> de la reine and Mme. d'Aulnoy's Mémoires de la cour d'Espagne.
> Evaluates rôle of Barogo ou le Ramoneur-Prince (see Dumesnil, 662)
> as that of "tremplin" at most. Refutes Hugo's claim that he always
> starts with abstract idea to illustrate on stage; finds remembrances
> of above three works at play's origin. Suggests other minor
> influences, but attributes best qualities of play to Hugo himself:
> "Décidément, il y a un peu plus dans Ruy Blas que l'imitation
> d'Edward Bulwer." See also contributions on subject by Lancaster
> (679), Lanson (680), Moore (694) and Lyons (689).

703. "Ruy Blas." Le Jour-Echo de Paris, 30 mai 1938.

Calls centenary performance the clou of the Paris theatrical season.

704. "Ruy Blas in Pittsfield." New York Times, 10 Oct. 1933, p. 24.

This first performance on any stage of Brian Hooker's modernized version of Ruy Blas "thrills large audience" in Pittsfield, Mass., with Walter Hampden in dual rôles of Ruy and Don César. To be played at Majestic Theatre in Brooklyn following week, then at Cort Theatre in Manhatten on Oct. 23.

705. Saal, Hubert. "France in Washington: The Romantic Epoch Festival." Newsweek, 28 May 1979, p. 81.

In reviewing festival at Kennedy Center, Saal remarks: "The homage to romanticism by the Comédie Française was appropriately 'Ruy Blas' by the firebrand Victor Hugo, whose rallying cry was 'Liberty in Art, liberty in Society.' His play . . . could have had no more realistic interpretation than that given by this oldest of repertory companies. . . ."

706. Sablé, J. "Ruy Blas ou les jeux du destin." L'Ecole, 12 janv., 9 févr. 1963.

707. Sénart, Philippe. "Victor Hugo: Ruy Blas." La Revue (des Deux Mondes), 1er janv. 1969, pp. 159-61.

Reprise at Comédie-Française reawakens enthusiasm for Hugo that Sénart felt as an adolescent. Sénart forgets the teachings of his former professor, the late President Pompidou, and responds fully to all he had been taught to scorn—"l'enflure, le clinquant, le toc, toute la fausse joaillerie dont le talent gitan de Hugo se contentait." Suggests that the play's captivating charm goes beyond surface veneer: "Oui, Ruy Blas est une outre gonflée de vent, mais quelle jolie musique, ô cuivres! ô timbales!"

708. Showalter, English, Jr. "De Madame de la Pommeraye à Ruy Blas." La Revue d'Histoire Littéraire de la France 66 (avril-juin 1966): 238-52.

Suggests influence of story of Mme. de la Pommeraye from Diderot's Jacques le fataliste on Helen Williams' 1801 novel, The History of Perourou, or the Bellowsmender, mentioned by Lytton as his source for The Lady of Lyons. Wonders if either original French version of Perourou story or Diderot's tale influenced Hugo in Ruy Blas. Claims that Hugo definitely borrowed from Wailly's Angelica Kauffmann for more "vraisemblance," but finds that "le génie de Hugo n'a pas réussi pourtant à faire un chef-d'oeuvre de cette matière ingrate. De nos jours, son invraisemblance et une certaine fausseté dans le drame même nous déplaisent. Non que les mythes romantiques aient perdu leur force: c'est l'idéalisation des personnages qui nous rebute. . . . La pièce souffre enfin d'un changement dans le goût." Of all these literary works on the same subject, l'Histoire de

Madame de la Pommeraye, in Showalter's opinion, "reste la plus vraie." See also Rigal (702), Lanson (680), Lancaster (679) and Moore (694).

709. Simiot, Bernard. "Ruy Blas." Hommes et Mondes 24 (avril 1954): 121-25.

Reserved praise offered in this review of Vilar's production of the play. Says Hugo still has a lot to offer our century and, though Ruy Blas is far from "un chef-d'oeuvre," we applaud "sa jeunesse, son élan, sa générosité, sa lumière, ses sentiments simples."

710. Simon, Gustave. "A propos de Ruy Blas." Le Temps, 28 août 1918, p. 3.

List of twelve works Hugo said he consulted before writing Ruy Blas, including Mme. d'Aulnoy's Relation du voyage en Espagne. Simon checked holdings of Bibliothèque Nationale and found all available to Hugo at time in question.

711. _____. "A propos de Ruy Blas. Documents inédits." Le Temps, 26 août 1918, p. 3.

Lettres inédites from Anténor Joly to Hugo on founding and direction of the Théâtre de la Renaissance, which was to open in 1838 with Ruy Blas. Contract for the play was tied to a required number of performances of Marie Tudor and Lucrèce Borgia at the new theatre.

712. Souchon, Paul. "L'Année de Ruy Blas." Annales Politiques et Littéraires, 10 mars 1939, pp. 259-61.

713. _____, ed. "Autour de Ruy Blas. Lettres inédites de Juliette Drouet à Victor Hugo." La Revue des Deux Mondes, sér. 8, t. 45 (15 mai, 1er juin 1938): 337-73, 604-32. (Also published separately. Paris: A. Michel, 1939.)

Through Juliette's letters to Victor Hugo and the narration connecting them, we see Juliette's love, patience, regret at having the rôle of queen taken from her through Mme. Hugo's efforts and at losing Hugo to theatre. Shows progression in his writing the work, reading it to actors, directing rehearsals, bearing the play's public success and critical failure. Appendix quotes the preface to show Hugo's intentions, cites Rousseau's Confessions as a source, includes critical quotations, dates of composition and performance through the triumphal 1938 centenary performance. No bibliography. Not a scholarly work, but affords a vivid view of the circumstances surrounding play.

714. Strona, O. "Ruy Blas (principali edizioni 1869-91)." Discoteca (Milan) (gen.-febbr. 1970).

715. Ubersfeld-Maille, Annie. "Ruy Blas: Genèse et structure." La Revue d'Histoire Littéraire de la France 70 (sept.-déc. 1970): 953-74.

Studies two "schémas internes" of Ruy Blas to clarify chronology
of its genesis and meaning. First, "schéma de base" is "la triade
femme-maître-valet," the origin of which author traces to childhood
experience of Hugo's seeing marionettes in the Jardin du Luxembourg.
Second is "l'homme démasqué," a scene which long preoccupied Hugo,
according to Victor Hugo raconté. Don César identified as example
of "non-consentement, l'homme de liberté," in contrast to Ruy Blas,
and also as "l'image fraternelle." Schémas also help identify
work's theme on political level--people versus aristocracy. Article
forms part of author's critical edition of Ruy Blas (58).

716. Vandegans, André. "Reflets hugoliens dans Escurial." La Revue
d'Histoire Littéraire de la France 69 (mars-avril 1969): 262-68.

Interesting study of influence of Le Roi s'amuse and Ruy Blas on
Ghelderode's 1928 Escurial. Modern playwright admits he was
attracted to Hugo's theatre; but he has also passed through
le théâtre de cruauté so that his characters and message are more
complex, ambiguous. Escurial is a darker play than Le Roi s'amuse
and Ruy Blas, and it gives more place to psychology, history, and
philosophy: "Escurial reflète deux grands drames romantiques,
mais en les dépouillant, en les concentrant, en creusant
impitoyablement des figures que Hugo nous avait laissées à l'état
de moins inquiétants simulacres."

717. Vandérem, Fernand. "Le Cas Ruy Blas." Le Figaro, 27 janv. 1934,
p. 5.

Ruy Blas has just been put on the "programme scolaire," and Vandérem
evaluates the play: "Car si l'on n'y rencontre pas la grâce
discrète et fluide d'un Racine, combien de vers, dans Ruy Blas,
dont, pour l'éclat, la fougue, les trouvailles, on chercherait
vainement l'analogue chez les classiques."

718. Vier, Jacques. "Plaidoyer pour Ruy Blas." L'Ecole (15 mars 1952).
(Also in his Littérature à l'emporte-pièce, I, 50-57. Paris: Editions
du Cèdre, 1958.)

Explains why he likes the play. Sees in it exiled Hugo as Ruy
Blas. Analyzes the "philosophie historique" and "symbolisme social"
of the play. Finds: "De tous les drames romantiques de Hugo,
c'est le seul survivant."

719. Vilar, Jean. "Ruy Blas. Notes pour les comédiens." Théâtre
Populaire, no. 6 (mars-avril 1954), pp. 45-48.

Director's notes for actors in T.N.P. production of the play: "Ruy
Blas est une pièce bien faite et intense. . . . Il faut la jouer
romantique. Pas de pudeur." Calls attention to fact that "Ruy Blas
est aussi une pièce où l'accessoire est un tyran. Oui, c'est à
la fois l'oeuvre d'un poète et un drame réaliste." Interesting
views from a talented director.

720. Warning, Rainer. "Hugo: Ruy Blas." In Das französische Theater vom Barok bis zur Gegenwart. Edited by Jürgen von Stackelberg. II, 139-64. 2 vols. Düsseldorf: A. Bagel, n.d. [1968].

Says Hugo's plays are unplayable today, and not just his dramaturgy is to blame, but also his theory. Finds in Ruy Blas all the configurations of melodrama and the whole play based on the hero Ruy Blas's absurd lack of vision. Ultimately, Hugo's theatre is a failure because Hugo was not clear about who his audience was to be and what problems his dramas had to solve: "Nur so klärt sich der Widerspruch zwischen der auffälligen Heterogenität des Werks und der ebenso auffälligen Homogenität seiner--von einem vermeintlich gesicherten geschichts--philosophischen Bestand ausgenenden-Theorie."

## Les Jumeaux

721. Berret, Paul. "L'Affaire des Jumeaux de Victor Hugo." Le Mercure de France 250 (15 févr. 1934): 17-27.

Investigates why play was never completed. Explains it mainly because Hugo borrowed plot and characters from "le mélodrame en prose d'Arnould et Fournier, L'Homme au Masque de fer, joué au théâtre de l'Odéon le 3 août 1831. . . ."

722. Duvivier, Maurice. "Le Masque de fer d'après Hugo et Vigny au Festival de Coussac-Bonneval. Une fable mystérieuse, tragique et scandaleuse." Les Cahiers Littéraires de l'O.R.T.F., année 8, 19 (1970).

723. Henriot, Emile. "Le Masque de fer, Hugo et Vigny." Le Temps, 14 nov. 1933, p. 3. (Also in his Courrier littéraire, XIXe siècle: Les Romantiques, pp. 59-66. Paris: A. Michel, n.d. [c 1953].)

Suggests that Hugo left Les Jumeaux unfinished because Vigny had already fully treated the subject in "La Prison" of 1821. Points out striking similarities between the two works, and indicates that Hugo knew Vigny's work well enough to write an article on it.

724. Kirton, W. J. S. "Les Jumeaux and the Inadequacy of Hugo's Dramatic Formulae." French Studies 28 (Oct. 1974): 408-20.

Sees in the play's ambiguities evidence of Hugo's transition to more mature political and social views and his need for changed dramaturgy: "The contradictions Les Jumeaux contains, the abandonment of the manuscript, and the fact that Hugo never returned to it all suggest that the play was a casualty of his developing attitudes in the crucial years around 1840, that he had outgrown the facility of his early dramatic technique, and that the vessel proved inadequate for the substance it was to contain."

725. Levaillant, Maurice. "Les Jumeaux de Victor Hugo. Documents inédits." Le Figaro, 21 oct. 1933, pp. 3-4.

Interesting article on problems of play--its history, why it was never finished, possible endings. Enthusiastically claims that, if it had been completed, the play would have been beautiful with excellent poetry and quotes Jules Lemaître's favorable comments in 1889. In conclusion Levaillant says the play should be compared to Torquemada: "Ici et là, Victor Hugo peignait deux formes de fatalité; ici, la fatalité des événements; là celle du fanatisme, qui n'est peut-être pas qu'une erreur de l'amour."

## *Les Burgraves*

726. Aderer, Adolphe. "Les Barbus graves." Le Temps, 23 févr. 1902, p. 2. (Also in his Hommes et choses de théâtre, pp. 34-39. Paris: Calmann-Lévy, 1905.)

Feuilleton article on Duvert and Lauzanne's parody as weakened echo of battle of classics, romantics and l'école du bon sens. Funny preface and good verse parody of beginning of Les Burgraves, he finds. Too literary, however, and scarcely gay. Considers it ironic that "les vieux" here are Hugo and Dumas and "les jeunes" Ponsard and his cohorts.

727. _____. "Les Burgraves." Le Temps, 22 févr. 1902, p. 2. (Also in his Hommes et choses de théâtre, pp. 29-33. Paris: Calmann-Lévy, 1905.)

Examination of the première of Les Burgraves. Recounts versions told by Gautier, the témoin in Victor Hugo raconté, and Léon Chevrau. Claims play failed only because l'école du bon sens formed a cabal against it after the third performance. Resumes press reaction and states that Lucrèce succeeded less on its own merits than as reaction against giant Hugo.

728. _____. "Un Prologue inédit des Burgraves." Le Temps, 25 févr. 1902, p. 2. (Also in his Hommes et choses de théâtre, pp. 40-46. Paris: Calmann-Lévy, 1905.)

His third article occasioned by 1902 reprise of Les Burgraves. Prints excerpts from previously unpublished prologue Hugo cut from play. Singles out for praise "un superbe récit sur les guerres des burgraves et de Frédéric Barbarousse." Finds these pages "dignes de celles qui étaient déjà connues."

729. Ascoli, Georges. "L'Arrière-plan politique des Burgraves." Neophilologus, 23, 4 (1937-38): 261-66.

This brief article examines Hugo's political development and the evolution of his conception of a Franco-German union, which Ascoli sees at heart of the play.

730. Attoun, Lucien. "Les Burgraves." Les Nouvelles Littéraires, 1er déc. 1977, p. 28.

Review of Antoine Vitez's production at the Théâtre de Gennevilliers. Admires the experimental nature of this stripped-down version (five actors play 27 rôles), but finds that this play "est tout aussi (peu) jouable que ne l'est Hernani ou tout le théâtre d'Hugo."

731. Bainville, Jacques. "De La Mandragore aux Burgraves." L'Action Française, 2 mars 1913. (Also in his Une Saison chez Thespis pp. 85-88. Paris: Editions Prométhée, 1929.)

Review of performances of both plays (Les Burgraves at Comédie-Française). Bainville admires Hugo's idea but regrets that he lacked ability to carry it out successfully in play: "C'est le tragique ridicule, le mélodrame bouffe, la parodie indiquée à tous les vers. Avec cela, l'idée des Burgraves n'était ni médiocre, ni méprisable. . . . Hugo ne semble pas avoir eu la vigueur nécessaire pour en faire la reine de son drame. La vision historique, l'intention politique qu'il avait eues un jour sur les ruines d'un burg rhénan s'étaient envolés. Mais quelle tentative. . . ."

732. Baldensperger, Fernand. "Les Grands Thèmes romantiques dans Les Burgraves de Victor Hugo." Herrig's Archif (Archiv für das Studium der Neueren Sprachen und Literaturen) n.s. 121 (1908): 391-410.

Long, scholarly article outlining German inspiration in Les Burgraves. Most Romantic of the themes exploited are the idea of fatality as worked out in the Schicksalsdrama and "la vieille résistance au 'fait social'" as in Die Raüber and Wilhelm Tell. Indicates resemblances between Hugo's play and Grillparzer's L'Aïeule and influence of Schiller's Wallenstein. Sees Scott's Ulrica as model for Guanhumara and stresses that all characters are Romantic rather than classical in conception. Public not fooled, Baldensperger says, by Hugo's references to Aeschylus; audiences saw "le caractère plus épique que dramatique" in the play.

733. Berret, Paul. "Guanhumara dans Les Burgraves de Victor Hugo." Bulletin de l'Université de Lille, sér. 2, année 6 (avril 1902): 137-43.

Sees Urfried in Scott's Ivanhoe as prototype for Guanhumara and traces their similarities. Stresses transformation of Hugo's vengeful character into "un coeur droit, fidèle, sympathique, qui peut s'émouvoir et qui sait pardonner." Credits Scott with giving Hugo in 1823 "la conception générale d'une oeuvre qui tient le milieu entre l'Iliade et la Tour de Nesles." This desire to create an epic led Hugo twice to the theatre, to Notre Dame de Paris and finally to La Légende des siècles.

734. Berton, René. "La Première Représentation des Burgraves." Le Figaro, supplément littéraire, 12 mars 1927, p. 2.

Good review of events leading up to and at première. Offers this comment on play itself: "Certes, la pièce est chaotique, mal équilibré et, par instants, incompréhensible: mais un prodigieux souffle lyrique l'anime." To explain échec, Berton suggests: "Le public commençait à être lassé des succès ininterrompus de Hugo. . . ."

735.  Brisson, Pierre.  "Reprise des Burgraves."  Le Temps, 4 avril
1927, p. 2.

On reprise at the Comédie-Française to celebrate centenary of
Romanticism after Cromwell was judged still unperformable.  Brisson
is disappointed in Les Burgraves and views it as unplayable also:
"C'est la dernière en date de ses oeuvres dramatiques, et sans
doute la plus faible.  On y voit, poussés dans leur déformation
extrême, les procédés du genre. . . . Les vers ici sont du Hugo
le plus facile. . . . L'ensemble reste pâle et sans grandeur
épique."  See Thibaudet's (770) response.


736.  Carrère, Jean.  "L'Epopée dans l'art dramatique.  Les Burgraves."
La Revue Hebdomadaire, année 11, t. 4 (15 mars 1902):  337-47.

To explain the failure of this play in both 1843 and 1902, Carrère
measures the plot against the poem and finds the former lacking:
"C'est un mélodrame de l'Ambigu exécuté par un poète du plus grand
génie. . . . Hugo, délibérément, a voulu transporter l'épopée sur
la scène, il a voulu condenser en trois actes tout un cycle
héroïque, et cette confusion de deux éléments de beauté absolument
dissemblables quoique également puissants l'a obligé à sacrifier
l'un à l'autre.  C'est l'épopée qui a survécu, et le drame en est
mort."


737.  Claretie, Jules.  "Comment furent joués Les Burgraves."  Le
Gaulois du dimanche, 1er-2 mars 1902, p. 1.

Excerpt from his book published for the centenary, Victor Hugo,
souvenirs intimes.  Claretie, director of the Théâtre-Français in
1902, chose Les Burgraves to celebrate Hugo's birth because in it
he finds the poet's loveliest, most modern verse.  This article
treats largely the conditions surrounding the première, the success
of Lucrèce, the parodies and Daumier's caricature.


738.  Cru, Paul.  "Victor Hugo et l'Allemagne à propos du centenaire des
Burgraves (1843)."  Bulletin des Etudes Françaises (Collège Stanislas de
Montréal) 3 (janv. 1943):  20-29.

Says Les Burgraves written when Hugo "était encore plein de son
admiration d'artiste pour ces vieux pays rhénans. . . ."  Asserts
that Hugo had intuition of new art, first expressed in Les Burgraves
and realized fully only later by Wagner, but that French were not
yet ready for work of either genius:  "On peut donc voir dans
l'échec des Burgraves et de Tannhauser que le public français est
souvent trop conservateur en ce qui concerne les choses de l'art,
et du théâtre en particulier."


739.  Dac, Henri.  "Les Burgraves."  Univers et Monde, 3 mars 1902.


740.  Debidour, Antonin.  "Une Source probable des Burgraves."  La Revue
d'Histoire Littéraire de la France 40 (janv.-mars 1933):  38-48.

Details of resemblances given between Hugo's play and Le Tribunal
Secret (1823) of Léon Thiessé, a tragedy in pure Voltairian tradition.  These borrowings indicate that there were not always such

wide divergencies between classical tragedy and <u>drame romantique</u>.
Yet this debt touches only upon the melodramatic part of play: "la
partie épique, l'évocation grandiose de la lutte entre les
Burgraves-Titans et le Jupiter-Barberousse appartient en propre à
Victor Hugo, et de cette première fresque de <u>La Légende des Siècles</u>
nul ne lui a fourni le modèle."

741. Duchesne, Alfred. "<u>Le Rhin</u> et <u>Les Burgraves</u> de Victor Hugo." <u>La
Revue de Belgique</u>, sér. 2, année 34 (15 févr. 1902): 162-86.

Critic dislikes the play for combining disharmoniously the ode,
drama and epic. Yet sees this play and <u>Le Rhin</u>, also of 1843, as
dividing Hugo's life into twò parts: "jusqu'en 1843 le poète
s'était contenté à l'actualité et aux questions sociales; après
1843, il se lança dans la politique active. Jusqu'en 1843 il avait
été surtout un poète lyrique, après 1843, il réalisa l'oeuvre
épique la plus considérable du XIXe siècle."

742. Dufeu, R. "Texte commenté: Job (Victor Hugo, <u>Les Burgraves</u>,
1ère partie, scène 7)." <u>Les Humanitiés</u> (Classes de lettres. Sections
modernes) année 8 (sept. 1964): 13-17.

<u>Explication de texte</u> of Job's explanation of his position to <u>le
Mendiant</u>. Conclusion: "Tout contribue dans ce passage . . . à
donner une impression intense de grandeur, de force surhumaine,
implacable, invincible, indéracinable comme le roc lui-même et
à faire de ce texte une belle page épique où Hugo a su retrouver
le frémissement qui parcourt nos chansons de geste. Egalement,
tous les procédés chers à Hugo, . . . tout ce que la puissante
personnalité du poète a considéré comme 'efficace' pour frapper un
public qui, au moment des <u>Burgraves</u>, commence d'ailleurs à se lasser
de ces ficelles un peu trop grosses et trop anciennes [s'y trouvent].
. . . L'échec de l'oeuvre . . . ne nous étonne pas tellement."

743. Estang, Luc. "La Première des <u>Burgraves</u>." Le Journal des Débats,
4 févr. 1902.

744. Flat, Paul. "<u>Les Burgraves</u>." La Revue Bleue 69 (8 mars 1902):
310-13.

Largely unfavorable review of 1902 production. Emphasizes plastic
nature of Hugo's vision, shallowness of his thought, <u>invraisembl-
ances</u> of this <u>mélodrame</u>. Says Musset is Shakespeare's real French
descendant and even Vigny's dramas are superior to Hugo's.

745. Giraud, Jean. "Etude sur quelques sources des <u>Burgraves</u>." <u>La
Revue d'Histoire Littéraire de la France</u> 16 (juill.-sept. 1909): 501-
39.

In a formidable display of sound scholarship, Giraud presents
convincingly sources of <u>Les Burgraves</u> he has discovered. Rejects
Schreiber's manual as influence. For facts, touches of local color
and "saisissants tableuax d'histoire," Hugo read Kohlraush's
history of Germany. Mentions also Schiller's <u>Die Raüber</u> and <u>Wilhelm
Tell</u> and Grillparzer's <u>L'Aïeule</u> but says Hugo did not imitate them.
Even suggests the <u>Aeneid</u> as possible source. It is, however,

especially Hugo himself that Giraud finds in Les Burgraves in echoes of the poet's plays. Hugo accomplished what he set out to do in Les Burgraves, Giraud concludes, in creating his version of Aeschylus's Oresteia.

746. Glaesener, Henri. "La Malédiction paternelle dans le théâtre romantique et le drame fataliste allemand." La Revue de Littérature Comparée 10 (1930): 41-73.

Examination of paternal curse in such French dramas as Cromwell, Le Roi s'amuse and Les Burgraves to measure influence of German fatalistic drama. Concludes: "les dramatistes français . . . s'efforcent de mitiger ce que, dans les pièces de Werner et de Grillparzer, la notion d'anathème offre de trop cruel, de trop implacable, de trop terrible. En particulier Pixerécourt, dans le Monastère abondonné, et Hugo, dans les Burgraves, adoucissent et corrigent la notion de l'antique Fatalité par la notion chrétienne d'une Providence qui sait pardonner au pécheur repentant."

747. Hérold, A. Ferdinand. "Reprise des Burgraves." Le Mercure de France 42 (avril 1902): 228.

Favorable review of 1902 centenary performance: "Victor Hugo y réalise magnifiquement le drame épique et légendaire, et les vers des Burgraves sont peut-être les plus grandioses qu'il ait écrits avant ceux des Châtiments et de la Légende des Siècles. . . . Les Burgraves sont un très beau drame, le plus beau qu'ait créé la force merveilleuse de Victor Hugo."

748. Isay, Raymond. "Hugo, le dernier Burgrave, ou le secret de Victor Hugo." La Revue (des Deux Mondes), juill.-août 1949, pp. 465-89.

Isay said that centenary of Les Burgraves fell during German occupation of France. Presents details of literary history surrounding the work and offers interesting views on sources. Besides "l'inspiration eschyléenne" and Napoleonic Barberousse legend, Isay suggests that "secret" guilt over Eugène's thwarted love for Adèle and consequent madness led Hugo to a concept of fatalité that dominates "l'oeuvre si complexe, si discutée, riche d'éclatante poésie, chargée de sens et de secret, des quarante ans de Victor Hugo."

749. Johnson, Douglas. "Burlesquing the Burgraves." TLS, 3 Feb. 1978, p. 128.

Review of Vitez's production at the Théâtre des Quartiers d'Ivry, also presented at the Round House in London, Jan. 23-28, 1978. Judges the attempt to "present the atmosphere of the drama rather than try to interpret the text" unsuccessful; Hugo's text becomes all but unrecognizable. Yet praises the idea for its "boldness."

750. Larroumet, Gustave. "Reprise des Burgraves à la Comédie-Française." Le Temps, 3 mars 1902, p. 1.

In this basically unfavorable review, Larroumet does find kind words
for Hugo's poetic style: "La pièce, en tant que pièce, ne s'est
pas trouvée meilleure aujourd'hui qu'autrefois. De ce chef, le
public de 1843 avait bien jugé. . . . Certes, ce public avait le
grand tort de traiter avec la même sévérité le fond, qui est
d'extravagance pure, et la forme, qui est de toute beauté."

751. Lemaire, Hippolyte. "Les Burgraves." Le Monde Illustré, année
46 (8 mars 1902):  163.

Another generally unfavorable review. Lemaire has enjoyed reading
the play since his youth, but feels Hugo's fears about translating
epic dream world to concrete stage representation are justified.
Even great Mounet-Sully disappointing as Job.

752. Lugli, Vittorio. "Nota ai Burgraves." Rendiconto delle sessioni
della R. Accademia delle Scienze dell'Istituto di Bologna, Classe di
Scienze morali, ser. 4, vol. 7 (1943-1944):  81-89. (Also in Jules
Renard ed altri amici, pp. 73-80. Messina:  G. D'Anna, 1948.)

Calls play "un'opera di pura poesia" at time when man of the hour
is prose author Balzac. Gives history and plot of play and suggests
it is "un'opera precorritrice" of Wagner, Villiers de Lisle-Adam's
Axel, perhaps Claudel, certainly the rest of Hugo's work. Recognizes
"la scarsa teatralità dell'opera" but tries to suggest its value as
epic, worthy of inclusion in La Légende des siècles.

753. Mambrino, Jean. "Les Burgraves par le Théâtre des Quartiers
d'Ivry." Etudes 348 (mars 1978):  372-73.

Admires Vitez's efforts to make relevant for a modern audience
Les Burgraves, a play which Mambrino considers "au stade du mélo
conventionnel" and written "trop hâtivement." Quotes extensively
from his interview with Vitez, who sees the play as "un Faust
inversé."

754. Massin, Jean. "De Pécopin aux Burgraves." In Victor-Marie Hugo,
Oeuvres complètes, VI, 543-66. Paris:  Club français du livre, 1968.

Good introduction to play, especially on genesis and play's relationship with other works of Hugo:  "On entrevoit alors comment a
pu naître le noyau des Burgraves. Insertion d'un drame individuel
dans l'épaisseur d'une réalité familiale, débouché du conflit vital
entre deux frères sur une lutte politique qui met en cause une
civilisation et une histoire. . . . Par ailleurs, il est clair que,
dans les années 1840-1843, Victor Hugo s'interroge sur la validité
de son esthetique dramatique, telle que les préfaces de ses drames
antérieurs l'avaient formulée. . . . Victor Hugo tente de renouveler
ses formes dramatiques en y insufflant l'épopée. . . . Mais le pas
décisif se trouvait bel et bien franchi dans les Burgraves, comme
la prophétie du prophétisme futur."

755. Mendès, Catulle. "Les Burgraves." Le Journal, 28 févr. 1902,
p. 3.

On centenary performance.

756. Messager, Jean. "Les Burgraves en musique." Le Figaro Artistique, n.s. no. 39 (12 juin 1924), p. 4.

Musical adaptation of Hugo's play by Léo Sachs to be shown at the Théâtre des Champs-Elysées. Messager encourages public to attend what he believes will be an excellent performance: "M. Léo Sachs, qui est avant tout un musicien romantique, devait être attiré par la grandeur du sujet et, aux dires des initiés, il a su en traduire fidèlement la pensée. . . ."

757. Moreau, Pierre. "Une Source possible des Burgraves." La Revue d'Histoire Littéraire de la France 36 (oct.-déc. 1929): 592-95.

Witty article comparing texts of Hugo's play and Népomucène Lemercier's Clovis. Hugo published long study of the latter in the Conservateur Littéraire in 1820, so obviously knew the play well.

758. Perrot, G. "Les Burgraves à Montmartre." Bulletin de la Société d'Histoire et d'Archéologie des IXe et XVIIIe arrondissements 3 (1901-1905): 269-71.

759. Pinatel, Joseph. "Une année de théâtre: 1843." L'Ecole 5 (20 nov. 1954): 133-36.

760. Pommier, Jean. "Un Drame rhénan: Les Burgraves." L'Alsace française 5 (1930): 374.

761. Ponsard, Francois. "Les Burgraves et l'Ecole du bon sens." Le Gaulois, 24 févr. 1902, pp. 1-2.

Son of Lucrèce's author offers an apology for his father's work and l'école du bon sens as his rather ironic contribution to the centenary celebration. Stresses the long, cordial relationship between Hugo and Ponsard despite differences of "conception théâtrale": "Je serais heureux de prouver . . . que mon père . . . n'en manifesta pas moins, chaque fois qu'il eut à se prononcer, toute son admiration pour le génie de l'auteur des Burgraves."

762. Regard, Maurice. "Les Burgraves et La Revue des Deux Mondes. Document inédits." In Problèmes du romantisme, numéro spécial de La Revue des Sciences Humaines, n.s. nos. 62-63 (avril-sept. 1951), pp. 244-48.

Two letters written by François Buloz, director of La Revue des Deux Mondes and also Commissaire Royale, indicating his delicate situation at première of Les Burgraves. Finally gets Charles Magnin to see the play and write article on it; review praises the play but expresses also some adroitly worded reservations. Article did not help fate of Les Burgraves. Second letter to Magnin says Alfred de Musset found the play admirable.

763. Rigal, Eugène. "Les Burgraves." In his Victor Hugo, poète épique, pp. 22-31. Paris: Société française d'imprimerie et de librairie, n.d. [1900].

Investigates the epic characteristics of this play and links it to
La Légende des siècles, Dieu and La Fin de Satan. Sees signs of the
epic in previous dramas--don Carlos before Charlemagne's tomb and
Ruy Blas's speech to the Council. The means of tragedy and opera
that Hugo uses to animate the epic are, however, not successful
here: "Les Burgraves marquaient le déclin d'un dramaturge en
annonçant magnifiquement la venue d'un puissant poète épique."

764. Russell, Olga Webster. Etude historique et critique des Burgraves
de Victor Hugo. Avec variantes inédites et lettres inédites. Paris:
A. Nizet, 1962. Pp. 280.

Thorough, carefully documented study of the play, based on detailed
analysis of manuscripts. Chapters on preparation, genesis of
preliminary manuscript, genesis of final manuscript, play's meaning,
historical sources, literary sources for themes, literary sources
for characters and scenes, play's dramatic and poetic value and
play's fortune. Solid bibliography. Appendix contains lettres
inédites placed with manuscript in Bibliothèque Nationale and study
of variants. Russell stresses fact that Hugo always intended this
work to be epic drama. Concludes: "Oeuvre de transition, dans une
époque de transition, le drame des Burgraves survit, par la grandeur
de la vision qu'il exprime, ainsi que par la beauté solide et
éclatante de sa poésie. Le fait de ne plaire à aucune faction est
la marque de ce qui précède un nouveau développement."
a) Hunt. French Studies 18 (July 1964): 281-82.
b) Riffaterre. Romanic Review 55 (Oct. 1964): 220-21.
c) Seebacher. La Revue d'Histoire Littéraire de la France 65
   (juill.-sept. 1965): 517-18.

765. Saradin, E. "La Représentation des Burgraves." Le Journal des
Débats, 28 févr. 1902.

766. Seebacher, Jacques. "Le plus beau saut périlleux du théâtre
français. Monter Les Burgraves, pièce immontable, à la manière
inimitable d'Antoine Vitez, c'est parier sur l'impossible." Les
Nouvelles Littéraires, 24 nov. 1977, p. 12.

Surmises that Vitez's production at the Théâtre de Gennevilliers
would not be appreciated by audience of the Comédie Française or of
old T.N.P. But, Vitez's "enterprise d'une exemplaire probité
hallucinée et dérisoire" accomplishes Hugo's goal--"le retournement
du public en peuple."

767. Sénart, Philippe. "Les Burgraves. Théâtre de Gennevilliers."
La Revue des Duex Mondes (févr. 1978): 436-38.

Very negative review of Vitez's production: Vitez "vient de
prouver par l'absurde l'impossibilité de jouer les Burgraves. . . .
Vitez parodiant Hugo qui déjà, peut-être, se parodiait lui-même,
nous sommes renvoyés d'une dérision à l'autre."

768. Simon, Alfred. "A la barbe des Burgraves." Esprit n.s. 2 (janv.
1978): 95-97.

Simon praises Vitez for trying to make Les Burgraves real "théâtre populaire . . . une création collective," but says Hugo's theatre in general and this play in particular are impossible to act today. Yet Simon poses an intriguing question: "Et si le théâtre de Hugo était en effet le vrai théâtre de la mort de Dieu? . . . le seul vrai théâtre de l'absurde, peut-être: théâtre sacré sans sacrement, . . . la splendeur verbale étant l'instrument de cette hémorragie mortelle."

769. Stirling, André. "Les Burgraves." Effort Clartéiste, année 7 (mai 1935): 56-59.

Reprise of play at Comédie-Française stirs author to review criticism on and pariodies of Les Burgraves. His own opinion stresses epic qualities and Hugo's lack of moderation: "Telle est la marque de son génie, ennemi de toute mesure gréco-latine et assez voisin de ces héros germaniques qu'il a choisis d'instinct pour y souffler son verbe."

770. Thibaudet, Albert. "Les Burgraves dans le théâtre romantique." Les Nouvelles Littéraires, 23 avril 1927, p. 4.

Very perceptive review article in special issue indicated to Hugo on centenary of Romanticism. Thibaudet takes issue with Brisson (735) on reaction to reprise of Les Burgraves. Thibaudet loves the play and whispers to himself, "C'est sublime!" Attaches play to three systems--Romantic convention, myth of Emperor's return, and 'la vieillesse"--to understand its impact. Regretfully admits, however, that plays' admirers are in the minority and that the future is dim for verse drama: "Pour la première fois depuis Richelieu on cesse de jouer des pièces nouvelles en vers, le public cesse d'en demander, d'en supporter; le drame romantique est devenu lui aussi un vieux burgrave. . . ."

771. Tout-Paris. "La Première des Burgraves, 1843-1902." Le Gaulois, 26 févr. 1902, p. 1.

A rather superficial recounting of the première through anecdotes and traditional literary history.

772. Ubersfeld, Anne. "Un Espace-texte." Travail théâtral 30 (Jan.- March 1978): 140-43.

After indicating all the textual "meanings" not explored in Vitez's production of Les Burgraves at the Théâtre des Quartiers d'Ivry, Ubersfeld says Vitez is faithful to Hugo in mounting Les Burgraves as abstract theatre: "C'est la dérision du théâtre; . . . explorer pour les faire éclater les limites du théâtre." Approves "cette double postulation simultanée vers le rire et vers l'émotion, typique du public nouveau. En ce sens, ces Burgraves sont une étape d'une importance extrême pour l'éducation d'un spectateur à l'oeil neuf."

773. _____. "Formes nouvelles du grotesque, Les Burgraves, mise en scène par Antoine Vitez." Nouvelle Critique 111-12 (févr.-mars 1978): 63-65.

A similar review of Vitez's production. Finds play "grotesque
'romantique' comme le veut Bakhtine," but it "trop difficile . . .
pour promouvoir une autre forme de théâtralité, celle qui nous
impliquerait directement, nous, spectateurs."

774. Vianey, Joseph M. "La Légende et l'histoire de Frédéric
Barberousse dans Les Burgraves de Victor Hugo." Mémoires de l'Académie
des sciences et lettres de Montpellier, sér. 2, t. 5 (1909): 49-69.

Excellent, well researched article on Hugo's successful presentation
of a legendary, epic figure. Vianey concludes: "Malgré des
anachronismes et des détails contestables, Hugo a donc bien rempli
son dessein: il a réussi à nous faire comprendre ce que fut
réellement la belle figure de Barberousse et pourquoi la légende
l'embellit encore, ce que furent ses luttes contre les burgraves
et pourquoi l'imagination populaire en demeura toujours si frappée.
Ce grand sujet a rencontré, comme il le souhaitait, un grand poète."

775. Vilarem, Edouard. Les Burgraves. Lodève: E.-F. Corbière, n.d.
[1901]. Pp. 31.

Lecture originally. Vilarem states at the beginning: "J'ai
toujours considéré les Burgraves comme le chef-d'oeuvre du théâtre
romantique." Examines sources, application of Hugo's theories,
psychology of Job and Hatto, eloquent style, and moral lessons in
play. Cannot explain the play's failure in 1843, "un mystère
incompréhensible" for him. Looking forward to coming reprise (1902)
at Comédie-Française.

776. Ward, Patricia A. "Les Burgraves." In her Medievalism of Victor
Hugo, pp. 67-74. Pennsylvania State University Studies, no. 39.
University Park, Pa.: Pennsylvania State University Press, 1975.

Identifies in Les Burgraves the motif of pardon and redemption and
Hugo's vision of the Middle Ages as a political metaphor for desired
peace and unity. Examines multiple sources, dramatic techniques,
critical opinions on the play. Concludes: "Its failure on the
stage suggests that Hugo had not found the proper vehicle for his
vision of the past. . . . Like Notre-Dame de Paris, Les Burgraves
illustrates Hugo's ambivalent attitude toward the Middle Ages, but
by the 1840s he articulated more sharply the parallels he saw between
the past and the political and social injustice of the present."
See more comprehensive treatment in Russell (764).
a) Bryant. Romanic Review 69 (1978): 150-51.
b) Cook. Nineteenth Century French Studies 6 (1978): 289-91.
c) Grant. French Forum 1 (1976): 88-89.
d) Williams. French Review 49 (1976): 793.

777. Wolff, Maurice. "La Genèse des Burgraves et Le Rhin de Victor
Hugo." Le Figaro, 11 août 1927, pp. 4-5.

Article on relationship between Le Rhin and Les Burgraves prompted
by recent reprise of play "avec un éclatant succès au Arènes [sic]
de Saintes." Describes 1838 trip to the Rhineland as mainspring for
both works. Speaks of Les Burgraves as a "monument d'une sauvage

grandeur, temoin de la formidable puissance épique autant que
dramatique de Victor Hugo."

## *Le Théâtre en liberté—* General Criticism

778.  Barrère, Jean-Bertrand.  "Victor Hugo dans l'île de Serk.
Mai-juin 1859:  un épisode de la création en exil."  La Revue des
Sciences Humaines 74 (1954):  117-65.  (Also in his Victor Hugo à
l'oeuvre: le poète en exil et en voyage, pp. 103-57.  Paris:  C.
Klincksieck, 1965.)

Attempts to demonstrate parentage of inspiration during Hugo's
"séjour idyllique" on Isle of Serk in 1859 of parts of Le Théâtre en
liberté and other creations of that period--Les Travailleurs de la
mer, Dieu, La Fin de Satan and Les Chansons des rues et des bois.

779.  Gaudon, Jean.  "Sur une pièce imaginaire de Victor Hugo."  La
Revue d'Histoire Littéraire de la France 69 (nov.-déc. 1969):  1021-22.

Refers to 1939 article of Montargis (336), presenting two pièces
inédites of Hugo, Le Château du diable and Le Suicide.  Second
never printed because of suit over ownership of literary rights.
According to Gaudon, it is only a poor fragment from section
Spleen in Le Théâtre en liberté, dating from 1853-1854.  Gaudon
advises reader to forget "ce Suicide imaginaire."

780.  Jamati, Paul.  "Dans l'atmosphère des Châtiments."  Europe, année
31 (sept. 1953):  84-87.

Claims tone and theme of L'Epée, "ce joyau du Théâtre en liberté,"
are the same as those in Les Châtiments--a revolutionary appeal to
insurrection.  Comparison of verses from both works, Jamati suggests,
indicates L'Epée is really Les Châtiments "transposés pour le
théâtre."

781.  Le Senne, Camille.  "Le Théâtre en liberté."  Le Siècle, 8 nov.
1910.

782.  Paraf, Pierre.  "Victor Hugo et le Théâtre Libre."  La Nouvelle
Revue, sér. 4, t. 43 (sept.-oct. 1919):  70-75.

Effusive appreciation of Hugo's Théâtre en liberté especially of
Mangeront-ils?:  "Lorsque prend fin notre séduisante rêverie dans
la forêt, notre âme en sort enivrée de clarté, pleine des senteurs
sauvages et ardentes de la vie.  Et l'auteur d'Hernani ne nous
apparaît que plus grand d'avoir su . . . créer, tel Shakespeare,
allégé de toute érudition historique et de tout élément de temps
ou de lieu, le théâtre libre et éternel de l'humanité."

783.  Schneider, Pierre.  "Victor Hugo:  Sublimis, sub limine."  Les
Temps Modernes, année 6 (avril 1951):  [1761]-93.

More on poetry than drama but does consider and praise the Théâtre
en liberté as the last work before end of exile. Emphasizes Hugo
as Priapus and includes quotations from Mangeront-ils? and Sur la
lisière d'un bois.

784. Schwab, Raymond. "Hugo annoté par Pierre Louÿs." Les Marges 56
(10 juill. 1935): 69-71.

Schwab investigates text of the Théâtre en liberté annotated by
Pierre Louÿs, who appears to have been especially interested in the
reliquat, the character Maglia, Hugo's theme of "life is a stage"
and his "métamorphoses de l'image."

785. Truffier, Jules. "Le Théâtre de Victor Hugo: Le Théâtre en
liberté." Conferencia 14 (1$^{er}$ août 1920): 187-200.

This lecture tries to situate the Théâtre en liberté in Hugo's work
as a whole and to offer evaluation and appreciation of it. Quotes
Aristotle and Corneille to arrive at "la formule et la critique du
Théâtre en liberté." Contends that this series of plays from exile
period shares some basic characteristics with plays of 1827-1843
period. "Absurdités" and brilliant lyrical passages dominate all
Hugo's theatre. Truffier says that Mangeront-ils?, Sur la lisière
d'un bois, La Grand'mere and L'Epée have been played with varying
success; so he talks about lesser known plays and projects like
Les Gueux, Comédies injouables qui se jouent sans cesse and Les
Deux Trouvailles de Gallus, all of which he finds delightful.

786. Vigo-Fazio, Lorenzo. Il Teatro in libertà di Victor Hugo. Lecco:
E. Bartolozzi, n.d. [1953]. Pp. 24.

Format like that of his book on Hugo's major dramas (323). More a
plot presentation with details of genesis, composition and
production (if any) than a literary analysis per se. In prologue
summarizes strengths and weaknesses of Le Théâtre en liberté: "Tutto
ciò costituisce il pregio massimo, dal punto di vista della poesia,
ed il difetto più grave, da quello del teatro, di questi sette
componimenti, nei quali l'azione sovente ristagna, ed il dramma cede
il posto alla lirica."

787. Volinson, I. J. "Victor Hugo's Dramatic Work in the Sixties."
In Research Papers of the Gorki Institute for World Literature. N.p.,
1956.

In Russian.

## Mille Francs de récompense

788. Abirached, Robert. "Une Arme souveraine." Le Nouvel Observateur,
18-24 mai 1966, p. 40.

Favorable review of Marcel Maréchal's reprise of Mille Francs de
récompense at Théâtre des Célestins in Lyon. Finds this production
a faithful translation of Hugo's ideas, accenting their

"signification sociale et politique." Calls the play "un mélotype: manichéanisme des personnages, pathétique, rebondissements, clairon et larme à l'oeil, tout y est." Praises masks used for Hugo's black characters, scenery, and acting. Concludes that the show proves Hugo can be played today seriously and well for public's enjoyment.

789. Butheau, Robert. "Marcel Maréchal met en scène à Lyon Mille Francs de récompense de Victor Hugo." Le Monde, 29 avril 1966, p. 14.

Features an interview with director Maréchal, who wants his production to present the play as "un mélo politique et progressiste." Calls Glapieu "un Jean Valjean qui . . . dénonce la misère du peuple et caricature la bourgeoisie." Plans to use Brechtian techniques to highlight play's modernity.

790. Cézan, Claude. "A Metz: Une première de Hugo." Les Nouvelles Littéraires, 23 mars 1961, pp. 1, 9.

Review of Hubert Gignoux's "première mondiale du mélodrame hugolien," Mille Francs de récompense. Features interview with director on techniques of staging play for today's audience. After brief résumé of play's history, Cézan indicates that production was well received by the public.

791. Dumur, Guy. "Mille Francs de récompense de Victor Hugo, mise-en-scène d'Hubert Gignoux, avec la Comédie de l'Est, au Théâtre de l'Ambigu." Théâtre Populaire, no. 42 (2e trim. 1961), pp. 95-96.

This critic does not like Gignoux's handling of play as a parody of mélodrame. Criticizes director for skirting important final scene of play, in which Glapieu is arrested. Dumur says Galpieu's arrest shows his goodness, his exact sense of justice and "la méchanceté de la société"; but Gignoux's version weakens these elements. Dumur most interested in the "personnage plus inquiétant, chargé de jouer deus ex machina et choeur antique, ce clochard reprise de justice, Glapieu, nullement sentimental, lui, mais spirituel et cynique."

792. Hugo, Victor-Marie. "Une Drame inédit de Victor Hugo: Mille Francs de récompense." Présenté par Maurice Levaillant. Le Figaro, 21 avril 1934, p. 5.

Act I, scene 1 given in entirety. Accompanying illustration shows a few lines from original manuscript.

793. Lemarchand, Jacques. "Le Théâtre--Mille Francs de récompense." Le Figaro Littéraire, 19 mai 1966, p. 16.

Another favorable review of Maréchal's production: "Une fois de plus Victor Hugo, aidé par les comédiens du Cothurne, a 'eu' son public--et c'est très bien ainsi." Admires especially successful "apparences 'brechtiennes.'"

794. Levaillant, Maurice. "Un Drame inconnu de Victor Hugo." In
Mélanges d'histoire littéraires offerts à Daniel Mornet, pp. 199-208.
Paris: Nizet, 1951.

 On Mille Francs de récompense. Details of composition, followed
by Levaillant's suggestion that play sprang from double inspiration
of Les Misérables and Ruy Blas: "Glapieu est un Jean Valjean qui
se souviendrait d'avoir été Don César." Cites as two ideas animating
the play Hugo's stand against harsh penal legislation of the Second
Empire and attempts to renovate his theatrical technique. Play not
totally successful because of overabundance of mélodrame and
"personnages de convention." Yet Levaillant finds in Rousseline
foreshadowing of Becque's Les Corbeaux.

795. _____. "Questions de littérature et d'histoire. Le Dernier
Drame en prose de Victor Hugo." Le Figaro, 21 avril 1934, p. 4.

 On Mille Francs de récompense. Says play is Les Misérables adapted
to stage: "Glapieu est un Jean Valjean qui se souviendrait d'avoir
été don César." Although it not a masterpiece, Levaillant describes
it as "un drame curieux, vivant, attachant jusqu'en ses étrangetés
dont quelques-unes anticipent les modes d'aujourd'hui."

796. Marrey, Jean-Claude. "Une Pièce oubliée." L'Avant-Scène, no.
248 (1er sept. 1961), pp. 3-8.

 Celebration of Mille Francs de récompense. Excellent photos of
Christian Cassadesus's production at Théâtre de l'Ambigu. Whole
text of play follows introduction. Last page devoted to quotations
from review of play, most of them favorable.

797. Mignon, Paul-Louis. "France." World Theatre 10 (Autumn 1961):
261-62.

 Short, favorable review in English and French of Mille Francs de
récompense: "The vigorous lyricism and the verbal brilliance
peculiar to the great poet lent lustre to melodrama wittily parodied
by the author. Hubert Gignoux and members of the company of the
Comédie de l'Est certainly did justice to the spirit of this play."

798. Saurel, Renée. "Mille Francs de récompense." Les Lettres
Françaises, 20-26 sept. 1967, p. 25.

 Televised production of play, directed by Gignoux and acted by the
Comédie de l'Est. Music, scenery, acting all praised. Reviewer
insists that Hugo's play is a "beau spectacle," undeserving of
neglect: "Mélodrame, oui, et naïf, mais d'une naïveté géniale, et
d'autant plus émouvant que le vieux monde dénoncé par le major
républicain est loin d'être anéanti, et qu'il faudra longtemps pour
que s'ouvrent toutes grandes les ailes de l'âme du peuple, comme le
souhaitait Hugo."

## L'Intervention

799. Attoun, Louis. "L'Intervention." Les Nouvelles Littéraires, 18 mai 1978, p. 29.

Praises Ewa Lewinson's production of L'Intervention at the Théâtre de la Cité Internationale. Lewinson, Vitez's assistant and collaborator, allowed her students at the Ivry theatre to choose the text themselves. Attoun calls the Théâtre en liberté a sort of dramatic Les Misérables. Lewinson breaks the text's melodramatic logic to attain the limits of the absurd and render the spectacle "intelligent."

800. Guillemin, Henri. "Une Comédie inédite de Victor Hugo." La Revue (des Deux Mondes), nos. 22-23 (15 nov., 1er déc. 1950): 193-210, 385-404. (Also in his edition of Victor-Marie Hugo, Pierres. Geneva: Editions du milieu du monde, 1951.)

First publication of Hugo's L'Intervention, a "pochade rapide à laquelle le poète de soixante-quatre ans s'est amusé huit jours à Guernesey. . . . Hugo avait son côté Musset que l'on ignore trop." In brief introduction Guillemin lauds "la fantaisie" of the play but discovers also a more serious "arrière-pensée politique." Identifies a "secrète allusion" to Juliette and memory of Léopoldine at the end.

## Mangeront-ils?

801. Brisson, Adolphe. "Mangeront-ils? de Victor Hugo." Le Temps, 3 mars 1919, p. 3.

This play's première at the Comédie-Française evokes laudatory comments: "Elle tourne au profit du poète et atteste une fois de plus l'abondance, la variété, la souplesse, la force créatrice de son génie. . . . Hugo, quoiqu'il les fréquente peu à Guernesey, connaît les hommes. Toutefois, il les juge perfectibles. . . . Ces vérités ou ces mirages il les vêt de l'éblouissante étoffe de son verbe, tour à tour sompteueux, finement nuancé, plein d'appels de clairons, de murmures, de songes, de méditations lucides et d'ineffables chansons d'amour."

802. Carlier, Jean. "Mangeront-ils? de Victor Hugo." Combat, 12 févr. 1952.

Features interview with Christine Tsingos on choice of Mangeront-ils? to stage at the Théâtre Gaîté-Montparnasse.

803. Christ, Yvan. "Victor Hugo: Mangeront-ils?" La Revue (des Deux Mondes), mai-juin 1968, pp. 451-52.

Lukewarm appreciation of reprise at Alliance Française. Praise for director Serge Ligier and his "troupe excellente." Of play itself says: "Le thème est d'une stupidité accablante et ce que

l'on distingue de la versification d'Hugo ne l'est pas moins. . . .
La pesante farce du père Hugo ne pouvait être jouée que comme une
farce. . . . Le triomphe du gueux--Hugo est là tout entier. . . .
L'expérience peut-être applaudie, non point encouragée."

804.  Fert, L.  "Une Première de Victor Hugo à la Comédie-Française."
Le Gaulois, 25 févr. 1919.

On Mangeront-ils?.

805.  Gautier, Jean-Jacques.  "A l'Alliance Française:  Mangeront-ils?,"
Le Figaro, 9 mai 1968, p. 30.

Very favorable review of production and play:  "C'est peut-être dans
le Théâtre en liberté, et en particulier dans ce Mangeront-ils?,
que l'auteur d'Eviradnus et de La Légende des siècles s'est le plus
approché du ton shakespearien dans son mélange outré de lyrisme,
de burlesque, de verbalisme songeur, de jeux de mots énormes, de
répliques cocasses, de verve et de trivialité, avec de brusques
envolées vers des nuées poétiques ou de soudaines plongées vers des
vérités premières qui ont l'apparence de la pensée."

806.  Kemp, Robert.  "Notre-Dame d'en haut."  Le Monde, 20 févr. 1952,
p. 9.

Unfavorable review of Mangeront-ils? at Gaîté-Montparnasse.  Critic
had to leave at intermission because play was so bad:  "Je n'ai pas
pu endurer cet écoulement d'alexandrins, pâles répliques des beaux
vers imagés de la Légende des siècles, des vers amoureux d'Hernani,
des vers pétulants que lance don César dans Ruy Blas. . . . Je
croyais entendre des 'à la manière de' Banville ou Rostand; et pas
bons."

807.  Lalou, René.  "De Shakespeare à Victor Hugo--Mangeront-ils? au
Théâtre du Tertre."  L'Education Nationale, année 13 (24 oct. 1957):
23-24.

Reviewer asserts:  "Mangeront-ils? est, avec La Forêt mouillée dont
Rostand devait s'inspirer pour Chantecler, le plus savoureux exemple
de ce que Victor Hugo entendit par 'Théâtre en liberté.'"  Describes
Aïrolo as "une sorte de Hernani joyeux."  Praises actors for their
"esprit de poétique bouffonerie."

808.  Riffaterre, Michael.  "Un Exemple de comédie symboliste chez
Victor Hugo."  L'Esprit Créateur 5 (Fall 1965):  162-73.

Interesting analysis of Mangeront-ils?, which author sees as "la
lutte du Mal et du Bien."  Hugo's problem, then, is "comment trans-
poser dans le mode comique les thèmes graves de sa poésie métaphysique sans détruire leur contenu philosophique?"  One remedy is in
juxtaposition:  "La gaîte alterne avec l'inquiétude métaphysique."
Another is use of parody to signal author's presence.  Cites
parodies in Mangeront-ils? of plays of Racine, Beaumarchais,
Corneille, and of traditional ode; finds that "la parodie . . .
permet . . . [la] fantaisie et [l']intention philosophique:  elle
fait le pont entre le symbolisme et le comique."

809.  Schneider, Louis.  "Mangeront-ils?, pièce de Victor Hugo."  Le
Gaulois, 26 févr. 1919.

On première.

810.  Vandérem, Fernand.  "Mangeront-ils?"  La Revue de Paris, 15 mars
1919.  (Also in his Le Miroir des Lettres, II, 23-24.  Paris:
Flammarion, 1921.)

Although première brilliantly mounted and enthusiastically received,
play appears more dated to this critic than Ruy Blas.  It is from
Hugo's later period and seems to be "du romantisme rechauffé."
Vandérem sees Aïrolo as kin "par sa truculence" to don César de
Bazan.

## Les Deux Trouvailles de Gallus

811.  Allem, Maurice.  "Les Trouvailles de Gallus."  La Muse Française,
10 juill. 1923, pp. 521-27.

Review of play's 1923 première at the Comédie-Française.  Romantic
theme of pity for the fallen woman and her redemption through love
seen in second and "more important" of the two trouvailles.  Extensive
plot summary followed by praise for "passages riches de verve,
d'éloquence et de poésie."  Chides Hugo for childishness and
verbosity in some parts.

812.  Brisson, Pierre.  "Les Deux Trouvailles de Gallus."  Annales
Politiques et Littéraires 81 (juill. 1923):  19-20.

813.  Domenico, Oliva.  "La Marquise Zabeth dell'Hugo (trad. di G.
Civinini)."  Rivista di Roma 15 (sett. 1911):  303-05.

On Italian version of Les Deux Trouvailles de Gallus.

814.  Doumic, René.  "Les Deux Trouvailles de Gallus."  La Revue des
Deux Mondes, sér. 7, 15 (15 juin 1923):  943-46.

On première.  Finds in this work Hugo's same old Romantic bric-a-
brac; but it is saved by poet's "verbe magnifique . . . vers superbes
ou charmants . . . somptuosité verbale."  Claims play not made for
stage and says third act least good--"nous voilà en pleine convention
et en plein mélo. . . ."  Says play well staged and acted.

815.  Fischer, Max et Alex.  "Les Deux Trouvailles de Gallus."  La
Liberté, 4 juin 1923.  (Also in their Dans deux fauteuils.  Notes et
impressions de théâtre, pp. 242-47.  Paris:  E. Flammarion, n.d. [1924].)

Première impels brothers to look up Hugo's sources for title of
play--fables of Phaedrus and La Fontaine.  Reread them and found
them "ingénieuses et jolies"; so they would prefer to talk about
them rather than about Hugo's effort, which they find weak in
comparison.  They quote Jules Lemaître and agree with his opinion:
"'Dès qu'on essaie de les réaliser sur la scène, de donner un corps

à ces froides et éclatantes chimères, les drames de Hugo sonnent si
faux que c'est une douleur de les entendre. . . .'"

816. Flers, Robert de. "Les Deux Trouvailles de Gallus." Le Figaro,
4 juin 1923, pp. 1-2.

Very favorable review of première. Prefers first trouvaille,
which he calls "un bijou." Sees influence of Shakespeare's
A Midsummer Night's Dream: "Mais malgré cela et quoiqu'il n'ait
pensé à la scène en écrivant ce poème dialogué, il est curieux de
remarquer combien ce qui n'était pour lui qu'une brillante fantaisie
a conservé le caractère et les traits distinctifs de tout son
théâtre."

817. Girard, Maxime. "Les Deux Trouvailles de Gallus." Le Figaro,
2 juin 1923, p. 3.

Approves both production of première and Hugo's text: "Nous y
retrouvons le génie incomparable du poète; son lyrisme, son invention verbale; cet art qu'on n'a pas égalé de construire et
d'assouplir le vers."

818. Simon, Gustave. "A propos des Deux Trouvailles de Gallus." La
Revue de France, année 3, t. 2 (15 avril 1923): 870-77.

Detailed history of composition, publication and attempts at
performance of this play. First trouvaille dates from 1848-1850,
second from 1869. Simon publishes original verses and outline.
Catulle Mendès and Georges Courteline "étaient les deux plus
fanatiques admirateurs des Deux Trouvailles de Gallus."

819. Souday, Paul. "Au théâtre." La Revue de Paris, année 30, t. 4
(1er août 1923): 674-85.

Highly laudatory review of Les Deux Trouvailles de Gallus:
"L'antiromantisme actuellement endémique a rendu quelques auditeurs
insensibles à l'étincelante fantaisie et à la profondeur genereuse
de . . . [cet] hymne a l'amour, d'abord idyllique et charmant, puis
douleureux et tragique; voilà ce que sont les Deux Trouvailles de
Gallus, dans une forme éblouissante."

820. "Théâtres. Comédie-Française: Les Deux Trouvailles de Gallus."
Le Temps, 3 juin 1923, p. 5.

On première. Says the play not put on previously for good reason,
that these "deux petites fables de Victor Hugo . . . n'ont qu'un
rapport lointain avec l'art dramatique. . . ." Yet author finds
some justification for performance: "On ne peut cependant qu'être
reconnaissants à ceux qui, par culte hugolâtre nous permettent
d'apprécier une fois de plus l'abondance, la richesse, la force et
la beauté du vers romantique."

821. Vandérem, Fernand. "Les Deux Trouvailles de Gallus." La Revue
de France, 15 juin 1923. (Also in his Le Miroir des lettres, VI, 171-
72. Paris: Flammarion, 1925.)

Vandérem finds play "insupportable et creux. C'est le Victor Hugo humanitaire, le Victor Hugo apôtre, qui parle ici, et non le pur poète en pleine fraîcheur et force de talent." Does indicate, however, a few lovely verses.

## *Torquemada*

822. Behr, Dr. Fr. Victor Hugos Torquemada inter vergleichender Berucksichtigung der übrigen Dramen des Dichters. Abhandlung. Jahrbuch. Weimar Gymnasium Programm 931. Weimar: n.p., 1910. Pp. 11.

823. Cassou, Jean. "Torquemada." Europe, 15 juin 1935, pp. 75-87.

Hugo seen as great metaphysical thinker, likened to Job, and protagonist Torquemada to le Mal. Identifies this quality in Hugo as possible reason for failure of his dramas like Torquemada: "On peut rire de ce drame effrayant, qui est le drame même. Car les métaphysiciens désespérés sont tragiques, mais non dramatiques. . . . Avec Victor Hugo, une action se noue, une partie se joue. Est-ce cela qui fait rire? Un drame, bien sûr, peut toujours être traduit en comédie. Mais peut-être les raisons de ce rire sont-elles plus profondes et plus perfides."

824. Mécréant, Marc. "Les Sources de Torquemada." La Revue d'Histoire de la Philosophie 32 (oct.-déc. 1942): 329-38.

Locates many sources for the play. Interesting suggestion of play's origin: "C'est vraisemblablement chez Voltaire que Victor Hugo a trouvé l'idée d'écrire un drame sur l'Inquisition." Hugo relied upon one particular work for information, according to Mécréant: "En conclusion, de toute cette étude ressort que la source principale--et de loin--reste l'Histoire de l'inquisition d'Espagne de Llorente. Cet ouvrage nous a permis de constater une fois de plus avec quelle minutie Victor Hugo se documentait."

825. Peyret, Jean-François. "Dialogue d'exilés?" La Revue des Sciences Humaines, n.s. no. 156 (oct.-déc. 1974), pp. 641-51.

On Hugo and Brecht. Article a sort of Brechtian dialectical analysis of Torquemada, in which "l'histoire de Don Sanche et de Rose n'est qu'une métaphore de l'histoire des juifs." Concludes: "Imaginons Torquemada sans sa fable: qui sait! ce serait peut-être une pièce de Brecht. Ce qui est certain, c'est que Brecht aurait répugné à conserver cette fable dont le dénouement dramatique paraît assurer l'achèvement d'un procès qui reste en cours."

826. Zumthor, Paul. Victor Hugo, poète de Satan. Paris: R. Laffont, 1946. (Hugo's theatre, pp. 309-10.)

Sees inspiration of Torquemada as very close to that of La Fin de Satan: "On y relèverait tous les thèmes que nous connaissons, et d'abord cette hantise d'anéantir l'enfer; . . . Hugo se pose le problème avec une profondeur à laquelle nous ne sommes guère

habitués:   comment la foi peut-elle tuer par charité?"   Zumthor
indicates, however, that Hugo fails to attenuate anguish of
problem by creating a new myth in the play.

# Author Index

The numbers after each name refer to
item numbers in the bibliography.

# Subject Index

The numbers after each subject refer to
item numbers in the bibliography.

Religion in plays, 246

Rességuier, Jules de, 699

Le Roi s'amuse:
  centenary, 559
  English translation, 64
  general, 253, 550, 559, 562,
    563, 568, 569, 570, 716
  manuscript, 563
  première, 222, 553
  reprises, 552, 554, 555, 557,
    558, 561, 564, 567
  Rigoletto, 550, 568
  sources, 560, 562, 563, 565, 566

Romantic theatre, 71, 79, 133, 135,
  140, 148, 161, 187, 188, 210,
  214, 278, 285, 307, 540

Romanticism:
  dramatized scenes of, 90
  history of, 230, 233, 237, 292,
    319, 321
  in theatre before Romantics,
    265
  revolution in "sentiments . . .
    et . . . idées," 208
  social, 258
  triumph of, 245, 549

Roumania, 262

Ruy Blas:
  centenary, 670, 676, 678, 692,
    698, 703
  characters, 98, 218, 645, 646,
    675, 685, 694
  editions, 25, 46, 47, 48, 49,
    50, 51, 52, 53, 54, 55, 56,
    57, 58, 671, 712, 714
  English adaptations, 527, 634,
    642, 668, 704
  film adaptation, 651, 656, 657
  general, 330, 452, 635, 636,
    637, 638, 647, 654, 655, 664,
    666, 675, 686, 687, 689, 690,
    693, 699, 700, 701, 706, 713,
    715, 716, 717, 718, 720
  le grotesque, 689
  inédits, 638, 711, 713
  parodies, 648, 650, 653
  première, 222, 670

  reprises, 634, 639, 640, 641,
    644, 649, 652, 654, 658, 659,
    661, 663, 667, 668, 669, 676,
    678, 681, 692, 698, 703, 704,
    705, 707, 709, 719
  Romantic aesthetic, 643
  sources, 660, 662, 665, 672,
    673, 677, 679, 680, 683, 684,
    685, 687, 688, 691, 694, 697,
    702, 708, 710, 715.
  Spanish influence, 190, 260,
    495
  style, 674
  translations:
    English, 60, 61, 64
    Russian, 62
  Zola on, 696

S

Sainte-Beuve, 73, 273, 365

Satan and Satanism, 363, 826

Schiller, 138

School readings, 284

Shakespeare 231, 252, 418

Society, theatre and, 171

Spain, 151, 190, 207, 250, 251,
  260, 403, 495

Strindberg, August, 298

Le Suicide, 336, 779

T

Talma, see under Cromwell

Le Théâtre en liberté:
  general, 781, 782, 784, 785,
    786, 778
  sources, 780

Le Théâtre libre d'Antoine, 69,
  158

Themes in plays, 122, 157, 166

**About the Compiler**

RUTH L. DOYLE is Assistant Professor of Modern Languages at Central Missouri State University in Warrensburg.